Pastoral
Transformations

Pastoral Transformations

Italian Tragicomedy and Shakespeare's Late Plays

Robert Henke

DELAWARE

Newark: University of Delaware Press
London: Associated University Presses

Associated University Presses
440 Forsgate Drive
Cranbury, NJ 08512

Associated University Presses
16 Barter Street
London WC1A 2AH, England

Associated University Presses
P.O. Box 338, Port Credit
Mississauga, Ontario
Canada L5G 4L8

The paper used in this publication meets the requirements of the American National Standard for Permanence of Paper for Printed Library Materials Z39.48-1984.]

Library of Congress Cataloging-in-Publication Data

Henke, Robert, 1955–
    Pastoral transformations : Italian tragicomedy and Shakespeare's late plays / Robert Henke.
        p.   cm.
    Includes bibliographical references (p.   ) and index.
    ISBN 0-87413-620-2 (alk. paper)
    1. Shakespeare, William, 1564–1616—Tragicomedies. 2. Pastoral drama, English—History and criticism. 3. English drama—Italian influences. 4. Tragicomedy. I. Title.
PR2981.5.H46   1997
822.3'3—dc20   96-33001
                                                                        CIP

PRINTED IN THE UNITED STATES OF AMERICA

For Suzanne

Contents

Acknowledgments

It is a pleasure to thank those who have helped me to write this book. The project began as a 1991 doctoral dissertation at the University of California, Berkeley. As supervisor, Paul Alpers always balanced tough criticism with support and encouragement, and provided a model for the life of the social, not solitary, mind. Joel Altman was both rigorous and enthusiastic. As the dean of Italian-English Renaissance drama studies, Louise George Clubb was (and continues to be) a fount of knowledge, wisdom, and inspiration.

In the course of the many and substantial revisions undertaken since 1991, several colleagues carefully read all or part of the evolving manuscript and furnished me invaluable comments and suggestions: Michael Finke, Daniel Javitch, Emma Kafalenos, Arthur F. Kinney, William Matheson, Stephen Orgel, Randolph D. Pope, Leo Salingar, Robert Wiltenberg, and Suzanne Wofford. I especially appreciate the careful readings and detailed commentaries provided to me by Robert S. Miola and Jane Tylus. Talks at the American Society for Theatre Research, the Sixteenth-Century Studies Conference, the Modern Language Association, and two seminars at the Shakespeare Association of America annual meetings, one led by Robert S. Miola and the other by Paul Yachnin, all allowed me to test out chapter revisions. I thank the editors of *Comparative Drama, Genre,* and *Comparative Literature Studies* for permission to reprint some material. The staff at University of Delaware Press and Associated University Presses, particularly Jay Halio, Julien Yoseloff, Christine A. Retz, and Wyatt Benner, have all been very helpful.

Especially because of the support and encouragement of my two chairs, Randolph D. Pope and Henry I. Schvey, and because of a paid leave in the spring semester of 1995, Washington University has provided me world enough and time to work on this book. In order to complete the final revision of the book, I used a month of my fellowship year at Villa I Tatti in Florence, Italy. I thank Walter Kaiser and the staff at I Tatti for providing an ideal site for pastoral reflection.

Fullest, if most inadequate, thanks go to my wife Suzanne, who has supported me throughout the project with good cheer, patience, and wisdom.

Pastoral
Transformations

1
Introduction

Genre and Mode

The famous title page engraved by William Hole for the 1616 *Workes of Ben Jonson*, which features emblematic representations of tragicomedy, tragedy, comedy, pastoral, and satire, provides a good starting place for a study of Renaissance tragicomedy. It seems inappropriate for Jonson's own corpus, which only includes in *The Sad Shepherd* an unfinished example of pastoral tragicomedy (and that written approximately twenty years after the 1616 Folio), although some critics have argued that it suits Jonson's interest in the generic overlap between comedy and tragedy.[1] The illustration depends on classical, mainly Horatian genre theory—a general inheritance of Renaissance writers—even as it provides in the new hybrid kind of tragicomedy a typically syncretic, Renaissance response to the classics. The importance of the title page extends beyond the purview of Jonson's own work, because it illuminates commonly held Renaissance notions pertaining both to tragicomedy and, more generally, to the functions of Renaissance kinds. Whereas Jonson is extraordinary among English playwrights in his theoretical exactitude and in his concern for precise generic codification, the engraving does represent general Renaissance assumptions about literary kinds that would have been shared by less theoretically keen playwrights like Shakespeare.

On the title page, an architectural design features four columns supporting an arch.[2] A hexameter on the frieze quotes a phrase from Horace's "Art of Poetry": "Singula quaeque locum teneant sortita decenter" [Let each particular variety hold the place properly allotted to it].[3] In a niche between the two left columns, the muse of "Tragoedia" fronts a damask curtain. She holds a crown and scepter, and wears cothurni and an ornately jeweled robe. Under Tragoedia is a wagon or

13

GVL   LOCVM TENEANT S   CEN

THE

WORKES

OF

Beniamin Jonson.

— neque, me ut miretur turba,
laboro:
Contentus paucis lectoribus.

LONDON
printed by W.
Stansby, and are
to be sould by
Rich. Meighen.

PLAVSTRVM

VISORIVM

An° D. 1616.

plaustrum drawn by a horse. Barely discernible, a man gesticulates inside the *plaustrum*, to which a goat (the legendary prize for victory in ancient tragedic competitions) and wine flask are attached. The depiction of the playing space for Tragoedia refers to Horace's remarks on tragedy and the ancient tragedic actor Thespis, "said to have discovered the tragedic Muse, a type unknown before, and to have carried his pieces in wagons to be sung and acted by players with faces smeared with wine-lees."[4] The representation of Tragoedia, then, speculates a historical origin for the form and suggests something about primitive tragedic practice. The muse of "Comoedia" appears to behold Tragoedia from a niche between the two right pillars and stands before a plain curtain; she wears a wreath in her hair, carries a stave, and is dressed in classical slippers or *socci*, a humble tunic, and a *cliton*, over which she holds a cloak. Beneath her, in the middle of an ancient outdoor amphitheater that is given the Latin name of *visorium*, a chorus of men and women circle a sacrificial fire. The columns framing the two prestigious classical genres support an arch, at the top of which stands "Tragicomoedia." The hybrid form ingeniously mixes the costumes of the earlier forms; she wears the tragedic crown and scepter, but her tragedic, jeweled robe covers the comedic *cliton*, and she bears the comedic cloak and *socci*. She presides over an architecturally developed, urban *theatrum*, probably modeled after the Roman Theater of Marcellus, with three arcaded orders and a stage with returning wings. Tragicomoedia is flanked by the two representative figures of Renaissance pastoral: the wild goat-man, or satyr, who carries a reed pipe and a stave; and the countrified shepherd, replete with crook and cornet and dressed in jerkin, breeches, hose, and boots. The title page, then, indicates some kind of relationship between tragicomedy and pastoral. If we consider the incorrect but felicitous etymological confusion between "satyr" and "satyre," and remember that Renaissance writers could imagine the wild, extraurban satyr an apt "satirist" of courtly and city vices, the engraving may also indicate a relationship between tragicomedy and satire.[5]

The illustration suggests a historical relationship between the three major kinds.[6] Tragoedia came first, performed in the primitive *plaustrum* by itinerant actors like Thespis. Comoedia's apparent regard of tragedy could plausibly indicate historical retrospection, for she takes the more historically advanced fixed amphitheater as her playing space. Tragicomoedia, with its sophisticated Vitruvian *theatrum*, occupies a much later historical period. If the last kind combines the sartorial codes of the early kinds, it is also their historical offspring. The belated historical occurrence of classical pastoral and satire—Hellenic and Roman respectively—befits their grouping with tragicomedy.

The illustration, I believe, supports a distinction between the tragicomedic *genre* and the pastoral *mode*—one that is crucial for an accurate understanding of the subject of these pages: Renaissance tragicomedy with a pronounced pastoral component (a *subgenre* of Renaissance tragicomedy). My point will require some explanation of terms, so that I can move beyond the umbrella category "kind." Renaissance theorists also used the word "kind" to categorize and analyze literature instead of the modern terms "genre" and "mode," but our distinction between generic and modal functions is appropriate to Renaissance literature, which had the ideas if not the names.[8] "Genre," it should first be said, should not refer to the ahistorical, rhetorical relationships that may be established between the authorial persona and the audience, which constitute the lyric, dramatic, epic, and novelistic *mediums*. "Genre" instead should refer to kinds arising in history, such as tragedy, comedy, elegy, sonnet, and epigram, and thus subject to the pressures of history. However consciously manipulated by the writer, a genre has a history and a tradition, never more important than in modern and postmodern reversals of generic expectations. The distinguishing features of a given genre may be many—Alastair Fowler lists fifteen possible elements of the "generic repertoire"—but they must include formal as well as substantive considerations: features of "outer form" such as structure, size, style, meter, and plot, as well as features of "inner form" such as values, emotional mood, and attitude.[8] A less historically bound term (though still conditioned by historical changes), "mode" does not involve a realized external form. It emphasizes substance or "inner form" in its identification—tone, attitude, effect, and point of view— may be briefly announced by a characteristic formula, and admits of ready combination with other genres or modes. Modes derive from the historical genres, but may be incarnated in new genres: for example, a novel such as Faulkner's *Absalom, Absalom!* is modally tragic, as ultimately derived from the historical genre of Greek tragedy. Modes are more flexible and historically vagrant than genres and are capable of surprising incarnations.[10] Whereas genre terms are usually expressed in the nominal form, modal terms are expressed adjectivally. It is worth noting that dramatic kinds admit of both generic and modal use: one may speak of "tragedy" and the "tragic," "comedy" and the "comic," and "tragicomedy" and the "tragicomic." Here, "tragicomedic" will designate that which pertains to the genre tragicomedy, and "tragicomic" will refer to modal features. I will accordingly use "tragedic," "tragic," "comedic," and "comic." In describing the behavior of kind, I will alternate between generic and modal adjectives, depending on the phenomenon described. For example, I will refer to "tragedic" action, dramaturgy, catharsis, response, characteristics, codes, set decor, social status, structure, etc., because I wish to mean that which derives from the genre tragedy. But I will refer to "tragic" emotions, tonality, perspective, experience, intensity, etc., because in the latter cases I am referring to modal phenomena.[10]

I am suggesting that we consider Renaissance tragedy, comedy, and tragicomedy as *genres*—each of which can become modal—and pastoral and satire as *modes*. Although Renaissance and contemporary critics may disagree about the formal constituents of these three dramatic genres, matters of external form must be addressed, whereas the notoriously labile modes of pastoral and satire cannot be profitably analyzed by external, structural features. Now each of the three genres is originally associated not only with a given historical period but with a specific theater and its audience, and so may imply a given set of theatrical practices. We cannot learn much about such practices from the illustration, except that tragicomedy seems to involve the sophisticated deployment of tragedic and comedic codes, as figured in the hybrid costume of the late genre. Tragicomedy would then require an audience sophisticated and experienced enough to recognize the codes of the historically prior dramatic genres. The genre of tragicomedy could scarcely combine the entire genres of tragedy and comedy and their accompanying structures, but could easily combine tragic and comic, as well as pastoral and satiric modes.

This particular generic practice, of course, connects Renaissance with modern tragicomedy, which freely juxtaposes tragic and comic points of view, but cannot alone constitute the Renaissance genre. The combination of tragic engagement and comic detachment in a given play, and the production of unpredictable audience responses merely indicates that the work is modally tragicomic, which could be said of much Renaissance drama. To be more historically specific about Renaissance tragicomedy as conceived in the Jonson title page, we must include the generic practice of conjoining the tragicomedic genre with the pastoral mode. As tragicomedic, pastoral would function as a kind of hinge between tragedy and comedy. If this practice of "pastoral tragicomedy" seems to rule out much interesting Renaissance tragicomedy, we might extend the purview of the illustration by considering the ambiguity of the satyr figure. That the satyr could serve as well as the shepherd as the representative pastoral figure indicates the flexibility of the pastoral mode in the Renaissance. In Shakespeare's *Tempest*, then, the pastoral mode uses the satyrlike Caliban as an important figure. The satyr, who with the wild man lives "just beyond" the pastoral fountain or meadow, represents a wilder and less civilized version of pastoral than does the shepherd.[11] Alternatively, the satyr of the engraving might suggest the mode of satire, which works to mitigate the purely tragic effect. The illustration then could refer to satiric Renaissance tragicomedies such as John Marston's *Malcontent* (entered in 1604 in the Stationer's Register as "Tragicomoedia"). Marston's play, G. K. Hunter has shown, responds to the generic idea of Renaissance tragicomedy, but in the person of Malevole shifts the focus from the pastoral shepherd to the urban or courtly "satyrist."[12] Of course, Milton's "Lycidas" aptly shows that the pastoral modality is often accompanied by a satiric countermode because the visionary utopianism of pastoral naturally casts a satiric perspective on the court and the city.[13]

The following assertions about Renaissance genres and modes, which will form the basis of my study of Renaissance tragicomedy in the pastoral mode, may be made from the engraving: (1) Genres are historical institutions and not eternal essences; they arise from historical pressures of both literary and nonliterary natures. (2) New genres may be formed by combining the modal properties, as well as structural elements, of historically prior genres. (3) Theatrical genres are intimately related to their historically changing theaters and audiences, and so involve specific practices directed to those audiences—what I shall call audience-based dramaturgical strategies. (4) Flexible and transportable, modes are subservient to genres and may take on very different appearances depending on their historical and generic incarnations. (5) Genres and modes carry rhetorical force as befits their frequently allegorical and animated depiction in the Renaissance: tragic, satiric, pastoral, and comic points of view may engage each other in both contestatory and synthetic ways.

This study undertakes to compare late-sixteenth-century Italian tragicomedy and Shakespeare's late plays *Cymbeline, The Winter's Tale,* and *The Tempest*. The comparison is not primarily based on the assumption of direct Italian-English "influence" but on the presence of independent yet parallel historical, cultural, and theatrical developments.[14] The Jonson title page is relevant to both Italian and Shakespearean tragicomedy, which independently share a historical belatedness, the use of pastoral as a hinge between tragedy and comedy, and a similar modal multiplicity. We will begin by surveying the historical emergence of tragicomedy in Italian theater and in Shakespeare.

THE EMERGENCE OF LATE CINQUECENTO TRAGICOMEDY

The development of tragicomedy in late-Renaissance Italy does indeed roughly follow the historical progression suggested in the Jonson title page. Emerging after a certain crisis of tragedy and comedy, tragicomedy both looks retrospectively at the two major genres and exploits the renewed success of courtly pastoral drama. Following the fifteenth-century discovery and editing of several lost Plautine and Terentian plays, comedy was the first ancient genre to receive major practical and theoretical attention. The productions of Ariosto's *La cassaria* in 1508 and *I suppositi* in 1509 in Ercole I's court of Ferrara were crucial historical events, marking a significant and influential adaptation of classical comedy into the Italian vernacular. Often performed in the time of carnival, early-Cinquecento comedies by Ariosto, Bibbiena, Aretino, and Machiavelli added to their classical structures realistic depictions of contemporary urban Italian life, privileged the carnivalesque *beffa*, or prank, and tended to favor bawdy and harsh tonalities. Mostly at the expense of the clergy and of various bourgeois characters, Machiavelli and Aretino included heavily satiric registers in their plays. Until the mid 1550s, when the Tridentine reforms and the Spanish occupation of much of Italy began to mark Italian cultural life, anticlerical and anti-Spanish satire was possible in theaters such as that of the Sienese Accademia degli Intronati and the Congrega dei Rozzi.[15]

Whereas humanist textual inquiries combined with a vigorous medieval comedic tradition in the generation of Cinquecento comedy, Italian Renaissance tragedy remained a more strictly academic genre. Almost exclusively emanating from aristocratic circles, tragedy was less able than comedy to transform classical models into a viable mirror of sixteenth-century life. In the absolutist climate of northern Italian courts, it was much easier to represent bourgeois, urban vices than to stage the evils of political tyrants. After Giangiorgio Trissino's *Sophonisba* (published in Rome in 1524), the most seminal event regarding Italian tragedy was the 1541 production of G. B. Giraldi Cinthio's *Orbecche* in Ferrara. More than any other Italian Renaissance tragedian, Giraldi

joined theoretical to theatrical concerns. He adapted his tragedies following *Orbecche* to the perceived tastes of the theatrical audience, which
actually led tragedy in the direction of tragicomedy. He added sentimental, tragicomic tonalities to those of Senecan horror, allowed tragedy to
treat of fictional events, and permitted, in the *tragedia di lieto fine*, a happy
ending for the virtuous characters. A flowering of neo-Aristotelian
tragedic theory coincided with Giraldi's revival of tragedy, although it
did not necessarily follow Giraldi's dramaturgical adaptations. Following Giraldi's important 1543 treatise on tragedy and comedy was
Francesco Robortello's 1548 Latin edition of Aristotle's *Poetics*, which
produced a flurry of commentaries on Aristotle by Minturno, Castelvetro, and others.[16] By the 1550s, tragedy had joined comedy as a classically legitimate, theoretically informed genre, if one less infused by
social reality.[17]

In the Counter-Reformation climate following the Council of Trent
(1543–63), comedy began to shed its bawdy and satirical strains for the
sentimental and pathetic registers of what has been called *commedia
grave*.[18] Structurally too, comedy took on tragedic practices as commentators, lacking an Aristotelian treatise for comedy, rifled the *Poetics* for
information about comedic structure.[19] By the 1570s, the most energetic
and successful productions of comedy were performed not by amateur
actors of the *commedia erudita* but by the emerging professional acting
troupes, or what has come to be called the *commedia dell'arte*. Although
the *commedia dell'arte* actually performed a wide range of genres and
styles, especially after its inclusion of actresses in the 1560s, it continued to serve up the bawdy fare that the earlier *commedia erudita* had
included, and began to be widely attacked by ecclesiastical and municipal authorities.[20] Many dramatic theorists in the courts and the academies perceived a need to "ennoble" the ancient art of comedy.

Post-Tridentine pressures also challenged the appropriateness of
tragedy in a Christian milieu, on two grounds: its Senecan-style violence and the centrality of pagan fate, which was perceived as danger-
ously close to Calvinist determinism. (The historical transformation
of tragedic fate into providence would, in fact, constitute an important
practice of Counter-Reformation tragicomedy.) Without the political
resonance that tragedy would carry in Renaissance England, limited to
a courtly, aristocratic class, inordinately committed to the dictum of
generic purity, Italian tragedy had exhausted itself, so to speak, by
the latter part of the century. The most significant production of tragedy amounted to a kind of nostalgic museum display: the mounting of

Oedipus the King in the newly constructed Palladian Teatro Olimpico in Vincenza in 1585. By the end of the century, the predilection for monumentality and sumptuousness in tragedic production had been taken to such excessive and expensive lengths that Angelo Ingegneri argued that tragedy could only survive if its productions were radically simplified.[21]

Neoclassical commentators increasingly viewed pastoral drama as the third kind of a classical triad. But pastoral inherited a long, diverse tradition of rustic, bucolic drama as well as a tradition of courtly pastoral theater that peaked from 1480 to 1506, and was slower than comedy and tragedy to be rationalized by neoclassicism as a codified genre. As we shall see in chapter 4, by midcentury academic and courtly dramatists became interested in theorizing the third kind. Torquato Tasso's pastoral play *Aminta* (probably written in 1572) firmly established the prestige of the mode, initiating a period of such success that in 1598, Ingegneri could attribute the survival of theater itself to the *scena boscherreccia*.[22] The *commedia dell'arte* also began to perform not only scripted pastoral classics like *Aminta* itself but its own version of pastoral, whose lyric and sentimental registers could be adroitly performed by the new actresses. Satire, of course, did not prosper in the censorious atmosphere of the Counter-Reformation and of Spanish hegemony, when the works of Machiavelli and Aretino were put on the index. Whereas the 1546 Congrega dei Rozzi pastoral play *Il batecchio* may contain a veiled critique of Florentine hegemony over Siena, later pastoral expresses its critique of the court as a movement into the depoliticized pastoral space.[23] The satiric mode, however, preserved a half-life in the satyr, an evocative if marginalized figure in most Italian pastoral plays who often critiques the vices of court or city.

Italian tragicomedy emerges after the crisis of tragedy and comedy in their pure forms, in part as a defensive response to the successful *commedia dell'arte*. A courtier, diplomat, and professor of rhetoric named Battista Guarini, who succeeded Tasso in the Ferraran court of Alfonso II in the dual roles of diplomat and poet, followed *Aminta* with the composition and eventual production of *Il pastor fido*, a massive "pastoral tragicomedy" that would soon achieve great success throughout Europe. The play was written between 1580 and 1585 and then circulated in manuscript among friends, who gave Guarini comments that he used in revising the play. As early as 1584, attempts were made to produce it.[24] Various problems beset the production of Guarini's masterpiece, chief of which was his own directorial perfectionism and inherent distrust of actors. The play was not performed until 1596 in Mantua, and even then was not seen by its creator, summoned away by a family illness.

By the late 1580s, enough copies of the manuscript had been pirated by actors from rehearsals that Guarini prepared to publish the play, fearful of textual contamination. By then, news of Guarini's pastoral tragicomedy had reached a displaced Cyprian nobleman and professor of moral philosophy at Padua named Giason Denores. Without explicitly naming the play or the playwright, in 1586 Denores attacked Guarini on two fronts in his instructively titled work *Discorso di Iason DeNores intorno à que' principii, cause, et accrescimenti, che la comedia, la tragedia, et il poema eroico ricevono dalla philosophia morale, e civile, e da' governatori delle repubbliche.*[25] First, Denores argued that because only tragedy, comedy, and epic were properly grounded by the ancient Greeks in moral and civil philosophy, pastoral poetry has no value for the citizen or courtier. Pastoral is bound to the slight eclogue form and belongs with the epigram, elegy, and ode as minor forms governed by purely rhetorical and not philosophical and political principles. Second, because tragedy and comedy are each uniquely formed by such principles, they can never be combined in one work. Any such combination would constitute a "monstrous" offense to classical decorum and would confuse the didactic principles of each genre. Taking on the pseudonym of "Verato," a famous contemporary actor, the proud and contentious Guarini attacked Denores in his 1588 *Il Verato.*[26] Denores sallied back in his 1590 *Apologia*[27] to which Guarini responded in a second treatise, longer but just as venomous, completed in 1591 but not published until 1593.[28]

Sparked by the debate with Denores, then, as Guarini was preparing the 1590 edition of the play (published in Venice), he was compiling an impressive body of theory on pastoral and tragicomedy, a body of theory that doubtless influenced his dramaturgical revision. The composition of *Il pastor fido*, in fact, provides one of the best examples of the generative relationship between theory and practice in the late Renaissance. Guarini's theoretical and practical writings provide the best contemporary, if slightly antecedent, gloss on the Jonson title page. In the extended debates with Denores, Guarini does three important things: he addresses the historical belatedness of tragicomedy and argues for the historicity of genres; he provides a detailed and sophisticated account of audience-based tragicomedic practice; and he explains the peculiar connection between the tragicomedic genre and the pastoral mode. Like Jonson (to whom he has been compared), Guarini is more theoretically inclined than most of his contemporaries, but he articulates generally held assumptions about Renaissance genres and modes, assumptions relevant to contemporary tragicomedy both within and without Italy.[29]

First, Guarini contests Denores's Platonic belief that genres are ahistorical essences determined by unchanging philosophical principles. For Guarini, tragicomedy is a form that responds to the particular historical moment of late-sixteenth-century Italian theater, when academic tragedy seems to have run its course and the *commedia dell'arte* is posing a new challenge to *commedia erudita* playwrights. A form for its time, tragicomedy emerges for specific historical reasons in response to the attitudes and sensibilities of new audiences. A late humanist sense of historical retrospection shapes Guarini's new hybrid, which appropriates not the entire apparatus, but modes, structures, and elements of the older genres, just as Jonson's Tragicomoedia selectively appropriates properties of Tragoedia and Comoedia.

Second, Guarinian tragicomedy emerges in response to the attitudes and sensibilities of new audiences. It derives from academic and courtly Italian arenas that were particularly sophisticated in theoretical and practical matters of dramaturgy. Guarini's dramaturgy begins to consider, in a more thorough and nuanced manner than that of anyone before, varieties of cognitive, emotional, and ethical audience response. In so doing, he provides a much more variegated, audience-based notion of dramatic genre than is implied in Denores's view, which restricts itself to the didactic dimension.

From Denores's 1586 *Discorso* to the early-seventeenth-century exchanges between partisans of Denores and Guarini, the *Pastor fido* debates treated the issues of both pastoral and tragicomedy, and, either explicitly or implicitly, the relationship between them: the third salient issue raised by Guarini. Whereas Denores conceived of pastoral as a minor and fixed genre, tied to the ecologue form, and argued that pastoral could be adapted to the dramatic medium, Guarini untethers pastoral from generic constraints and frees it as a mode, so that it can be used in generically capacious ways and can be staged in the theater. As Joseph Loewenstein has argued, "pastoral becomes modal in the Renaissance."[30] Opting, with most of his contemporaries, for the shepherd rather than the satyr as the representative figure of the pastoral mode (although the satyr still serves an important function), Guarini spins off the various generic possibilities of pastoral, which can take a "forma o Comica o Tragica o Tragicomica" [comedic or tragedic or tragicomedic form] (*Il Verato*, 3:265).[31] A detailed discussion of the style, affective register, social dynamics, set design, and actions possible in pastoral shows how the pastoral mode can play a crucial role in the dramaturgical "technology" of the tragicomedic genre, in a way that seems to confirm the alignment of the Jonson title page.

Italian tragicomedy was mainly a courtly phenomenon, and the powerful, mysterious, and providential harmonies wrought in the final act of tragicomedies like *Il pastor fido* surely reflected the power of ducal courts like that of Ferrara—or the illusion of power in the waning light of the northern courts. Closely related to tragicomedy and performed in between the acts of tragicomedy as well as the other dramatic genres were the marvelous, powerful, and internationally renowned *intermezzi*, which similarly reflected ducal power.[32] The diminution of comedy's farcical extremes and the mythological distillation of satire into the satyr reflect post-Tridentine moral reforms and censorship, although in ways that paradoxically are dramaturgically innovative. The satyrs of *Aminta* and *Il pastor fido* become fascinating and contradictory figures: they vestigially retain the plebeian dimensions of early Cinquecento pastoral, as well as *arte* tonalities, and provide the plays' principal satire of the Petrarchan and courtly ethos. The process, advocated in Guarinian tragicomedy, of "tempering" comic and satiric extremes translates a historical process into a dramaturgical practice.

THE EMERGENCE OF EARLY-STUART TRAGICOMEDY

In the next chapter, I will consider the direct transmission of Italian tragicomedy to English soil between 1604 and 1608, especially in the cases of John Marston's *Malcontent*, Samuel Daniel's *Queenes Arcadia* and John Fletcher's *Faithful Shepherdess*. But Guarini and his Italian contemporaries become directly important to some early-Jacobean playwrights, because generic and modal tendencies similar to those of late Cinquecento theater were also developing in England. Like the generic tendencies of Italian Renaissance drama, they roughly reflect the basic historical scheme suggested on the Jonson title page, at least in regard to the belatedness of Renaissance tragicomedy in relation to tragedy and comedy. And Shakespeare's own career follows these trends, although of course crucial differences obtain between the Italian and

Shakespearean situations. If a diminution of tragedy, comedy, and satire characterizes the period of the late plays as it does late-Cinquecento
theater, one must hasten to add that great tragedies, comedies, and satires continued to be written by English contemporaries throughout
Shakespeare's career (as was not the case in late-Cinquecento theater),
and that their modal forces are much stronger and less harmoniously
blended together in English relative to Italian theater. Still, a brief examination of generic tendencies in Shakespearean drama will suggest
a surprising number of homologies, mutatis mutandis, between the Italians and Shakespeare.

Although Shakespearean comedy is at every point full of more complicated registers than practically every Italian comedy, if we consider
the span from *Comedy of Errors* and *Taming of the Shrew* to *Twelfth Night*
we may perceive the slight diminution of low-comic, bawdy, satiric registers in favor of the sentimental and pathetic. The repentance of Claudio
in *Much Ado About Nothing* (however unsatisfying it may be to contemporary audiences) and the pathos of Sebastian in *Twelfth Night* are given
greater prominence than in the earlier comedies. In the latter play, the
carnivalesque pranks of Sir Toby Belch and his cohorts give place to the
pathos-filled recognitions of the last act. As with the progression from
Mandragola to late-Cinquecento comedies such as the Sienese Accademia
degli Intronati's *La pellegrina* (probably written in the 1560s, but not
performed until 1589), Shakespearean comedy tends to privilege pathos and romantic love to an increasing extent, at the expense of the
harder comic edges of, say, *Love's Labour's Lost* and *The Taming of the
Shrew*. As such, Shakespearean comedy follows the general historical
trend of Italian comedy, if less because of a crisis in the major genres
than because of a will, respondent to shifting audience tastes, to generic diversity and experimentation. In the tonally and ideologically
multivalent world of Shakespearean comedy, one could of course point
to many divergences from this general trend. Still, the gradual elevation of pathos can be traced through to the late plays, performed in part
for a "gentlemanly" private-theater audience that had begun to surfeit
on the satiric drama of the children's companies. In the generically and
historically retrospective late plays, the low-comic characters (Cloten,
Autolycus, Caliban) played by Robert Armin are notably diminished
in relation to the pathos of the final reconciliations—and this debase-
ment is staged more conspicuously than in the earlier comedies.[33] As
with Italian tragicomedy, this is a tragicomedic, dramaturgical practice
responsive to historical developments and new audiences.

Similarly, Shakespeare's turn from the unfinished *Timon of Athens* to *Pericles* and the late plays reflects the relative decline of satire and satiric drama relative to its golden age of 1599–1605, when the children's companies performed satirical comedy and satirical tragedy before sophisticated private-theater audiences. The production of satire continued, and satiric modalities figured highly in the tragedies of Webster and his contemporaries, but dramatic satire declined, especially after the Children of the Queen's Revels gave up their Blackfriars' lease in 1608. The late plays represent this historical development by framing satire in a pastoral context, as in Belarius's critique of the court in *Cymbeline*, and by mythologizing satire as the "satyr" in the satyr dance of *The Winter's Tale* and as Caliban in *The Tempest*. In the 1599 *As You Like It*, Shakespeare is more interested in the satiric mode than he is in the late plays: Touchstone and especially Jacques are licensed "satirists" who explicitly reflect on the satiric persona, and much of the dramatic interest of the play consists in the alternation between satiric and romantic or pastoral points of view.

Although great Jacobean tragedies such as *The Duchess of Malfi* (1613–14) were still to be written, the great age of Shakespearean tragedy seems to peak with *Othello*; many critics have seen in *King Lear* and *Antony and Cleopatra* harbingers of the tragicomic and romance modalities of the late plays.[34] Prospero's long narrative to Miranda (*The Tempest* 1.2.36–186) may be seen to represent the historical modulation (in Shakespeare's own career) of fate-based tragedy into providential tragicomedy.[35] He tells a tragically coded tale of courtly conspiracy and usurpation, creating tragic horizons of expectation that provoke Miranda's "Wherefore did they not that hour destroy us?" (1.2.138) but swerve to tragicomedic providence with the interventions of Gonzalo and the beneficent sea. The late plays reprise, and do not altogether efface, many tragic modalities of Shakespeare's earlier work, but they favor a providential over a tragedic horizon of expectation and they modulate the pity and fear typical of tragedic emotional response into intermediate tragicomic tonalities. A reader of Florio's Montaigne, Shakespeare treats providence in a more critical manner than do the post-Tridentine Italians. The providentiality of the late plays is not undercut to the extent that Jonathan Dollimore claims it is in the tragedies, but it is less absolutely applied than in the Counter-Reformation Italian theater. Still, it has important dramaturgical significance, as providence becomes a kind of hidden playwright.[36]

The pastoral mode resurfaced and flourished in the years just pre-ceding Shakespeare's late plays, and it seemed to respond to both courtly and popular tastes (as it also did, in fact, in late-Cinquecento Italy, by virtue of the *commedia dell'arte*'s popular adaptation of the pastoral mode).[37] In writing his 1605 *Arcadia Reformed* (published a year later as the *Queenes Arcadia*) for a performance at Oxford University, Samuel Daniel was not merely imitating the famous Guarini but responding to the courtly taste of Queen Anne and others in James's court for pastoral. Nor did *The Faithful Shepherdess* merely indicate foreign borrowing; the play reflected the revival of Spenserian pastoral mainly associated with Fletcher's cousins Giles and Phineas. The 1605 edition of Sidney's pas-toral romance *The Arcadia*, which later served Beaumont and Fletcher for the plot of their "Arcadian tragedy" *Cupid's Revenge*, also reflected renewed interest in pastoral. The appeal of a more popular version of pastoral to urban theatergoers, some of whom were newly gentrified transplants from the country, is indicated by the Jacobean success of the anonymous play *Mucedorus*, reprinted first in 1606 and performed in 1609 or 1610 by the King's Men in Whitehall before James.[38]

Shakespeare's late plays respond to the early Jacobean revival of pastoral, but in a distinctly modal manner, unhitching pastoral from many of its fixed external characteristics and giving it a somewhat dif-ferent form each time.[39] The plays are not only "pastoral" in that they involve an escape to the wild or "green" world, as does *A Midsummer Night's Dream*, but because there is an examination of both realistic and idyllic experience in the pastoral locus. Although only *The Winter's Tale* has actual shepherds—both real and disguised—the Wales scenes of *Cymbeline* provide a fine example of "hard pastoral": a difficult life in a forbidding natural environment conspicuously differentiated from the ease and corruption of the court.[40] Especially if one considers that Ital-ian pastoral was sometimes extended to maritime locales, *The Tempest* suggests itself as pastoral drama by various indexes, including Gonzalo's golden-age reverie (2.1.139–60), the play's implicit debate between nature and civilization, and the familiar pastoral opposition between the innocent nymph and the libidinous satyr. It may fairly be said that, independently of direct influence, Shakespeare's late plays represent the fullest realization of Guarini's theoretically revolutionary contention that pastoral is modal and not generic. But as the Italian pastoral tragicomedies and those of Guarini's English imitators are not, Shakespeare's late plays are also freed of the full external apparatus of pastoral; they distill the mode into symbolically resonant natural places and representative speakers, each expressing a pastoral point of view.

The pastoral center of Shakespeare's late plays aligns them with what we know to be a direct adaptation of Guarini's new genre, Fletcher's *Faithful Shepherdess*. After the dismal failure of the play in the Blackfriars theater in 1608–9, Fletcher prefaced the 1609–10 edition with an arch note, "To the Reader," in which he provided a brief theory of pastoral tragicomedy that carries clear verbal echoes of Guarini's theoretical writings.[41] In the next chapter, we shall analyze the note in detail; for now, three aspects of Fletcher's theory may be underlined: the conjunction of the pastoral mode and the tragicomedic genre; the claim (against Denores) that pastoral is more than a low popular mode, because shepherds as understood in literary tradition are poetically learned and of high social status; and the admissibility of gods in tragicomedy, and by extension of supernatural and marvelous phenomena. In a recent critical anthology on English tragicomedy from 1610 to 1650, Gordon McMullan and Jonathan Hope persuasively argue that Fletcher's note "To the Reader" does not represent the predominant form of tragicomedy in England established by Beaumont and Fletcher after 1609, which is not pastoral and features few divine or supernatural interventions.[42] Because of, inter alia, the virtual absence of pastoral, the realistic action, the undiminished vitality of satire, and the use of a simple rather than Italianate complex plot, the prominent tragicomedies of Beaumont and Fletcher such as *Philaster* and *A King and No King* do not look backward to Guarini and the Italians but create something new and more properly English. Paradoxically, Fletcher's "To the Reader" is in fact a better gloss on Shakespeare's late plays than on the tragicomedies of Beaumont and Fletcher themselves. If "To the Reader" points backward to the Italians rather than forward, so do Shakespeare's late plays in large measure, dramaturgically speaking. Guarini and the Italian context, then, is more relevant to Shakespeare than to Beaumont and Fletcher.

As in Italy, generic tendencies culminating in the emergence of tragicomedy reflect cultural and historical pressures, if not in a simple manner that admits mapping of historical events onto dramatic texts. According to Franco Moretti, Tudor/Stuart tragedy staged the necessarily brief moment of English absolutism, which was not the embodiment of the analogical, divinely ordered world picture discussed by Tillyard but was rather an attempt to forestall emerging empirical and rational modes of representation. Tudor/Stuart tragedy, for Moretti, staged the fall of the absolutist king, a figure with total power but without the capacity to account rationally for that power, and so dramatized the breech between will and reason. This was a brief historical moment because absolutist power could not long sustain the palpable absence of rational legitimization. The increasing incoherence of Jacobean and Caroline absolutist claims in relation to a skeptical Parliament made it more and more difficult to stage an absolute monarch. As Moretti argues, Jacobean tragedies following 1605 do not feature a strong monarch but rather a labyrinthine court of intrigue and deception, more suitable to tragicomedic than to tragedic action and atmosphere.[43]

Although the English court never controlled the professional theater as much as Italian ducal courts controlled late-Renaissance Italian drama, James immediately effected a closer relationship between court and theater upon his accession in 1603, reconstituting the Lord Chamberlain's Men as the King's Men and attaching to the royal household the other major theater companies. James may not have been a more enthusiastic patron of the theater than Elizabeth, but the number of professional company plays performed at court significantly increased during his reign—*The Winter's Tale* and *The Tempest*, for example, each received at least two performances at Whitehall. An important aspect of the "courtly aesthetic" that intensified its pressure on English theater was the interest, transmitted through Inigo Jones and others, in Italian innovations in theater technology: the Vitruvian-Serlian and Palladian traditions of theater architecture, Italian experiments in scene machinery, and the marvelous and complex Italian *intermezzi*.[44] Clearly the English masque, dramaturgically similar to tragicomedy in a technological-royal resolution of discord, was directly influenced by the *intermezzi* as well as by native English traditions. (This was not only true for the Italophile Samuel Daniel but also for the classicist Ben Jonson, despite his protestations to the contrary.)[45] The masque's containment and diminution of the antimasque's low and grotesque comedy are very similar to the diminution of comic excess in tragicomedy as theorized by Guarini. Such a practice parallels, Leah Marcus has argued, James's royal appropriation of rural and "carnivalesque" country festive traditions in the face of Puritan opposition, as rationalized in a 1618 declaration known as the *Book of Sports*.[46] Royal policy, Marcus argues, reflects James's (as well as Jonson's) personal agon: James was inordinately delighted by the grotesque buffoonery of his fools David Droman and Archer Armstrong and other coarse entertainments, and would have appreciated in the masque's taming of misrule an effective

image for self-dominance.[47] The tragicomedic diminution of low comic
buffoonery, then, finds its reflection in James's appropriation of popular festivity and in the court masque's dramatization of temperance.

With James may also be associated the relative decline of satire.
The anti-Scots satire of *Eastward Ho!*, performed by the Children of the
Queen's Revels in 1605, resulted in the imprisonment of Jonson,
Chapman, and Marston. When the same company offended both James
and the French ambassador in 1608, it was disbanded by James, ending
a decade-long run of the satiric plays performed by children's companies in the private theaters. When Shakespeare's company redeemed
the lease of the Blackfriars theater, they did not perform predominantly
satirical drama.

Just Italian tragicomedy is conditioned by the Counter-Reformation, so early-Stuart English tragicomedy is a form of its time. After
long years of anxiety about monarchical succession, the fear of tragic
foreign invasion and civil wars was dispelled by James's peaceful
accession in 1603. To many, James's early years betokened imminent
national renewal and prosperity after a dark and anxious time—a suitable context for reconciliatory, providential forms like tragicomedy and
the masque that dramatize conflict only to resolve it. The miraculous
discovery of the near-catastrophic Gunpowder Plot—accomplished in
part by the scholar-king's capacity to interpret a riddling, anonymous
letter—seemed to lend credence to the claims of royal providentiality.
James's own account of the incident is telling in its allegorical use of
generic terms. He wrote, "The Almighty . . . will . . . put it in his Majes-
ties heart to make such a conclusion of this Tragedie to the Traitors, but
Tragicomedie to the King and all his trew sujiects."[48] Whereas tragedy
is a punitive genre here, tragicomedy signifies both felicity after near
catastrophe and the unified community formed by James and his faithful subjects. Although never successful in any more than a nominal
way, James's pet project of uniting the two crowns of Scotland and
England and his efforts to secure political and religious harmony on
the international arena via dynastic marriages are both parallel to the
synthesizing work of the tragicomedic playwright, who attempts to
wrest unity out of tragic, comic, pastoral, and satiric modes. (Guarini,
as we shall see in chapter 9, connects dramaturgy and politics, if not as
explicitly as does Denores.)

The term "tragicall comaedie" surfaces in a historical document
closely related to *The Tempest*, one of the Bermuda pamphlets describing
the calamitous but ultimately fortunate 1609 expedition of Sir Thomas

Gates and Sir George Summer to Virginia. The Council of Virginia's *True Declaration of the State of the Colonie in Virginia* asks,

> What is there in all this tragicall comaedie that should discourage us with impossibility of such an enterprise? When of all the fleete, one onely ship, by a secret leake was endangered and yet in the gulfe of Despair was so graciously preserved. Quae videtur paena, est medicina, that which we accompt a punishment against evill is but a medicine against evill.[49]

Here, "tragicall comaedie" does not indicate the ironic production of ambivalent response as does "tragicomedy" in the late-twentieth century. What appeared to be a tragedic punishment of evil is revealed, from a providential perspective, to supply salutary, tragicomedic medicine. In the Council of Virginia's allegorical use of generic terms, as in the Jonson title page, tragicomedy follows tragedy, constructing itself on the appearance of the prior genre. As a term designating a sudden, providential turn from apparent disaster to collective felicity, "tragicomedy" then had a powerful resonance in the period. This is not to say, however, that playwrights working in tragicomedy were limited to the ideological meanings commonly associated with the term.

This brief survey of cultural and theatrical homologies in Italy and England surrounding the emergence of tragicomedy should, I hope, increase the plausibility of comparative inquiry beyond the province of directly influenced cultural transmission. In this study, I argue that Shakespeare's tragical-comical-satirical-pastoral plays *Cymbeline*, *The Winter's Tale*, and *The Tempest* should be seen in the light of the generic practices of tragicomedy in the pastoral mode, as I have begun to construct it from the Jonson title page and from my survey of historical tendencies in Italian and Shakespearean forms. As a label, the neutral term "late plays" is probably best, for there is always danger in announcing that one has finally discovered the true generic identity of these odd creations. To say that these plays *are* tragicomedies, as if literary genres behaved like members of a biological class, would be to compromise their generic and modal complexity. Still, I do hope to show that "tragicomedy," understood in its historical context, tells us much more about the plays' dramaturgy than the nondramatic, modern, and modal term "romance."

Irrespective of direct Italian-English influence, Shakespeare's late plays compare with Italian tragicomedy in several major respects: their belated and resumptive relationship to recent tragedy and comedy, their audience-based dramaturgical practices that largely have to do with the diminution of tragic and comic registers and the marginalization of satire, their tragical-comical-satirical-pastoral modal alignments, and their use of pastoral or "satyre" as a tragicomic mode, which has many and various dramaturgical consequences. Largely because of the common humanist response to Aristotelian/Horatian genre theory, generic practices and modal characteristics were internationally disseminated in the Renaissance (although of course also determined by historical and cultural pressures specific to each tradition and each writer), and so provide fruitful objects for comparative inquiry. In particular, pastoral poses similar questions and problems in Italy and in England, and so provides a good comparative fulcrum.[50]

COMPARATIVE METHODOLOGY

Although one may speak of the "indirect influence" of Italian tragicomedy on Shakespeare via Marston, Daniel, and Fletcher and, less patently, through the *commedia dell'arte*, a comparative study of Italian and Shakespearean tragicomedy cannot work according to the influence and imitation model that might govern a comparative study of Spenser and Ariosto, or of Milton and Tasso. The case for my comparative inquiry will best be made by contrasting my methodology with other comparative treatments of Shakespeare and Italian drama, most of which have concerned comedy.

Traditionally, comparatists have asked whether specific Italian Renaissance plays "influenced" specific English plays. There are, of course, several clear cases of causal influence, such as John Marston's use of Sforza Oddi's 1576 *I morti vivi* in his 1601 *What You Will*. Positively identifiable elements such as plots, character types, names, and verbal resonance constitute the major quarry of traditional comparison. In the best example of such a study, David Orr cautions his reader that influence studies must largely be a negative endeavor, since they must continually demonstrate that similarities in Italian and English plays could not have arisen from common classical, medieval, or contemporary sources.[51] At least half of the examples that meet Orr's criteria are those of late-sixteenth-century Italian comedies (by Sforza Oddi, Giovanni Battista Della Porta, and others) directly adapted in the Latin drama written and performed in English universities. The mediatory function of English university drama, most prominently represented in the role that "far-famed Laelia" might have had in the circuitous road from the Intronati's *Gl'ingannati* to *Twelfth Night*, is unfortunately a largely untapped field.

Orr's rigorous positivistic study is extremely useful, but incorrectly limits comparative inquiry by not distinguishing between dramatic *imitatio* and that of other genres and mediums. Much more than the mediums of lyric, epic, and romance narrative, drama is collaborative and is transmitted through other than merely textual means. One does not have to abandon the notion of dramatic authorship in the Renaissance to concede that playwrights worked in collaboration with specific actors, remembering their particular skills and performance histories when composing playscripts. Orr rejects the transmission of *commedia dell'arte* characters from Italy to England, because "they depend on archetypal similarities which can be explained by native English influence."[52] Archetypes, however, cannot explain the many precise references in English Renaissance plays to the specific nature and behavior of *arte* characters such as Pantalone and Zanni.[53] During the several documented exchanges between Italian and English professional actors, in Paris or elsewhere, one can easily imagine actors discussing and even performing for one another the fictional characters to whom they had hitched their professional fortunes.[54] A second productive area of Italian and English comparison, therefore, has examined characters such as the braggart soldier, the Arlecchino, and the transvestite woman from Lelia of *Gl'ingannati* to Viola of *Twelfth Night*, the specific behaviors of which depart from classical practice and seem to indicate Renaissance innovations likely transmitted from Italy to England, possibly through university drama and the *commedia dell'arte*.[55]

If a family of characters constitutes a text unbounded by any specific play and transmitted through both textual and nontextual means, why could not other elements of theater be transmitted in ways that defy positive identification? Louise George Clubb has proposed that Renaissance theater was produced from an extended system of theatrical moving parts or "theatergrams," such as "units, figures, relationships, actions, topoi, and framing patterns" common to both the *commedia erudita* and the *commedia dell'arte* and thus transmissible through a variety of international conduits, both textual and theatrical.[56] Clubb's method, which is largely synchronic and emphasizes comedy and pastoral, is to examine the entire system of Italian theatrical moving parts and to show striking and persuasive similarities with Shakespeare's overall system, many of which cannot be retraced back

to a common classical or medieval heritage. Both for deliberative playwrights and for improvisatory actors, English as well as Italian comedy (and to a lesser extent pastoral and tragedy) was produced by the
combination, displacement, fission, and reversal of theatergrams. The
production of comedy, then, comes not from the imitation of one playwright by another, as might be the case in Renaissance lyric and epic,
but by a more anonymous cutting, pasting, and overturning of sys-
temic parts. In its frank pilfering of *commedia erudita* scripts, the *commedia
dell'arte* surely worked this way. Shakespeare's notorious theatrical op-
portunism, range, and copiousness becomes for Clubb his supreme in-
ventive and transgressive mastery of Renaissance theatergrams.

Thus Shakespeare and the Italians share an important theatrical
practice, one that Clubb terms "combinatory dramaturgy." Ultimately
deriving from the revered Terence's practice of "contaminating" two or
more Greek plots in his New Comedy inventions, Renaissance
contaminatio eventually included the mixing of genres as well into various tragical-comical-historical-pastoral combinations worthy of
Polonius, the fullest expression of which is my subject: Renaissance tragicomedy.[57] Complementary to the practice of *contaminatio*, which Clubb
sees Shakespeare inheriting from the Italians, is that of *complicatio* as
discussed by Leo Salingar in his seminal work on Shakespearean comedy.[58] As early as *Comedy of Errors*, argues Salingar, Shakespeare seems
to follow the Italians in valuing a complicated and dense plot to a much
greater extent than did classical playwrights. Shakespeare, according
to Salingar, was interested in Italian dramatic strategies, at least in the
great period of comedic production. If Shakespeare was interested in
the dramaturgy of Italian comedy, it is likely that the dramaturgy of
other Italian forms would have interested him as well.

The largely synchronic nature of the theatergram method, however,
suggests certain limitations for the comparative study of the Renaissance tragicomedy in the pastoral mode, which the Jonson illustration
has indicated to be a genre particularly sensitive to the pressures of
history. Certainly one could identify many pastoral theatergrams common to the Italian tragicomedies and to Daniel's *Queenes' Arcadia* and
Hymen's Triumph, Fletcher's *Faithful Shepherdess*, and Jonson's late, fascinating attempt at a pastoral tragicomedy, *The Sad Shepherd*. And in
the next chapter I will address the astonishing similarity of *The Tempest*
to a group of contemporary pastoral scenarios performed by the
commedia dell'arte. Taken together, the scenarios provide most of the plot
elements and many of the theatergrams of Shakespeare's masterpiece.

Still, although providing some interesting dramaturgical analogies to *The Tempest* such as the deployment of the unities, the Arcadian scenarios cannot account for the dramaturgical complexity of Shakespeare's play. A comparative study of Renaissance tragicomedy requires a diachronic as well as a synchronic view. For tragicomedy, more important than a common system of theatergrams are a cluster of dramaturgical practices common to Italy and England, practices that are historically specific and largely conditioned by audiences: the use of pastoral as a flexible mode; the exploration of intermediate ranges of audience response between those of tragic horror and comic laughter; the use of genre-coded places to alter audience horizons of expectation; the interplay between tragic, comic, pastoral, and satiric modalities; and the marginalization of the comic buffoon and the satyr figure. In plays representing the generic expressions of parallel historical moments and constituted by similar, tragical-comical-satirical-pastoral modal alignments, certain dramaturgical strategies may repeat themselves, regardless of direct influence.

A dramaturgical practice is different from an external property or "characteristic," which has provided the principle identificatory tool of several previous studies of Renaissance tragicomedy. These studies tend to consider genres like biological classes to which a particular example may or may not "belong."[59] But what counts is not so much the presence of a characteristic or a theatergram but what the playwright does with it, and that may considerably vary from country to country. Once one establishes international "family resemblances" of tragicomedic dramaturgical practice, one may go on to observe that Shakespeare's response to these practices is radically different from that of the Italians.[60] Unlike characteristics, practices admit of different solutions.

In plays based on similar modal alignments and generic practices similar theatergrams do arise, independently of direct influence. In the case of tragicomedy mediated by the pastoral mode, modal liminality or ambivalence may characterize these theatrical structures: the tragicomedic bear common to Italian pastoral drama, *Mucedorus*, and *The Winter's Tale*;[61] dreams of diminished terror (*Il pastor fido, Cymbeline, The Winter's Tale*); the calmed storm of *Il pastor fido*, Guidubaldo Bonarelli's *Filli di Sciro*,[62] the Bohemian seacoast scene of *The Winter's Tale*, and of course *The Tempest*; generically flexible deities such as Hercules (*Il pastor fido*) and Proserpine (*The Winter's Tale*); gnomic but ultimately benign oracles (*Il pastor fido, Cymbeline, The Winter's Tale*); and the figure of the satyr—either in its traditional guise in Italian drama, suggested by allusion in the "dance of the twelve satyrs" in *The Winter's Tale*, or blended with the wild man of literature and the American native (Caliban in *The Tempest*).

Not only the canonical plays of Tasso and Guarini, but the full range of pastoral tragicomedic practice in Italy must be taken into account in a comparative study of Renaissance tragicomedy, for Guarini's historically conscious dramaturgical practice incorporates other Italian practices. Because Guarinian tragicomedy is largely a response to the *commedia dell'arte*, both the *arte* as a social/ideological phenomenon and the particular pastoral tragicomedies performed by the professional theater should be considered. Also worth investigating is the violation of Aristotelian verisimilitude in many late-Cinquecento courtly pastorals, a liberty at odds with *Aminta* and *Il pastor fido* but not with Shakespearean pastoral from *A Midsummer Night's Dream* to *The Tempest*.

Guarini's practice must be related to his voluminous theory, which carries international implications beyond the particular example of *Il pastor fido*. Guarini's speculation emerges in the context of the first thorough body of aesthetic theory in the West, a theory more innovative and liberating than has often been assumed. Taken together, Guarini's responses to Denores reveal one of the most detailed and sophisticated dramaturgies in Renaissance drama, one acutely conscious of the ways in which genre signals mediate between playwright and audience by organizing various systems of signification, creating horizons of expectations, and eliciting various rhetorical effects in the audience. Anglo-American critics who have limited their reading of Guarini to an abridged translation would discover in Guarini's *Verati* a more capacious and innovative theory of tragicomedy than that which is usually attributed to him.[63] If, from our perspective, the Italians generated a significant body of theory but a dramatic corpus without the success of a Shakespeare, a Lope de Vega, or a Molière, and if the extraordinary success of the English stage is not matched by a coherent body of theory, consideration of the Italian theory (usually tied to concerns of practice and relevant to the professional as well as the amateur theater) can illuminate the "unwritten poetics" of English plays characterized by a similar system of kind.[64]

Although I am not arguing that Shakespeare directly knew Italian theory, there was, in fact, a great deal of English interest in Italian theatrical technologies in the early-Stuart years, and so it is probable that Fletcher was not the only one of Shakespeare's contemporaries to know of Guarini's avant-garde theories. We know a fair amount about Inigo Jones's transmission of Italian stage and scene technology from the Italian *intermezzi* to the English masque. Our well-documented account of Italian scenic technology needs to be supplemented by an equally detailed, properly theatrical understanding of tragicomedic dramaturgy, which tends to get reduced to accounts of its "lavish, poetic style" or subsumed in analyses of *intermezzi* technology, analyses that assume the misleading commonplace that the play itself was of no account for Cinquecento audiences.[65]

In both late-Cinquecento theater and early-Stuart theater there was a concern to combat neoclassical attacks on dramatic romance and on hybrid forms like tragicomedy with coherent and developed dramaturgies. Loosely compacted modal hybrids like *Cambyses* would no longer do. Just as Guarini defends tragicomedy against Denores on Aristotelian grounds, Fletcher seems to respond to barbs like that of Sidney's "mungrell tragicomedy" when he insists, in "To the Reader," that a tragicomedy provides more than characters "sometimes laughing, sometimes killing each other."[66] The unorthodox notion that Shakespeare was not indifferent to neoclassical theory has been proposed by Richard Proudfoot, who persuasively argues that the implementation of the unities in *The Tempest* and the concern for the unity of time in the Time speech of *The Winter's Tale* are quite possibly responses to Jonson's attack on the dramaturgical primitiveness of romance.[67] This attack is, of course, most prominently set down in the induction to *Bartholomew Fair* but was probably conveyed to Shakespeare, either directly or indirectly, in the period of the late plays. That Sidney and Jonson were joined by Gosson, Whetstone, and Nashe in criticizing the sprawling nature of dramatized romance suggests the ubiquity of the neoclassical critique and the concern that early Jacobean dramatists would have had to find proper theatrical instruments for staging romance material.[68] Only an ahistorical, romantic division between the "theoretical" Jonson and the "natural" Shakespeare would allow us to separate Shakespeare from his theatrical context, in which theories of Italian dramaturgy were circulating.

It is important to be precise about Guarini and his milieu, because most studies of Renaissance tragicomedy present a rather impoverished view of tragicomedic dramaturgy. Many of these studies date from the 1970s, at the height of the "metatheatrical" approach to theater. Consequently, we learn again and again that tragicomedy is distinguished by its artifice, self-consciousness, and display of its own theatrical mechanisms.[69] Notwithstanding tragicomedy's anticipation of baroque self-display, the pleasures of such metatheatrical devices may be more apparent to late-twentieth-century critics than they were to late-Renaissance audiences. Critics have also stressed the dramaturgical connections between Renaissance and modern tragicomedy and have explored the unstable oscillations between audience detachment and engagement anticipatory of a Pinter or a Beckett. Because one person's engagement, however, may be another person's detachment, this approach also lacks historical specificity. Marxist critics like Walter Cohen have provided important analyses of the social and economic contradictions mystified in the resolutions of tragicomedy.[70] They tend, however, to focus on plot, and in so doing also give an impoverished account of the various dramaturgical techniques with which tragicomedy achieves resolution. The road from conflict to resolution in tragicomedy is complex and subtle, especially in the mediatory use of pastoral, and needs to be carefully studied in its own terms before (or while) formulating political readings. For example, whereas I will attempt to argue that the nuanced adjustment of audience response constitutes an important tragicomedic technique, interesting in its own right, Marxist critics dismiss the pathos of tragicomedy as merely emotional pandering or "symptomatic" of political mystification.[71] The "symptomatic" approach to Renaissance drama risks simplifying the nuances and complexity of theatrical practice. Dramaturgical practices surely are related to cultural and political pressures, but as a theater practitioner Shakespeare could have been interested in a theatrical practice for the sake of a technical solution to a dramaturgical problem.

ANALOGOUS FORMS: THE MASQUE, ROMANCE, AND *PERICLES*

At this point, it will also be useful to consider the relationship of tragicomedy with the English masque, to contrast my approach with those of "romance" criticism, and to explain why I give less attention to *Pericles* than to the other late plays, despite its customary grouping with them.

As did Italian tragicomedy, the masque appealed to the tastes of Queen Anne and other members of James's court. Both forms dramatize discord and low-comic disruption, and may be seen to reflect Jacobean absolutism in their totalizing harmonies. If the English masque partially derives from the Italian *intermezzi*, tragicomedy is also related to the grand Italian mythological entertainments, for they played an especially important role between the acts of tragicomedies like *Il pastor fido*. Even in the more conservative Italian climate, however, tragicomedy is more socially and politically supple than the *intermezzi*. The dramatic form is not without hints of pastoral egalitarianism and is less neatly identifiable than the *intermezzi* with religious and/or political absolutism—the playwright's dramaturgy reflecting ducal power less obviously than the sumptuous *intermezzi* financed by the sovereign. Whereas wonder is certainly the chief audience response that the *intermezzi* and masque are designed to elicit, it is only one of the responses elicited in the internal and external audiences of the late plays, as critics who incorrectly conflate the masque and tragicomedy fail to see.[72] Whereas the *intermezzi* and the masque give free rein to the representation of mythological supernaturalism, tragicomedy carefully negotiates the claims of verisimilitude and the marvelous. The forms of the masque and tragicomedy are comparable in the degree to which theatrical technologies (stage decor, machinery, and music in the masque, dramaturgical devices in tragicomedy) appear to "solve" existential and political problems, but Italian and especially Shakespearean tragicomedy also dramatize the limitations of such technologies. If the masque's triumph over discord and evil appears to be sudden and complete, it is not so in tragicomedy, as the sudden dissolution of the wedding masque and then the exclusion of Antonio, Sebastian, and Caliban from Prospero's grand reconciliation at the end of *The Tempest* most clearly shows. If the not-so-hidden protagonist of the Stuart masque is King James, lent absolute power over his world within the Whitehall fictions, protagonists of tragicomedy such as Arbaces in *A King and No King*, Leontes, and Prospero have distinctly limited control over their fates.

My purpose here is not to substitute the term "tragicomedy" for "romance" as a biological classification for Shakespeare's late plays. Nor would I wish to undercut the rich "romance" interpretations of the late plays provided by such great critics as Northrop Frye, Leo Salingar, Howard Felperin, and Stanley Wells.[73] Both "tragicomedy" and "romance" will surely persist as interpretive paradigms for the late plays, the latter term probably more frequently than the former. My study aims to supply a more precise understanding of the former term, too often carelessly invoked in being stretched from Euripides to Beckett. There are, however, some advantages to "tragicomedy."

Unlike "tragicomedy," "romance" was not a term of dramatic nomenclature and so not a consciously considered dramatic genre. And indeed, most romance critics of the late plays use the term modally and not generically. From Edward Dowden's use of "romance" to convey what he saw as the plays' serene optimism to Fredric Jameson's notion that romance in general seeks to provide imaginary solutions to real but unprecedented social and cultural contradictions, "romance" says little about dramaturgical practice (the province of a genre, as suggested in the Jonson title page) but much about tone, attitude, and point of view.[74] As Barbara Mowat has pointed out, the late plays do inherit from medieval and Renaissance nondramatic romance the practice of narrative exposition.[75] More central to *Pericles* than to the three succeeding plays, however, narration hardly exhausts the plays' dramaturgy.

The late plays undeniably employ romance plots, or material, although the same can be said of *The Comedy of Errors* and *Twelfth Night*. Many of the important sources of these plays are romance poems, novels, or plays. Leo Salingar argues that roughly a third of the plays performed by English professional actors in the first twenty years of Shakespeare's life would have been stage romances, judging from the evidence of recorded titles.[76] In both Shakespeare's late plays and the Hellenistic, medieval, and Renaissance romance narratives available to Shakespeare and his audience the following "romance" elements can be found: an expanse of time and space greater than that of the comedies and tragedies (whether enacted or established by narrative, as in *The Tempest*); a generally schematic, typological presentation of character that turns away from the psychological realism of the tragedies; and the suspension of the laws of cause and effect by supernatural agency (if sometimes only apparently, as in *The Winter's Tale*). And of course many plot elements of the late plays—tempests, improbable adventures, a general woe-to-weal trajectory, the reuniting of severed families— derive from romance. As Salingar has shown, the trial and patience of the maligned and often exiled "exemplary" protagonist cut off from but eventually reunited with her or his family would have been very familiar to Shakespeare in his youth.[77] If the late plays, as I shall argue, are characterized by an insistently "pathetic" quality, this might derive from medieval exemplary romance. But the labor of Renaissance playwrighting, as Riccardo Scrivano has argued, lay precisely in giving dramaturgical expression to romance material, and here "tragicomedy" is more historically informative than romance.[79] Not to discipline romance material with the proper dramaturgical technology was to incur the criticism of Sidney, Nashe, Jonson, and others.

The insights of romance criticism need to be refocused by the terms of tragicomedic dramaturgy, which provide a historical framework. For example, if the marvelous and the supernatural are important elements of romance, tragicomedic dramaturgy carefully negotiates the verisimilar and the nonverisimilar, as I will discuss in chapter 4. If romance criticism has discussed, in either reverent or debunking terms, the providentiality of the late plays, the Italian dramatic theorists conceive of providence as a dramaturgical, tragicomedic translation of tragedic fate. Because pastoral, as Fredric Jameson has argued, is a "partial [segment] of the romance paradigm," many insights of romance criticism can be explained in the pastoral terms congenial to the late Renaissance, particularly the utopianism and satirical antiutopianism of the late plays.[79]

Romance criticism has moved a long way from Dowden's optimism, but it must to some degree work against itself in order to account for the dark and discordant aspects of the late plays. Asking the provocative question "When is Romance no longer Romance?" Howard Felperin argues that romance contains the seeds of its own critique, acknowledging its own artifice and the limitations of its own utopianism.[80] For Felperin, romance incorporates and continually offsets the pleasure principle and the reality principle. Harry Berger's brilliant and seminal debunking of sentimental *Tempest* interpretations is still a piece of romance criticism, because it depends on so many of its terms.[81] But the tragical-comical-pastoral-satirical modal alignment of the late plays (a feature of tragicomedy) effectively accounts for their inner tensions and multiple perspectives. Instead of arguing, with Steven Mullaney, that romance replaces satire in the late plays, I would prefer to see a redistribution and continual negotiation of different dramatic modalities; satire may be diminished, but it is still present.[82] Many of Shakespeare's adaptations, in *The Winter's Tale*, of Greene's romance *Pandosto* amount to translating romance material into the terms of dramatic modes, which lends a tragical-pastoral-comical alignment to the romance material. As Stanley Wells has shown, *The Winter's Tale* "is less of a romance than *Pandosto*," largely because of the increased agency lent the characters— tragedic in the case of Leontes, comedic in the case of Camillo.[83]

Sharply differentiated from the satiric *Timon of Athens* in tone, point of view, subject matter, and dramaturgy, *Pericles* initiates a postsatiric phase in Shakespearean drama, which draws extensively on the plot motifs of exemplary romance. It is thus sensible for critics to group the play with *Cymbeline*, *The Winter's Tale*, and *The Tempest*. I do, in fact, discern important elements of tragicomedic dramaturgy in the play: a tragicomedic despair-to-felicity plot reminiscent of the Council of Virginia quotation (see p. 31); an emphasis, not on heroic, tragic defiance nor on comic craftiness, but on patience and suffering typical of pastoral figures as well as exemplary romance protagonists; the eliciting of wonder rather than tragic terror; the replaying and reformulation of tragedy (in its most classic form, the oedipal incest myth); and, to be discussed in chapter 10, the purifying and sublimating of low, mercenary comedy in the brothel scene, which has all of the characters (a bawd, a pander, a supposed prostitute) of low comedy but none of the results or the tonalities. Still, I attend less to *Pericles* than to the other plays, because it lacks certain dramaturgical practices of tragicomedy as I have begun to define them. If, following the implicit theory of tragicomedic practice as indicated in the Jonson title page, the advanced genre is tied to an advanced theater, *Pericles* cannot be associated with the Blackfriars as can the other three plays. Written in 1607 or 1608, it preceded the King's Men's assumption of the Blackfriars lease by as much as a year, and so could not have been influenced by the anticipation of a new audience and new theatrical conditions. Secondly, it is not modally pastoral in anything but the vaguest sense. One might possibly argue that the fishermen in act 2, scene 1, are pastoral speakers in a very broad sense, reading the land symbolically and promoting a radical egalitarianism.[84] This is a short moment, however; pastoral is not established as a genuinely alternative point of view to the court or city as it is in the succeeding plays. The various places through which the episodic play rapidly moves are summarily established in the manner of medieval *decor simultané* staging, without the attitudinal and atmospheric fullness that characterizes the tragic, comic, satiric, or pastoral modes of the other late plays. Shakespeare increasingly tightens his dramaturgy from the episodic arrangement of *Pericles* to the sprawling but centripetal modal multiplicity of *Cymbeline* to the modally tripartite *The Winter's Tale* to the distilled unities of *The Tempest*. *Pericles* is the least dramaturgically sophisticated of the four plays, staying closest to its romance source by dramatizing romance narrative in the person of Gower himself. That it retains a crucial feature of Renaissance romance narrative as well as an archaic method of staging suggests that it lacks other sophisticated tragicomedic technologies implemented a generation after the period when dramatic romance held sway.

My study pursues the implications of my earlier five assertions about genres and modes as extrapolated from the Jonson title page.

(See p. 18.) Chapter 2 continues to lay the foundation for Italian-English comparison by examining the reception of Italian drama in Shakespeare's London via both "high" and "low" theater, and thus attempts to place tragicomedy in its historical context. It also investigates the adaptability of the Blackfriars theater to tragicomedic dramaturgy, and thus the relationship between a theatrical context and a genre. Chapter 3 argues that Cinquecento genre theory was potentially innovative and connected with practice. It distinguishes between different levels on which genre mediates between text/performance and reader/spectator: affective, cognitive, and ethical or social—a threefold scheme that organizes chapters 6 through 10. Because the pastoral mode is central to tragicomedic dramaturgy, the next two chapters explore historical and dramaturgical aspects of Italian pastoral and the ways in which pastoral serves a tragicomedic purpose in Shakespeare's late plays. Chapter 4 pursues pastoral drama in general, and chapter 5 the tragicomedic function of the pastoral satyr figure from the Greek satyr play to Italian pastoral drama to Caliban in *The Tempest*. Emphasizing the similarities between Shakespeare and the Italians, chapter 6 explores the *affective* audience responses elicited by tragicomedy: nuanced responses between the extremes of tragic terror and comic laughter. The next two chapters investigate the *cognitive* mediations of genres and modes. Chapter 7 considers the connection between place and genre— the ways in which generic and modal signals establish "horizons of expectation" for the audience.[85] Emphasizing the differences between Shakespeare and the Italians, chapter 8 considers the tragical-comical-satirical-pastoral modal alignment of Renaissance tragicomedy, and the various debates and dialogues between modal points of view possible in the genre, which do not produce as harmonious a synthesis in Shakespearean as in Italian tragicomedy. Chapter 9 turns to the social and ethical dimensions of Renaissance tragicomedy, and examines *The Winter's Tale* in the light of Guarini's theories about the social and political mediations possible in tragicomedy. Chapter 10 explores the social dimensions of comedic residue in Renaissance tragicomedy, from Guarini's uneasy relationship to the *commedia dell'arte* to low-comic registers in the late plays to the function of *arte*-like elements in *The Tempest*.

Any genre-oriented comparative study necessarily treats both similarities and differences between the various objects of comparison; strategic reasons dictate whether one emphasizes resemblances or divergences at any given point. I often emphasize similarities because they have received the least attention and help place Shakespeare in an international dramatic context. But the Italian theory and practice, it should be acknowledged, lacks the experiential and political fissures of Shakespearean drama. Guarini and other Italians retain a supreme confidence in the dramaturgy and the technology of the theater. The felicitous resolution of tragedic conflicts in the arena of pastoral tends to be largely a formal problem in the Italian arena. Notwithstanding the tensions between modes and their points of view dramatized in the Italian hybrid, Guarinian tragicomedy ultimately aims to blend the kinds in a unified resolution. In Shakespeare's late plays, the differences between the constituent modes remain sharper. Shakespearean tragicomedy is more modally tragic, more comic, and more satiric than its Italian cousin, and thus approaches modern tragicomedy in some respects. And pastoral is "harder," more capacious, and more capable of admitting tragic modalities in Shakespearean than in Italian tragicomedy. The modes of Shakespeare's late plays are not always as harmoniously mixed as they are in the Italian arena, so that the plays yield grotesquely tragicomic moments such as the mauling of Antigonus by a bear in *The Winter's Tale* and Imogen's mistaking Cloten's body for that of Posthumus in *Cymbeline*. Furthermore, because English theater was performed for an audience of a much wider social and economic range, it is more capable of dramatizing diverse and destabilizing political perspectives.

2

Italian-English Transmissions
and English Contexts

Shakespeare's interest in tragicomedy in the pastoral mode may certainly be explained independently of Italian influence. The Italian model does not "cause" early-Stuart pastoral tragicomedy but reflects largely independent yet parallel developments in genres, modes, and theater audiences. Still, it is important to consider the particular cases of direct Italian-English transmission and to place Shakespeare in the context of his English contemporaries Daniel, Marston, Fletcher, and Jonson, each of whom did consciously imitate Italian tragicomedy—if with varying degrees of license. And if Italian theatergrams may well have been transmitted via the *commedia dell'arte* stage as well as the *commedia erudita* page, we must examine the *commedia dell'arte* as a possible conduit of international transmission, particularly in regard to a popular species of pastoral tragicomedy that bears striking external resemblances to *The Tempest*. Finally, this chapter will explore the relationship between English tragicomedy and the Blackfriars theater: the conjunction of the most advanced genre with the most advanced theatrical space.

Shakespeare had many ways of learning about both Italy and Italian drama: from the performance of Italian plays in the universities and in London, from books in private libraries, from reports of English travelers recently returned from Italy or from Italian émigrés living in London (some of whom had fled Italy to escape religious persecution), and from conversations or accounts of conversations with Shakespeare's Italian counterparts, actors of the *commedia dell'arte*. Two London venues in particular might have provided meetings with Italians. On his way to the playhouse Shakespeare would have passed the Oliphant (possibly transformed into the Elephant of *Twelfth Night*), a Bankside inn that served an Italian clientele.[1] And as Roger Ascham describes in the *Schoolmaster*, many Englishmen practiced their Italian at St. Thomas of Acon, the Italian Protestant church in London.[2]

Shakespeare certainly knew John Florio, the most prominent Italian in London and son of the first minister at St. Thomas of Acon. By 1594, Florio had entered the service of Shakespeare's patron, the earl of Southampton, as an Italian tutor. His library, containing works of Giraldi, Bandello, Boccaccio, Aretino, Machiavelli, Ariosto, Sannazaro, and Castiglione, almost certainly included Italian plays, even those of relatively obscure Italian dramatists such as Luigi Groto. From a study of Florio's 1611 dictionary *The World of Words*, Frances Yates notes the high number of dramatic works that Florio must have known.[3] Most importantly, his library is said to have contained many *commedia dell'arte* scenarios.[4] If Florio's Italian-English dictionary *A Worlde of Wordes*, his renowned library, and his conversation furnished his friend Ben Jonson with Italian literary references and with details of Venetian life put to good use in *Volpone*, it is not hard to imagine Florio performing similar service for Shakespeare.[5]

Around the time of Shakespeare's arrival in London the influence of Italian literature among intellectually curious Englishmen would have been at its height. Italian tutors and university education had made Italian texts accessible to a larger public. Especially important in disseminating Italian literature to an English public was the press of John Wolfe. Wolfe was a printer and publisher who had combated the monopolies of privileged printers and eventually won the right to print particular patented texts. He had worked in a Florentine printing house and brought with him to England a font of Italian type. The notoriety of his reputation increased when, in the late 1580s, he published, in Italian and under fictitious imprints, the works of two authors banned by the Inquisition that would have been of great interest to English readers: Pietro Aretino's five comedies and Machiavelli's *Clizia* and *Mandragola*.[6]

A close associate of Wolfe was Giacopo Castelvetro, an Italian émigré who had been persecuted by the Inquisition (thus a likely worshipper at the Italian church led by Florio's father) and nephew of the famous Aristotelian critic Lodovico Castelvetro. Castelvetro's courtly and literary circle included the queen herself, to whom he dedicated an edition of the first two cantos, in Latin, of Tasso's *Gerusalemma Liberata*. He tutored many Englishmen in Italian, including James I and Queen Anne. Between 1584 and 1592 Castelvetro edited eight Italian books published by Wolfe. The most important of these joint ventures, for our purposes, was a duodecimo volume of Guarini's *Il pastor fido* and Tasso's *Aminta*, printed in 1591. According to the dedicatory letter written by Castelvetro to Sir Charles Blount, the plays were published in response to a felt demand among Londoners for Guarini's avant-garde play, which had been published in Venice only a year earlier. As Castelvetro writes, the fame of Guarini's play had quickly reached England, and many "choice wits" of London had asked Castelvetro to obtain copies for them. Unable to procure more than one copy from Italy, he decided to print the coveted work in England, along with Tasso's *Aminta*.[7]

The edition seems to have been well received in London. Gabriel Harvey, for example, was closely associated with Wolfe's press and avidly read the plays, judging by the copious annotations that he made in his copy. From his involvement in the Martin Marprelate controversy, from his literary polemics with Nashe, and through mutual acquaintances John Florio and John Eliot, Shakespeare was likely to have been aware of Harvey's literary opinions.[8] A more important conduit of Guarini to England was Samuel Daniel, whose literary relationship with Shakespeare is well established.[9] Daniel learned Italian from John Florio at Oxford in the early 1580s and became known for his extensive knowledge of Italian literature and interest in new continental experiments. His translation of the famous golden-age chorus from Tasso's *Aminta* was published in his 1601 *Works*. In 1590–91, his then patron Sir Edward Dymoke took the twenty-eight-year-old Daniel on a tour of Italy, where they met with Guarini.[10] As Elizabeth Story Donno remarks, "The two Englishmen must have felt as if they were the literary vanguard for their countrymen."[11] Daniel was the first to introduce the masque to the Stuart court, with his *Vision of the Twelve Goddesses*, staged on 8 January 1604: a full year before the first Jones-Jonson collaboration. Although Jonson somewhat disingenuously discounted his own debt to Italian court entertainments in his classicizing apologias for the new form, of the two rivals Daniel was the unabashedly "modern" writer. In a letter prefacing his edition of his masque, Daniel argued against Jonson for the modern writer's independence from the ancients, which for Daniel only heightened the importance of contemporary Italian authors.[12]

Daniel seems to have been closely involved in the first English translation of *Il pastor fido*, published in 1602. The first edition of the translation was entered in the Stationer's Register by Simon Waterson, a long-time publisher and good friend of Daniel, and was introduced by Daniel's commendatory poem to Sir Edward Dymoke. The translator of the play wrote another introductory poem, identifying himself only as a "kinsman" of Sir Edward.[13] In 1604, Daniel became connected with a private boys'-theater company that would be associated with Italian tragicomedy on two other occasions from 1604 to 1608. A February 1604 patent changed the name of the Children of the Chapel Royal to the Children of the Queen's Revels, and appointed Daniel as the licenser of the company. In that same year, the boys performed Daniel's tragedy *Philotas* at the Blackfriars theater. Daniel's favor with Queen Anne apparently gained him little, for he was called into the Privy Council and interrogated about perceived references to the Essex affair in the play. Recurring to what he perceived as a less political form and perhaps prompted by the evident success of the 1602 "Dymoke" translation, in 1605 Daniel wrote the first avowed imitation of Guarini's play in England. First performed in August 1605 as *Arcadia Reformed* and published in the following year as the *Queenes Arcadia*, a "Pastorall Tragicomaedie," the play was written for Queen Anne of Denmark and performed before her and her husband James I by students at Oxford along with three Latin plays. Daniel's play seems to have been the best received of the four; it was well pitched for its audience, Queen Anne, who was very enamored of *Il pastor fido*.[14] Daniel, then, introduced two fashionable Italianate forms to the Stuart court: tragicomedy and the court masque.

Both contemporary and twentieth-century critics have faulted Daniel for too closely imitating Guarini and thus affecting Italian literary airs, just as Roger Ascham lambasted young English travelers for aping Italian fashions. But even Guarini's closest English imitator forged an individual and critical response to the idea of tragicomedy. Guarini, Daniel remembered later in the introductory poem to the Dymoke translation, arrogantly deprecated the capacities of English verse relative to Italian poetry. In the dedicatory poem of the 1594 *Cleopatra*, Daniel issued an implicit retort to Guarini, wishing that Italians could better know English verse, so "that they might know how far Thames doth out-go / The Musick of Declynéd Italie. . . ."[15] Daniel's innovation, which anticipates that of Marston, is to extend the purview of satire beyond that imagined by the Italian playwrights, thus responding to a modal alignment later clarified in the Jonson title page. Daniel's Arcadia is full of the city and the court. Anticipating Shakespeare's "satyrist"

Autolycus in *The Winter's Tale*, Daniel's Techne attempts to corrupt the country rubes with various female luxury items produced in the city: "complexions, dressings, tiffanies, and tyres" (1.3.285). Alcon, the quacksalver, distinctly evokes the Italian mountebank, the epitome of mercenary theatricality who many recent theater historians (and in fact Ben Jonson as well, in *Volpone*) see as anticipating the professional *commedia dell'arte*.[16] Like Jonson's Scoto of Mantua, Daniel's mountebank in Arcadia assumes a "surly grave Doctorall aspect" to sell drugs that "come from farre" (3.1.1106): tobacco, in Alcon's case. Guarini's *Arcadia* does include a corrupted *femme de la cité*, Corisca, but Daniel goes further in the satiric mode by staging an element that is largely excluded from Guarinian tragicomedy—mercenary theater—and giving it a topicality resonant for the tobacco-hating king.

According to Ben Jonson, by middecade Guarini had become second only to Montaigne in influence upon English writers. In Jonson's *Volpone*, probably first performed in February 1606 at the Globe, the consummate comparatist Lady Politic Would-Be makes the following claim:

> All our English writers,
> I mean, such as are happy in the Italian,
> Will deign to steal out of this author, mainly;
> Almost as much as from Montaignié:
> He has so modern and facile a vein,
> Fitting the time, and catching the court ear.
>
> (3.4.87–92)[17]

If Sir Politic Would-Be represents the indiscriminate English traveler in Italy, his wife stands for the uncritical English reader of Italian texts. In the context of an early-Stuart quarrel between the ancients and the moderns, Jonson here surely was rebuking his rival Daniel and the *Queenes Arcadia*. Indeed, in the preface to his 1606 *Hymenaei*, Jonson looked back both to *The Vision of the Twelve Goddesses* and to the *Queenes Arcadia*, and criticized Daniel's use of "a few Italian herbes, pick'd up, and made into a sallade."[18] But Jonson's ire at what he, unfairly, perceived to be Daniel's slavish imitation of modern Italian drama did not prevent him from interest in the idea of Italian tragicomedy, for he later praised Fletcher's *Faithful Shepherdess* in a commendatory poem to the first quarto edition of the play.[19] And as we shall see, in the late *Sad Shepherd* Jonson himself critically responded to the generic "invitation to form" by contesting Guarini's and Fletcher's proscription of popular dimensions.[20]

Lady Politic Would-Be points to more than one English imitator of Guarini, and indeed the Dymoke translation seems to have had an appeal beyond the walls of the court or university. One of those closer to Shakespeare's theatrical milieu who was apparently interested in the latest experiments from overseas was the satirist and private-theater playwright John Marston. Marston, whose mother was the daughter of an Italian surgeon who settled in London, beautified his 1599 *Antonio and Mellida* with Italian madrigalesque exchanges and adapted Sforza Oddi's *I morti vivi* into his *What You Will*. Now Marston's *Antonio and Mellida* and *Antonio's Revenge*, which were performed in the private theaters by children's companies, are modally tragicomic in their parodic use of high-tragic style and diction. But as G. K. Hunter has shown, Marston seems to have been interested in the tragicomedic genre as well as the tragicomic mode. Marston was probably responsible for the designation of the 1604 *Malcontent* as a "Tragicomoedia" in the Stationer's Register. And according to Hunter, some passages in Marston's play are close echoes of the Dymoke translation—not surprisingly of some of the satirical passages.[21] Judging by the mercurial relationship between Jonson and Marston, it would not be hard to believe that Marston was a second target in the Lady Would-Be quote. Marston's innovation was to all but reject the pastoral mode of tragicomedy as figured in the Jonson title page and to pursue the satiric mode much more than Daniel ever would—indeed, about as far as one could take it. And unlike Daniel and the Italian playwrights in the Counter-Reformation climate of late-sixteenth-century Italy (who create a theocratic but not specifically political Arcadia in the closed aristocratic environment of the Italian courts) Marston transforms tragicomedy into a political vehicle by situating the action in the court of an usurped but vengeful ruler. This politicizing of Italian tragicomedy is a generic innovation certainly relevant to Shakespeare's late plays.

Probably in 1603 or early 1604, Marston's play was performed by the Children of the Queen's Revels (the company for which Daniel had served as licenser) at the private Blackfriars theater. In 1604, the play was appropriated by the King's Men and performed at the Globe with an induction written by John Webster.[22] Shakespeare's company was then apparently interested in Marston's "tragicomoedia" of Guarinian influence. And *The Malcontent* seems to have influenced Shakespeare's *Measure for Measure* (1604) with the caustic, satiric Lucio and its theme of the hidden ruler. Hunter argues that verbal echoes of the Dymoke translation may also be found in *All's Well That Ends Well* and detects aspects of Guarinian tragicomic effects in *Measure for Measure*.[23] The strong controller figure of *The Malcontent* and *Measure for Measure*, who behind the scenes reestablishes social roles as if they were parts in a play, certainly does represent a decline from the absolute power of the tragedic sovereign, and does anticipate the era of the weaker tragicomedic protagonist.[24] In their harsh ironic juxtapositions of tonalities and generic structures, *All's Well That Ends Well*, *Troilus and Cressida*, and especially *Measure for Measure* are modally tragicomic—indeed, probably more so than any other group of Shakespeare's plays.[25] Although Marston could well have furnished Shakespeare with an indirect account of Guarini's theories, what Shakespeare seems to have actually appropriated from Marston in this period is less the generic idea of Italian tragicomedy, which emphasizes the pastoral mode, than the tragicomic mode with a heavily satiric register.

It was John Fletcher, his younger colleague with the King's Men, who probably furnished Shakespeare the most important source of information about Guarinian tragicomedy, and who might have incited him to attempt tragicomedy in the pastoral mode. Shakespeare must have been interested in the dramaturgical approaches of a man with whom he would collaborate in *Two Noble Kinsmen*, probably *Henry VIII*, and possibly the lost *Cardenio*. Fletcher introduced pastoral tragicomedy to the commercial stage with his *Faithful Shepherdess*, written in 1608–9, performed at the Second Blackfriars around 1609 by the Children of the Queen's Revels, and published in 1609–10. It was a notorious failure with a private-theater audience that turned out to be less sophisticated and less attuned to the avant-garde than Fletcher had hoped, but a group of commendatory poems to the printed edition of the play shows that it was well liked by contemporary poets and playwrights. According to Philip Finkelpearl, Fletcher's interest in pastoral literature and tragicomedy seems to have derived from several sources: not only his cousins Giles and Phineas, but also George Chapman, a friend of Fletcher who wrote a pastoral tragedy in 1599 and a commendatory verse for *The Faithful Shepherdess*. Fletcher and his future collaborator Beaumont knew Marston well. And Fletcher's brother Nathaniel, who until 1606 served as chaplain to Sir Henry Wotton in Venice (where Guarini periodically lived and where many of his works were published) might have also informed him about the Italian genre.[26]

Embittered over the play's failure, Fletcher introduced the 1609–10 edition of *The Faithful Shepherdess* with an arch note "To the Reader," in which he castigates the unsophisticated tastes of his theatrical public. Conceiving genres to be closely connected with audience response, as does Guarini, Fletcher begins by announcing the name of the new form—pastoral tragicomedy—and the demands that it places on its audiences. Similarly to Guarini in his rejection of the low comedy, Fletcher disdains popular, traditional pastoral, with its "whitsun ales, creame, wassel and morris-dances" and real shepherds.[27] And yet Fletcher's proscription of popular elements is not only motivated by an antiplebeian animus but also by his belief that real country shepherds are incapable of eliciting the fictional, social, and tonal suppleness promised by the new form. Pastoral tragicomedy does not treat "country hired Shepheards" but fashions a "representation of shepheards and shephearddesses, with their actions and passions, which must be such as may agree with their natures, at least not exceeding former fictions, and vulgar traditions." Fletcher thus claims a certain degree of fictional license for his shepherds, "as all the ancient Poets and moderne of understanding have receaved them," recalling both Guarini's view that shepherds may be based on previous fictional accounts of them and his belief that tragicomedy is a form less tied to history than tragedy (*Il Verato*, 3:189). This is to at least partially understand Guarini's modalization of pastoral, by which the shepherd is not limited to a mimetic representation but functions as a symbolic speaker capable of imitating actions appropriate to various generic registers. Fletcher argues that his shepherds must be "the owners of flockes but not hyerlings," which squares with Guarini's view that a socially elevated position must be accorded to shepherds if they are to be capable of tragedic or tragicomedic action (244). Like Guarini, Fletcher opposes the mere juxtaposition of tragedy and comedy ("[shepherds] sometimes laughing together, and sometimes killing one another"), but seeks a calibrated *negotiation* of death superior to that of earlier "mungrell tragicomedy": "in respect it wants deaths, which is inough to make it no tragedie, yet brings some neere it, which is inough to make it no comedie." Sensitive to the neoclassical critique of the mixing of tragedy and comedy, Fletcher aims for dramaturgical precision.

In casting his bucolic protagonists as learned in various humanist arts, Fletcher may be drawing on the prologue to *Il pastor fido*,[28] but in making them privy to the magical "vertues of hearbs, and fountaines," Fletcher gives more emphasis than Guarini does to the nonverisimilar aspects of pastoral prevalent in both contemporary *commedia erudita* and the *commedia dell'arte*. In the magical devices of the Sullen Shepherd and Amarillis, Fletcher's play does dramatize supernaturalism, although diminished in power from that of tragedy (e.g., *Macbeth*) to an appropriately tragicomedic level. Whereas Guarini only allows full-fledged gods in the framing prologues and *intermezzi* (only admitting two humans with distantly divine descent in the play itself), Fletcher breaks neo-Aristotelian decorum with his River God, and justifies it in the note: "a God is as lawfull in this as in a tragedie, and meane people as in a comedie."

Fletcher apparently failed with *The Faithful Shepherdess* for the same reason that Beaumont failed with *The Knight of the Burning Pestle*, also performed by the Children of the Queen's Revels at the Blackfriars. By satirizing citizen manners and theatrical taste, Beaumont had overestimated the sophistication of the private-theater audience, neglecting the fact that some of the theatergoers actually *were* citizens. Similarly, by rarefying pastoral of all of its popular-festive strains except the vestigial supernaturalism mentioned above, Fletcher insufficiently attended to the heterogeneity of his audience. By including, in *The Winter's Tale*, realistic shepherds and the kind of popular pastoral traditions rejected by Fletcher, Shakespeare gauged his audience much better than Fletcher—and not only the Globe audience but that of the Blackfriars as well. To be sure, Shakespeare has it both ways, socially sublimating the shepherds in the final act in a manner akin to the aristocratic fantasy of a classless society operative in Guarinian tragicomedy. Shakespeare takes further than Fletcher the implications of pastoral as a mode not tied to external appurtenances. To use pastoral modally is to permit popular as well as courtly manifestations, and to have a much better chance of success with diverse audiences.

In their 1609 *Philaster* and their 1611 *A King and No King*, Beaumont and Fletcher certainly made successful adjustments and concessions to the tastes of both public- and private-theater audiences, at the same time when Shakespeare was writing *Cymbeline*, *The Winter's Tale*, and *The Tempest*.[29] Critical analysis of *Philaster* and *A King and No King*, as well as the other collaborations of Beaumont and Fletcher, has shaped our understanding of "Jacobean tragicomedy" according to various "metatheatrical" characteristics of tragicomedic dramaturgy: the continual manipulation of audience engagement and detachment, protean characters, rhetorical and emotional self-display, theatrical self-consciousness, and the resolution of potential catastrophe by improbable and paradoxical *coups de théâtre*. Certainly the masterpieces of Beaumont and Fletcher have much in common with Shakespeare's late plays and share some of their dramaturgical practices.[30] In particular, the royal protagonists of these plays all have significantly limited power relative to their world, such that their heroic diction is made to seem mere bluster. As tragicomedic rather than tragedic protagonists, they lack the dignity and pity of a Lear flailing at the heavens. In *A King and No King*, Arbaces wonders that his courtiers do not obey his wild commands— "Why, here they stand like death; / My word moves nothing" (1.1.312– 13)—just as the passionate Leontes is dumbfounded at the disobedience of Paulina in *The Winter's Tale* (act 2, scene 3).[31] Certainly the Shakespearean protagonists, Posthumus in particular, display shifts of passion, although not as exaggerated as those of Beaumont and Fletcher's heroes. Other disjunctions between pretension and reality supply many modally tragicomic features in the plays of Shakespeare and his younger colleagues during this period.

But whereas pastoral in *The Faithful Shepherdess* is a symbolically resonant world in the manner of Shakespearean pastoral, referred to as "purged," "holy," and "virtuous," Fletcher all but abandons pastoral in his collaborations with Beaumont. The long forest scene in act 4 of *Philaster* does not stage a symbolically and atmospherically alternative place to the court, a modal world elsewhere with pastoral attitudes and tonalities. Satire does not shift into a pastoral framework, as it does in Shakespeare. The court satirists accompanying the king on his hunt quickly remake the country into the court, as the analogous satiric figures Antonio and Sebastian do not successfully do in *The Tempest*, countered as they are by Gonzalo's not-so-foolish pastoral vision. Whereas Shakespeare tempers satiric extremes under the aegis of pastoral, Beaumont and Fletcher more directly follow the harsh satiric tradition of Jonson and Marston.[32] Unlike the boys in *Cymbeline* or the shepherds in *The Winter's Tale*, the country fellow of *Philaster* offers no new pastoral perspective but merely functions as an instrument of plot. When pastoral functions as a signifying microcosm, it evokes either escapism, as in Arbaces's "I will live / In woods and talk to trees" (1.1.263–64), or irony at the expense of the rustics, such as when Philaster wishes he had taken a mountain girl and "borne at her big breasts / My large coarse issue" (4.3.11–12).[33]

In general, Beaumont and Fletcher do not construct multiple, generically coded "worlds" that supply contrasting points of view; they concentrate on the single, suspenseful, well-made plot as their response to early-Stuart imperatives for a dramaturgically coherent tragicomedic form. The effect of the suspenseful plot is not to create wonder—one of the intended effects of Italian and Shakespearean tragicomedy—but rather surprise. Still, Beaumont and Fletcher do establish the dominant pattern of English tragicomedy from 1610 to 1642, and it will be important in the present study to note both similarities and differences between their work and that of Shakespeare.

Especially because of the importance of the Jonson title page, brief mention should be made of the other conscious imitation of Italian pastoral tragicomedy in England: Jonson's late, curious, and incomplete play *The Sad Shepherd*. Not published until after 1640, three years after Jonson's death, the play emerges in the context of the Caroline revival of pastoral drama (Henrietta Maria reprising Queen Anne's patronage of the fashionable form), which dates from the revival of *The Faithful Shepherdess* in 1633 at court and at the Blackfriars. Jonson seems familiar with Guarini's theory as transmitted through Fletcher: Marian's address to the shepherds as "no others' hireling" (2.5.16) echoes a phrase from "To the Reader" itself appropriated from the Italian theorist.[34] Jonson's correction, in the genre-defining prologue, of the "heresy" that pastorals cannot be comedic would certainly make sense as a response to Tasso and Guarini's emphasis on the tragedic potentiality of pastoral. He promises his reader or viewer a copious range of emotional tonalities such as rendered pastoral an appropriate tragicomedic medium: "You shall have love and hate and jealousy, / As well as mirth and rage and melancholy" (prologue 49–50). But Jonson's most significant response to Guarini as well as to his former rival Daniel is to recast pastoral in a popular form; as his dramatic material he uses the popular theme of Robin Hood, subject of much medieval popular drama, and he has his "low" characters speak a Yorkshire or Low Scots dialect. As with Italian pastoral, an index of the popular quality of the play is its frequent use of the supernatural, although, like Fletcher, Jonson only renders the evil characters capable of Ovidian metamorphoses. Popular pastoral can be included in this erudite play because of Jonson's own role in the Stuart appropriation of old holiday pastimes.[35] The royal appropriation of popular festivity drew on the aesthetic of nostalgia—best expressed by Robin as he remembers the old country traditions (1.4.40–47).

Each of the three most popular dramatists in the seventeenth century, then, attempted a version of tragicomedy in the pastoral mode. Only Fletcher disallowed popular strains, although the presence of supernatural phenomena (associated with popular, rather than the neo-Aristotelian, drama) and a few odd references render him less than completely consistent.[36] Now, this inclusion of popular strains in pastoral tragicomedy has more in common with Italian dramaturgy than it may at first appear, because Guarini's high-cultural form is largely defined in opposition to popular pastoral drama, ubiquitous in Italy from the mid-fifteenth century to the early-seventeenth century. In Guarini and Shakespeare's time it was the *commedia dell'arte*, in the Arcadian scenarios already mentioned, that inherited the popular and supernatural strains of the pastoral tradition, although actresses like Isabella Andreini lent the bucolic mode a courtly and proto-operatic register. No examination of Italian-Shakespearean theatrical transmission would be complete without considering the Arcadian scenarios, whose resemblance to *The Tempest* is striking enough to render plausible the hypothesis that Shakespeare directly knew them.

The *Commedia dell'Arte* and *The Tempest*

As Winifred Smith, Kathleen Lea, Allardyce Nicoll, Niniam Mellamphy, Andrew Grewar, and other scholars have shown, Shakespeare and his contemporaries were well aware of the *commedia dell'arte*.[37] They knew about its particular characters or "masks," which Shakespeare adapts in *The Taming of the Shrew*, *Love's Labour's Lost*, and *Two Gentlemen of Verona*; they are referred to in very specific detail, as in Jacques's reference to the "lean and slipper'd Pantaloone, / With spectacles on nose and pouch on side, / His youthful hose well sau'd" (*As You Like It* 2.7.158–60).[38] Shakespeare and his fellow actors may even been aware of the improvisatory techniques of the Italian professional theater, and the extemporizing of clowns like Kemp may not have been the only instance when Shakespeare's actors used *arte*-like improvisation.[39]

There are many references to the *commedia dell'arte* in the literature and plays of Nashe, Florio, Heywood, Kyd, Day, Whetstone, Jonson, and Shakespeare, but there is little documented contact between Italian and English professional theater practitioners.[40] Of the several records of Italian players performing in England between 1546 and 1578, the most intriguing for our purposes is found in the Revels Accounts for February 1573 to November 1574, which lists charges for equipment needed by Italian players "that ffollowed the progresse and made pastyme fyrst at Wynsor and afterwardes at Reading."[41] These professional Italian players must have performed a pastoral play, judging by the expense accounts for such items as "Thred and shepherdes hookes,

Lamskynnes for Shepperds, Horstayles for the wylde mannes garment, and a syth for Saturn." Especially since *arte* players performed scripted pastoral plays like Tasso's *Aminta*, they may have either played a scripted or an improvised play in England. But elements like the satyr (adorned classically, as a horse-man instead of a goat-man) and the nonverisimilar use of gods (Saturn) moved freely between scripted and nonscripted theater. No other records of Italian players in England surface until 1610, when Prince Henry's privy purse accounts indicate payments to an "Italian comedian."[42] That the absence of Italian players may not be assumed by the dearth of records is suggested, however, by a 1591 report to Francis Bacon of "a devise of Italian espiales and intelligencers to come shortly in the habite and color of Tumblers." As Lea argues, spies would be unlikely to impersonate Italian acrobats if they were an altogether uncommon occurrence.[43]

Shakespeare could have heard about the *commedia dell'arte* through means other than direct witness. Will Kemp, member of Shakespeare's company until 1599, made two trips to Europe, where he probably came into contact with Italian players: in 1586 with Leicester's Men and around 1600 in Germany and Italy. A 1590 pamphlet links Kemp with the Italian professionals, as well as a 1607 play, *The Travailes of the Three English Brothers*, in which an Italian Arlecchino acts an extemporaneous routine with a character designated as "Kemp."[44] English players traveling abroad, especially in Paris in 1598 and 1604, may have met itinerant Italian troupes.[45] English travelers such as Fynes Moryson and Thomas Coryate recorded vivid memories of Italian players and mountebanks. The private library of John Florio was probably not unique in containing a substantial collection of *arte* scenarios.

The first great publishing event in early modern European theater was not Ben Jonson's 1616 *Workes*, but Flaminio Scala's 1611 *Il teatro delle favole rappresentative*, a collection of fifty scenarios arranged in Boccaccian style according to fifty "days."[46] Scala was closely associated with Francesco Andreini of the famous Gelosi troupe, of which many Englishmen were probably aware. One of Scala's scenarios, *L'albore incantato* (The enchanted wood) is set in Arcadia and has as its dramaturgical center a magician and his supernatural powers. This scenario and the pastoral elements that enter into other "days" in the Scala collection resemble a larger group of contemporary pastoral scenarios. Ten pastoral scenarios come from a two-volume manuscript collection compiled by Basilio Locatelli, dated 1618–22 and located in the Biblioteca Casanatense in Rome. Eight pastoral scenarios are in the Corsini collection in

Rome, dating variously from the first half of the seventeenth century.[47] Although these collections postdate the composition of *The Tempest*, the preface to the Locatelli collection indicates that they compile material already in circulation among the professional troupes and evidently of interest to amateurs and academics as well as to professionals.[48]

The first scholar to argue for a relationship between the Locatelli/ Corsini scenarios and *The Tempest* was Ferdinando Neri in 1913. E. K. Chambers and Frank Kermode (the latter albeit somewhat skeptically) have argued for the likelihood that the Arcadian plays were a source for Shakespeare's play, and Lea has made a quite deliberate case.[49] The evidence is based on the possibility discussed above that Shakespeare was exposed to *arte* performance (either directly or indirectly) coupled with the striking internal resemblances between the scenarios and *The Tempest*. Positivistic source hunters must contend with the fact, however, that no single scenario contains all of these resemblances. The late date of the extant scenarios poses another problem, as Kermode acknowledges, although Locatelli's claim that these kind of plays had long been performed is borne out by the resemblance of the Arcadian scenarios to several earlier printed scripts: Luigi Pasqualigo's 1581 *Gl'intricati* and Bartolomeo Rossi's 1584 *La fiammella*.[50] As Louise George Clubb has shown, *Gl'intricati* bears striking resemblances to the magical pastoral world of *A Midsummer Night's Dream*; this is not to claim direct influence, but to point out that Italian and English theater share a common system of pastoral as well as comedic theatergrams.[51] Kermode is right to say that the "provenance" of the scenarios is "dubious," but this is true because they derive from material that was widespread and in existence (both in print and on stage) for some time—thus rendering the possibility of Italian-English transmission more rather than less likely.

Kermode faults Lea for stacking the evidence in her juxtaposition of the plot of *The Tempest* with a "normal" Arcadian scenario. He argues that her "preoccupation with *The Tempest* has affected her choice of incidents from the corpus."[52] Certainly Shakespeare's play is based on an old folk-tale motif present in many non-Italian sources, including Jakob Ayrer's *Die Schöne Sidea*. But because the resemblances between the scenarios and *The Tempest* are too striking to rule out Italian-English transmission, it will be worth describing the theatergrams of the scenarios. Inevitably my choice of elements is also influenced by my own concern with *The Tempest*, but unlike Lea I will restrict myself to only two scenarios—*Li tre satiri* and *Il gran mago*—drawing most of my material from *Li tre satiri*, and mentioning a few details from other scenarios in footnotes.

In all of the scenarios, a magician holds center stage, ruling over the island, casting spells, drawing magic circles, and calling upon supernatural forces, mostly of a chthonic and infernal sort. He can turn people into trees *(Li tre satiri)* and strike his enemies motionless with one gesture of his magic rod *(Li tre satiri)*. He is given to grand declarations of his power, boasting that he is obeyed both by the infernal powers and the wild creatures of the island *(Li tre satiri)*. Keenly aware of the Fates *(Li tre satiri)* and able to see into the future, he knows that the arrival of the strangers by shipwreck will threaten his rule. He foresees the conspiracy against him undertaken by the strangers after they have settled on the island *(Li tre satiri)*. Inimical to the erotic pursuits of the nymphs and shepherds *(Il gran mago)*, he thwarts their amorous desires with various malicious tricks.[53]

A shipwreck brings a group of Italians, usually the stock figures from the *commedia dell'arte*, to the magician's shore.[54] In *Li tre satiri*, Pantalone stands alone, lost and terrified on the shore, recounting the shipwreck and lamenting the loss of his companions. He is frightened by a whale, who finally spits out his companion Burattino. After various *lazzi* of "touching and fear" they recognize one another and rejoice. Hungry and thirsty, they call on Bacchus for help *(Il gran mago)*. The Italian buffoons visit a temple, emerge dressed as the gods Jove, Mercury, and Cupid, and, convincing the native populations of their divinity, receive offerings from them. They steal the sorcerer's magic book and discover its great effects, including the power to command the local satyrs *(Li tre satiri)*. In *Li tre satiri*, the magician is besieged on several fronts: Fausto, Gratiano's lost son who has been living on the island, convinces the satyrs that the magician should be punished for all the evil he has done. In *Il gran mago*, Pantalone, Gratiano, and Burattino regain their proper shapes (they have been turned into various animals), blame the magician for their metamorphoses, and decide to kill him. Like Caliban, the satyrs switch allegiances, first grudgingly serving the magician, then obeying the buffoons, and finally returning allegiance to the magician *(Li tre satiri)*. The buffoons, however, are more often the victims of supernatural magic than they are successful conspirators. When they greedily reach for a plate of macaroni that the satyrs have obediently brought them, flames burst from the food *(Li tre satiri)*.[55]

Learning of the buffoon's theft of his magic book, the magician of

Li tre satiri announces that he will avenge himself. He conjures the conspirators into a circle, wields his magic rod, and renders them motionless. In *Il gran mago*, he announces that he has foreseen all of their evil plans but now forgives them. When the travelers are all returned to their former shapes, there are several recognitions, including the recognition by one of the travelers of his son, who was lost as a baby and grew up on the island *(Li tre satiri)*. The magician consents to various marriages *(Il gran mago)*, including a union between the magician's daughter and one of the shipwreck victims. The travelers, including the newly married couples, announce that they will immediately return to Venice *(Li tre satiri)*.

Crude and schematic as these scenarios are, their supernaturalism and their comic business, in addition to the sheer detail of plot, point to Shakespeare more than to his contemporaries Fletcher and Jonson. The sudden, improvisatory character of many of Prospero's actions, to be further discussed in chapter 10, as plausibly point to a continental theatrical tradition as they do to issues of character or politics. Certainly one can notice that popular pastoral took strikingly similar forms in Renaissance Italian and Shakespearean theater, and the possibility of Shakespeare's exposure to the general system of *commedia dell'arte* pastoral is too strong to be discounted. If Shakespeare was exposed to the *arte* pastorals, they could have supplied many of the theatergrams of *The Tempest*, as well as several important dramaturgical devices: the unities of time, place, and action; an enchanted and tempestuous island; the negotiation of verisimilitude and the marvelous; and a *mago* tragicomically poised between low-comic and solemn registers.

THE BLACKFRIARS THEATER

Although the differences between the situations of Guarini's amateur, courtly theater and Shakespeare's professional, largely popular theater are more striking than the similarities, the relatively sophisticated, if heterogeneous, audience of the Blackfriars theater, which most critics agree exerted some degree of influence on the late plays of Shakespeare, resembled the kind of learned audiences out of which the generically self-conscious form of Italian tragicomedy emerged. It was an audience of fairly high "dramatic competence" that would have recognized, more quickly than the Globe theatergoers, the codes of genre variously manipulated in the late plays and might have been more ready

to appreciate generic innovations like tragicomedy.[56] Certainly, compared with northern playhouses such as the Red Bull, the Fortune, and
the Curtain, and even compared with the Globe, the Blackfriars audience was of higher social aspiration and would have appreciated drama
pitched to the tastes of "gentlemen." At the same time, the Blackfriars
patrons seemed to enjoy old plays like *Mucedorus* and popular elements
such as those included in *The Winter's Tale*, and would have been receptive to a more socially heterogeneous form of tragicomedy than pre-
vailed in Italy.

Not allowed by local residents to perform at the converted playhouse that his father had bought and prepared in the Blackfriars dis-
trict in 1596, Richard Burbage arranged a twenty-one year lease in 1600
to the Children of the Chapel Royal, renamed the Children of the
Queen's Revels in 1604. Their commercial fortunes and their grace with
Elizabeth and James continually waxed and waned until their license
was terminated in March 1608. In August 1608, the King's Men bought
back the lease of the Blackfriars theater from Henry Evans, the manager
of the Children of the Queen's Revels. The King's Men began prepara-
tions for supplementing their Globe performances with winter productions at the Blackfriars, but plague prevented them from utilizing their
new theater for approximately a year and a half—so that *Cymbeline*, not
Pericles, was the first play written by Shakespeare with an eye to a
Blackfriars performance.

From the mid 1570s on, entertainment at the "private" or indoor
theaters had been exclusively produced by companies of boy choristers. Although the children's theaters survived in some form after 1608,
their commercial fortunes sharply declined after 1608, and the King's
Men were the first to appropriate the gentlemanly audience of the private theaters, particularly those who attended the performances of the
Children of the Queen's Revels at the Blackfriars theater. This company,
we remember, performed Marston's *Malcontent* in 1603–4, was associated with Samuel Daniel around the time he wrote the *Queenes Arcadia*,
and produced Fletcher's *Faithful Shepherdess* in 1608. Like the 1580s private-theater audiences attending the pastoral, avant-garde plays of John
Lyly, the Blackfriars clientele was a testing ground for generic innovation—sometimes receptive, sometimes not. Whereas the private-theater
audiences of the 1575–90 and the 1599–1605 periods dependably went
in for the pleasures of wit, satire, and "girds at citizens," private-theater taste from around 1607 to 1613 seems to have been less certain,
judging from the independent failures of first Beaumont and then

Fletcher.[57] Therefore, it was a time when playwrights might well have been interested in testing out new varieties of audience response.

Notwithstanding Ann Jennalie Cook's rebuttal of Alfred Harbage's too distinct separation of popular and "coterie" theater, the audiences that attended performances of *Cymbeline, The Winter's Tale,* and *The Tempest* were relatively wealthier, on the whole more educated, and either more sophisticated or more culturally ambitious compared to the audiences of the Globe and especially to those of the northern playhouses.[58] Critics may doubt that the reacquisition of the Blackfriars had as significant an effect on the dramaturgy of Shakespeare's late plays as Gerald Eades Bentley claims; it is often pointed out in critique of Bentley that these plays were performed at the Globe as well as at court.[59] Still, because the King's Men performed in the Blackfriars for a greater part of the year than in the Globe (open for only four months of the year), and would soon derive the majority of their profits from private-theater audiences, it is hard to believe that play composition and play selection would not have been affected by the new venue. Samuel Schoenbaum, generally skeptical of Bentley's thesis, concedes that "the significance of the Blackfriars move lies more in its social and economic dimension, from which (needless to say) the aesthetic is not entirely separable."[60]

Because its minimum admission was six times the cheapest entrance fee to the Globe, compared to amphitheater audiences the theatergoers attending Blackfriars plays were decidedly wealthier and more sophisticated; they included courtiers, lawyers, and gentry. Private theaters drew upon the new influx of prosperous Londoners to the fashionable residential areas west of the squalid and crowded city.[61] As Keith Sturgess says, "'Gentlemen' is the characteristic address of the private-theatre prologue, and the 'gentle audience' is technically one composed of gentlemen."[62] Indeed, the progress of the shepherds of *The Winter's Tale* to "gentlemanly" status and their concomitant capacity to shed "gentleman-like" tears, I shall argue, constitutes a fundamental dynamic of tragicomedic dramaturgy. Although the reality did not always match the gesture, playwrights of the private theater could at least flatter their audiences with references to their good breeding, their sophistication, and their subtle judgment.[63] And if Jonson, in the acerbic reference to Guarini made in *Volpone,* suggests that tragicomedy is a "feminine" genre by attaching it to the fashionable Lady Would-Be, here too the private-theater audience might prove especially receptive to the new form: women gained easier admittance to the private than to the public theaters, and were recognized by the playwrights as important patrons.[64]

Still, the distinction between private and public theaters in the time of the late plays can easily be taken too far. Rather than joining the early Beaumont and the early Fletcher in supposing a great divide between the indoor and the outdoor theaters, Andrew Gurr acknowledges the confluence and interchange between the two arenas, especially during the liminal period of 1607 to 1613. After 1610, the Globe drew theatergoers that frequented King's Men performances at the Blackfriars, so that "the rich went to public and private playhouses alike, the poor more exclusively to the public."[65] If Jonson, indeed, could complain in 1609 of "six-penny mechanicks" and the "shop's foreman . . . that may judge for his sixpence"[66] at the Blackfriars, we may better understand the failures of Beaumont and Fletcher's early avant-garde attempts and Shakespeare's success in including both highbrow and lowbrow strains in his late plays. As has often been noted, scenic decor and stage properties were not much more elaborate in the indoor than in the outdoor theaters. Even the private and public acting companies themselves were converging to some extent; the reconstituted Children of the Queen's Revels in 1610 had six young adults, and two actors from the original Queen's Revels left in 1608 to join the King's Men.[67] And the indoor theater seems to have influenced public theater staging, at least in one respect. After 1607, the public theaters followed the private theaters in suspending performances between each act—a practice that might lend an air of neoclassicism to theatrical presentation. As we discuss some differences in private and public playing conditions, it would be better to think of a productive negotiation between the different strains than of an absolute divide.

Music was more central to the private than to the public theaters, and provides another important point of comparison between the amateur Italian and the private English traditions. Besides the frequent musical entr'actes performed when candles were trimmed, the boy choristers delivered their lines in an operatic manner, exploring finely nuanced vocal registers. The indoor theaters would not encourage the use of loud instruments such as the shawms (a sort of bagpipe), war trumpets, and military drums frequently employed at the outdoor theaters, but rather quieter ones such as the recorder.[68] *Aminta* and *Il pastor fido* were proto-operatic, the latter the subject of a number of seventeenth-century operas. As we shall see, Guarini advocates a range of style as nuanced as musical scales, and compares the composition of tragicomedy to the counterpointing in musical composition (*Compendio*, 3:400). Music carries strong symbolic weight in Marston's tragicomedy

The Malcontent, filled out in the Globe version with dialogue to compensate for "the not-received custom of music."[69] The play begins with the "vilest out-of-tune music" that reflects the *discordia* of court corruption and ends with a nearly tragedic, but ultimately tragicomedic, masque, replete with harmonizing music. The musical center of the late plays, fostered by the new theatrical venue, should be viewed in the context of tragicomedic dramaturgy

It is not hard to see how the kind of theater produced by the boys' companies would lend itself to comic or tragicomic, rather than tragic, registers. The pleasures of wit, parody, and exaggeration tended to replace the cathartic pleasures cultivated in tragedy. If the private companies treated tragedic subjects, as they did in Marston's *Antonio* plays and Chapman's *Bussy* plays, they would tend to "play with tragedy"—somewhat like the *commedia dell'arte* when they tackled tragedic subjects from the *erudita* repertory—creating plays of modally tragicomic registers. The self-conscious theatricality often noted in the private theater includes the consciousness of generic codes. Especially in the 1570s and the 1580s, the background of the boy companies was more academic than that of the adult companies: they performed less frequently than the adults and devoted the rest of their time to formal education. The result was that theatrical performance itself was seen as an extension of their education, and the rhetorical declamatory arts were stressed. The perception, at least among the private-theater playwrights such as Marston and Chapman, was that the boys delivered finer, subtler theatrical fare than did the adults, or "common players," who were given to "stampe, curse, weepe, rage, and then [their] bosom strike."[70]

The more intimate playing conditions of the private theaters facilitated tragicomedic dramaturgy. The Blackfriars was roughly one-half the size of the Globe and held one-third the audience capacity, about one thousand people. The furthest carry from actor to audience was sixty feet at the Blackfriars, compared to ninety feet at the Globe. Candles were used to illuminate the performances, sometimes in conjunction with natural daylight, sometimes to provide the sole lighting for evening performances. The expansive physical gestures and heightened vocal delivery required at the large and sometimes noisy Globe theater could modulate into more subtle, nuanced registers at the private theater. Instead of staging the grand tragic style appropriate for the roles of King Lear or Othello, the private theater might explore the varieties of passion and sentiment for which Beaumont and Fletcher are praised. As we shall see in chapter 6, both Guarinian tragicomedy and Shakespeare's late plays explore nuanced ranges of affective response in the audience. Granville-Barker's hypothesis about playing conditions in the indoor theaters points towards tragicomedic dramaturgy:

> The plots of the new plays might well grow more elaborate and their writing more diffuse, for it would be easier to keep an audience attentive and see that no points were missed. If violence is still the thing, noise will not be. The old clattering battles may gradually go out of favour; but processions will look finer than ever, and apparitions and the like will be twice as effective. Rhetoric will lose hold a little . . . and sentiment will become as telling as passion.[71]

The imperative to write plays that would be adaptable in the various venues of the Globe, Whitehall, and Blackfriars does mitigate Bentley's assertion that the late plays were written exclusively with the Blackfriars in mind. At the same time, the sentiment that pervades the boys' funeral for Fidele in *Cymbeline*, the pathetic responses to the narrated and enacted recognitions in *The Winter's Tale*, and the emotional reversal scene of *The Tempest* in which Prospero forgoes his revenge could all be effectively portrayed in the new theater.

In conclusion, the audience, playing conditions, and general climate of the Blackfriars, where Marston and Fletcher had undertaken earlier tragicomedic experiments in plays written for the Children of the Queen's Revels, lent itself to tragicomedy at the time when Shakespeare was writing his late plays. Having failed with *The Faithful Shepherdess*, Fletcher turned away from pastoral to develop, with Beaumont, a more English version of tragicomedy. Shakespeare had more success than Fletcher with a pastoral, and thus Italianate, version of tragicomedy in part because his retention of popular pastoral elements more successfully gauged the heterogeneity of the Blackfriars audience, as well as the diversity of performance venues. More fully than Daniel, Fletcher, and even Marston, Shakespeare successfully negotiated both high and low strains of tragicomedy, while appealing to new and emerging gentlemen such as himself, not with the kind of anticitizen raillery once popular with private-theater audiences but with the "gentleman-like tears" of Guarinian tragicomedy.

3

Theory and Practice in the Cinquecento

GENRE, THEORY, AND PRACTICE

Fletcher's interest in Guarini's theory does not provide the sole example of Italian theory influencing English theory and practice. Documented cases of Italian-English transmission mostly date from an earlier period. Scaliger's 1561 *Poetices librem septem* and Minturno's 1564 *L'arte poetica* influenced both Sir Philip Sidney's 1583 *The Defense of Poesie* and George Puttenham's 1589 *The Arte of English Poesie*. But English poets from Ben Jonson to Milton continued to read or hear about the Italian Renaissance commentators, whose interest in literary theory has only been surpassed by that of the late-twentieth century. Italian theory, based largely on discussions of genres, inflected international assumptions about generic practice, the more pervasive for not being fully articulated except in unusual cases like that of Jonson. Implicit theories and assumptions about genre are especially important in the historically advanced and "metageneric" genre of tragicomedy.

Late-Renaissance Italy produced the first extended body of aesthetic theory in the West, but it has usually been regarded as inhibiting rather than fostering experimentation and innovation. The term "neoclassicism" may, it is true, be justified for the period because practically all theorizing began with commentary on Aristotle and Horace, and attempted to provide a rational system of genres and principles by adding to or extrapolating from the classical authorities on matters where they remained silent. And some neoclassical principles such as the notorious unities were actually codified in the secondo Cinquecento. It has usually been thought that Cinquecento theory was "academic" in a pejorative sense because it was sharply divorced from practice or married to poems and plays that never reached a public beyond academic and courtly walls. Why didn't commentators addressing comedic theory turn to the most influential and enduring practical manifestation of the genre, the *commedia dell'arte*, which at that very time was emerging as a significant cultural phenomenon not only in Italy but throughout much of Europe?[1] It is convenient to associate the supposedly oppressive and inhibitive theorizing of the period with the presumably repressive effects of the Counter-Reformation in the cultural sphere. What was not put on the Index of prohibited books, in this view, was forced into the straitjacket of neoclassical theory and post-Tridentine moralizing.

But monolithic and censorious interpretations do no more justice to secondo Cinquecento theory than they do to the culture of late-sixteenth-century Italy, the breadth and influence of which has been acknowledged by historians from Ferdinand Braudel to Paul F. Grendler to Eric Cochrane.[2] Braudel points out that the 1559 peace of Cateau-Cambrésis was followed by a great flowering of Italian culture, whose international prestige contrasted the political subjection of Italy to Spain enforced by the settlements to the Italian wars. In particular, the period is distinguished by the proliferation of new forms: in music, for example, one can point to Palestrina's developments in polyphony and to Monteverdi's formulation of a new dramatic monody. Economically, some of the Italian states actually gained at the expense of Spain and the Low Countries. Hard-pressed because of military imperatives, Spain's Philip II made concessions to Genovese merchants that rendered them central figures in international trade until the early-seventeenth century.[3] And after 1550, the reestablishment of Mediterranean trading routes for pepper and other spices staved off the decline of Venice as a center of international commerce for another century.[4] Venice's economic prestige included its extraordinary printing industry, which was checked but not ultimately controlled by the post-Tridentine church. By the 1590s, Venice asserted its independence relative to Rome in its printing industry as in political, agricultural, and religious arenas, and the number of books printed almost matched the high of the 1560–74 period. Especially in northern Italy, the constrictive effects of the Index at the end of the century must be balanced against the expanded dissemination of different kinds of literature due to the still vigorous circulation of printed material, consisting proportionately less of religious works relative to the 1570s and 1580s.[5]

Surely there was a relationship between the renewed circulation of multiple literary forms in Venice and elsewhere and the development of new cultural forms in literature as well as in other arts. In the late Renaissance, well after the humanist "disinterment" of "pure" classical forms like epic, comedy, and tragedy, new forms like tragicomedy and opera issued from a kind of commerce and cross-fertilization of established forms and mediums.[6] This late humanist moment was one of historical *retrospection*: the ancient genres had already been established by the transgressive imitation of classical *exempla* and the speculative interpretation of ancient theory. Further generic development took place largely through the combination or transformation of existing genres; through the exploration of the boundaries between genres; and through the application of modes to new mediums, as in pastoral drama as well as ballet and opera. By the late-sixteenth century, the *commedia dell'arte*, especially active in Venice and other northern Italian cities, performed a variety of styles and genres, surely in response to the "what you will" of audiences that ranged from the piazza to the court. And late-Cinquecento literary theory, not hindered by the Index and the Inquisition in any discernible manner, often facilitated rather than inhibited such generic proliferation.[7] The generic "polyglossia" seen by Bakhtin as a characteristic of the period and applied by him and other critics to canonically transgressive writers like Rabelais, Cervantes, and Shakespeare also provides the context for practicant-theorists like the Ferraran poets Giraldi and Guarini, authors who were controversial enough in their own time because of their generic innovations. Guarini, who stayed in Venice for significant periods and who published five of his major works there, finds an apt analogy for the kind of generic cross-fertilization that naturally occurs in a cultural crossroads such as the Serenissima.[8] He compares the proliferation of genres occurring at the end of the sixteenth century to the generation of new biological species in Africa, where different animals are presumably driven by thirst to encounter each other at an oasis (*Il Verato*, 3:178). Tragicomedy, the new genre Guarini defends against conservative opponents, is proposed as the "child" of tragedy and comedy, and its production is compared to the generation of hybrid biological species (167). It was a fertile period of literary generation.

In the Italian Renaissance, a self-justifying circularity insured that theory could not be separated from practice. Many of the important literary theorists—Sperone Speroni, Giraldi Cinthio, Torquato Tasso, and Battista Guarini—were practicing poets and in fact often used theory (after the fact) to justify their own controversial practices.[9] The theoretical discussions and controversies of the Cinquecento were directed to practical issues germane to individual works: Ariosto's *Orlando Furioso*, Dante's *Divina Commedia*, Speroni's *Canace e Macareo*, and Guarini's *Il pastor fido*.[10] In turn, the theoretical ferment of the sixteenth century served as the "background condition" for practical experimentation. Theoretical controversies surrounding Ariosto's controversial romance, for example, surely informed the composition of *Don Quixote*.[11] The centrality of genre to Cinquecento critical theory assured a close relationship between theory and practice, because generic concepts both addressed theoretical issues and served as practical devices for poets and critics.[12] In the case of *Il pastor fido*, written in the midst of theoretical debates and accompanied in the definitive 1602 edition with extensive annotations, it is impossible to separate theoretical from practical concerns.

Most late-twentieth-century theory has developed from nondramatic forms, especially lyric poetry and the novel. Conversely, dramatic theory was at the heart of Cinquecento theorizing for several reasons: the critical prominence of the *Poetics*, mostly dedicated to tragedy, and the fact that theories of nondramatic kinds tended to be extrapolated from Aristotle's text; the classicizing prestige of "tragedy" and "comedy" for Renaissance humanists; the sheer expansion of theatrical activity in Italian courts, halls, academies, piazzas, and streets; and the humanist impulse to inform this activity with classically based dramatic theory. But the centrality of drama to Cinquecento literary theory was more than circumstantial. Because Renaissance theorists emphasized the rhetorical effects of literature upon its readers or audiences, the palpable presence of the audience in drama rendered it a particularly generative laboratory for practical, rhetorically based genre theories.

Neo-Aristotelian commentators like Lodovico Castelvetro (the London activities of whose nephew Giacopo we have reviewed) largely based their dramatic theories on perceived audience response. This was true not only in the obvious case of catharsis theory. For Castelvetro, matters of dramatic composition—length, the notorious unities, verisimilitude—are based on the needs and natures of audiences rather than on purely structural considerations.[13] If genres change according to historical shifts in the audience, as "moderns" like Giraldi Cinthio and Guarini asserted against "ancients" like Denores, then the dramaturgical strategies of historically advanced genres like tragicomedy anticipated audience expectations and responses. These Italian generic innovators actually anticipated the late-twentieth-century interest in the active, productive role of the theater audience. Contrasting a view of the theater spectator as a passive object of the playwright, director, or performer, Marco De Marinis claims the following:

> We can also speak of a dramaturgy of the spectator in an active or subjective sense, referring to the various receptive operations/actions that an audience carries out: perception, interpretation, aesthetic appreciation, memorization, emotive and intellectual response, etc. . . . These operations/actions of the audience's members are to be considered truly dramaturgical (not just metaphorically) since it is only through these actions that the performance text achieves its fullness, becoming realized in all its semantic and communicative potential.[14]

That genre concepts dominate Cinquecento theory does not at all imply a passive role for the audience—quite the contrary. Renaissance genres, in fact, mediated between the play and the audience by eliciting *emotional* responses in the audience, organizing *cognitive* systems of signification in creating "horizons of expectations," and provoking *ethical*, evaluative responses by virtue of their social coding. In the increasingly complex genre system of the late Renaissance, some theorists actually defined genres less by conventional signals such as diction, character, and subject matter than by the kinds of effects elicited in the audience—effects that could be discerned, or at least hypothesized, more readily for a theatergoer than for a reader. Brief accounts of these three mediatory functions of genre will prepare for succeeding chapters of this study.

Cinquecento commentators like Minturno and Castelvetro inherited Cicero's affective amplification of the Horatian "docet et delectat" formula. The ideal model for the Renaissance playwright became the Ciceronian orator, who "dicendo animos audientium et docet et delectat et *permovet*" [in speaking at once teaches and delights and *moves* the souls of those listening to him] (*De optimo genere oratorum* 1.3; emphasis mine). As we shall see in chapter 6, because of Aristotle's emphasis on the tragedic responses of pity and fear, the neo-Aristotelian tradition actually placed great emphasis on the emotional responses generated by the play (or by the actors) on the audience. Because Aristotle only directly addressed the emotional responses proper to tragedy, commentators were free to speculate and argue about the affective registers of other genres or modes. Sidney thus considers the emotional registers of various modes: "the lamenting Elegiack, which in a kind heart would move pity rather than blame"; the "bitter but wholesome Iambick, which rubs the galled mind"; the "Satirick, who . . . sportingly never leaveth till he make a man laught at follie."[15] The emotional effects of genres like tragicomedy that mix different modes would then be extremely varied and complex.

Common to all Cinquecento theorists and surely present in the English theorists Puttenham, Sidney, and Jonson is a keen awareness of the cognitive functions of genres and modes: the subject of chapters 7 and 8. As in James I's use of "tragicomedy" and the Council of Virginia's use of "tragicall comoedie" discussed above, Renaissance kinds indicated particular, historically conditioned perspectives on the world. The "resources of kind" enabled Renaissance writers to use genre tags (characters, diction, topoi, or themes appropriate to a given genre) as an expressive shorthand.[16] For example, the pastoral art/nature topos implicit in Lear's "Nature's above art in that respect" (*King Lear* 4.6.86) quickly summons up pastoral points of view and expectations, rendering the scenes on the heath all the more terrible in contrast to the possibility of pastoral idyllism.[17] To a greater degree than twentieth-century writers, Renaissance authors used genre tags and concepts as materials of communication, indicators capable of combination, alteration, and surprising incarnations.

The Horatian *utile* ensured that the ethical questions would at least be at the forefront of genre debates, if not guaranteeing that all playwrights would adopt Denores's extreme position that genres (or at least tragedy, comedy, and epic) taught specific political and ethical lessons. Guarini ranks with Castelvetro among those who championed the *dolce* over the *utile*, arguing that the function of poetry was to give pleasure and delight and not to teach ethical or political lessons. But Castelvetro is not always perfectly consistent in this matter, and Guarini's position must be seen in the polemical context of his exchange with Denores, who took the didactic line about as far as one could. We shall see in chapter 9 that Guarinian tragicomedy has an implicit politics. Furthermore, because Renaissance kinds were socially coded, their deployment carried important social implications. Both the pastoral mode and the tragicomedic genre became charged locuses of debate in this regard, because of the lack of classical specificity about their social coding.

To sum up, many Cinquecento theorists conceived of genres not categorically but functionally; they asked not what genres *were* but what they *did*. Guarini distinguishes between the instrumental ends of poetry, which concern structural principles and proper methods of imitation, and the architectonic ends of poetry, which have to do with the practical emotional, cognitive, and ethical effects elicited in the audience.

Of tragicomedy, he is mostly interested in the architectonic functions rather than the instrumental structures, and asks questions of his new hybrid such as "Che intende ella di fare? che fine ha? vuol ella rider o piangere? [What does it {tragicomedy} intend to do? What end does it have? Does it aim to cause laughter or crying?] (*I Verato*, 2:245). For Guarini, poetry is not a branch of politics or philosophy, as it was for Denores, but of rhetoric. And dramaturgy that followed the rhetorical model was practical and interventionary. Like rhetoric and medicine, it was concerned with specific, practical effects elicited in the audience.[18] The playwright, in fact, was often compared to a doctor in his careful treatment of his patient, and the signature trauma of tragicomedy became not death but the treatable wound. If tragicomedy, in avoiding tragic melancholy or comic dissolution, achieves an "eccellentissima temperatura" [excellent temperature], it conforms to the ideally regulated human constitution, "che tutta solamente consiste nella temperie de'quattro umori" [which entirely consists in the tempering of the four humors] (*II Verato*, 3:199).

INNOVATION

Cinquecento genre theory has often been viewed as a complex of Horatian and neo-Aristotelian rules that impeded experimentation and innovation. Horace and Aristotle, however, were invoked by both conservative and progressive forces and interpreted in widely varying fashions. Castelvetro claims to have discovered that the *Poetics* was incomplete and derives only from rough notes, and uses this discovery as a basis for significant extrapolations as well as frequent disagreements with Aristotle's text. As Daniel Javitch has shown, poets writing theory to justify their own poetic practices often attributed principles to Aristotle's *Poetics* not justified by a close reading of the document itself.[19] Whereas ancients like Denores, opposed to generic experiments like *Il pastor fido*, certainly marshaled Horace and Aristotle in order to inhibit innovation, moderns such as Guarini himself used the ancient authorities for precisely the opposite purpose: to defend dramaturgical experiments scarcely imaginable by Aristotle. According to Javitch, the codification and systematization of kinds practiced by Cinquecento theorists as often served to expand as to constrict the canon.[20] The Quattrocento and early-Cinquecento humanist models based on the imitation of individual writers (e.g., Homer, Vergil) yielded a narrow canon, whereas the achievement of a genre canon and theories of individual kinds by the later theorists allowed writers to transcend the practices of individual writers. Aristotelian or neo-Aristotelian principles, Javitch notes, often were invoked by the moderns to develop theories of new kinds such as the *romanzo* or tragicomedy and to defend them against the attacks of the ancients.

Guarini constructs his poetics not with specific details but with broad principles extracted, conjectured, or hypothesized from the *Poetics*. For Guarini, the *Poetics* yields "universal" concepts that must be distinguished from local and changeable rules: "Nella Poetica sono alcuni precetti universali, che per esser tratti dalla natura non si posson mutare; come sarebbe a dire l'imitazione, il costume, il verso, il decoro ed altri di questa sorta" [In the *Poetics* there are several universal precepts, which cannot change because they are taken from nature, for example imitation, custom, verse, decorum, and others of this kind] (*I Verato*, 2:233). Such general concepts as decorum, imitation, verisimilitude, and catharsis may smack of neoclassicism to our ears, but could actually be manipulated in ways that advanced experimentation and innovation.

Guarini extends the concept of stylistic decorum to his new generic hybrid and argues for a new tragicomic style that mixes the "grave" and the "polished." The Horatian notion of decorum is invoked by Denores against tragicomedy, but the decorous Jonson title page founds a system of genres and modes out of which one could construct complex combinations worthy of Shakespeare's Polonius. If the objects of tragedic and comedic *imitatio* were generally taken by Cinquecento theorists to be the external customs and manners of the court and city, the notion of *imitatio* could be stretched in the "third kind" of pastoral to include inner experience of an amatory or contemplative nature.[21] The quarrel over Dante's *Divina Commedia* turned on differing ideas of imitation; against Belisario Bulgarini's contention that Dante's poem violated Aristotelian mimesis by imitating unreal things, Giacopo Mazzoni distinguished between the *icastic* representation of objective things and the *phantastic* imitation of things feigned or imagined only in the mind.[22] Verisimilitude itself, in the new genre of tragicomedy, could admit more fictional, imaginary realms than those normally admitted in tragedy. The reconciliation of verisimilitude and the marvelous (an effect that poetry was supposed to elicit) generated innovations. And no concept, as we shall see, was more exploited than the suggestively ambivalent notion of catharsis. The new, constructed kind of tragicomedy, then, provides an important example of the practical, experimental

manipulation of "neoclassical" theories and of the ways in which theoretical debates about those theories could inform practice.

THE HISTORICITY OF GENRE; GENRE AS MATERIAL

If Petrarch's consciousness of historical distance bespeaks, for Thomas Greene, an emergent Renaissance historicity, Giraldi and Guarini
provide a late-Renaissance theory of generic historicity that enables their
practical experiments.[23] For Guarini, tragicomedy is historically advanced,
a genre for its time that strikes a middle way between the horror and
atrocity of tragedy and the bawdy laughter of comedy, especially as
practiced by the *commedia dell'arte*. It was a genre appropriate for post-
Tridentine Italy, when tragedic fate too closely resembled Calvinist pre-
destination and when the moral earnestness of the reforming church
could not well countenance the carnivalesque transgressions of earlier
Cinquecento comedy (e.g., Machiavelli, Aretino). But such constrictive
cultural conditions paradoxically could spur artistic innovation, as play-
wright/theorists explored several possibilities for a third, intermediate
genre: tragedy with a happy ending *(tragedia di lieto fine)*; Giraldi's *satira*,
a very free imitation of the Greek satyr play; tragicomedy; pastoral;
and sentimental comedy.

Denores does betray a nominally historical view when he recognizes the development of his three major genres from rough, unculti-
vated beginnings to the period when, as he sees it, Greek philosophers
and statesman informed them with serious, ethical principles (*Discorso*,
1:153). Once having achieved that state, however, they did not change,
and their essential forms were as available to the sixteenth-century
writer as they were to the Greeks. Guarini formulates, following Giraldi,
one of the most important early modern claims for the historicity of
genres. New kinds must be constructed according to the changing tastes,
dispositions, and outlooks of audiences. Against Denores's Platonic
position that genres correspond to fixed, ideal, and historically immu-
table types, Guarini argues that they change over time, responding to
the changing tastes, outlooks, and social configurations of their audiences: "E questa è la vera cagione delle differenze, e dei gradi, che sono
nelle favole più, e men Tragiche, perciocchè i poeti vedendo i gusti
diversi degli ascoltanti, alcuna volta componevano favole co'l fin lieto
per rimettere in parte quella acrimonia" [And this is the true reason for
the differences and the degrees of more and less tragic plays, because

the poets, seeing the various tastes of their audiences, sometimes wrote plays with a happy ending in order to make them less harsh] (*I Verato*, 2:260). It is precisely Guarini's rhetorical view of poetry that leads him to a historicist view of genres, which modulate in response to ever changing audiences. The rhetorical, historical determination of genres is especially clear in drama: "E veramente se le pubbliche rappresentazioni son fatte per gli ascoltanti, bisogna bene, che secondo la varietà dei costumi, e dei tempi si vadano eziandio mutando i poemi" [Indeed, if public representations are made for audiences, it is necessary that according to the variety of customs and times poems also change] (261). The kinds, then, are not inert structural forms, but are rhetorical and audience-based. To Denores's charge that Aristotle did not discuss tragicomedy, Guarini responds that Aristotle could have anticipated neither the changes taking place in epic, comedy, and tragedy (the three principal, philosophically informed kinds for Denores) nor the emergence of new kinds such as Dante's dream vision epic or Ariosto's *romanzo*: "e quante nuove, e vaghe forme di poesia abbiam noi oggi, che non s'usavano al tempo d'Aristotile" [and how many new and pleasant forms of poetry do we now have that were not used in Aristotle's time] (232). Although he cites classical precedents such as the satyr play and Euripidean tragedies with a happy ending, Guarini proposes tragicomedy as a peculiarly late-sixteenth-century genre.

If generic codes, structures, attributes, and tonalities are not determinative frames (as for Denores) but historical conventions, they may be shaped and crafted by the writer. Guarini's theorizing about kind is practical, because he does not envision kinds as Platonic, fixed forms but as the very *materials* of dramaturgical creation, exploitable for transformation by various combinatory strategies. Early modern theorists such as Guarini, then, anticipate the late-twentieth-century sense of the constructed, historical nature of literary genres.[24] This is never clearer, of course, than with a hybrid genre such as tragicomedy, and Guarini clearly works tragicomedy out of the material of tragedy and comedy. Guarini's frequently cited formula for composing tragicomedy (too often the sole citation in critical discussions of Guarini's theory), is instructive in this regard.

Chi compone Tragicommedia . . . dall una [Tragedy] prende le persone grandi, e non l'azione: la favola verisimile, ma non vera: gli affetti mossi, ma rintuzzati: il diletto, non la mestizia: il pericolo, non la morte. Dall'altra [Comedy] il riso non dissoluto, le piacevolezze modeste, il nodo finto, il rivolgimento felice, e sopra tutto l'ordine Comico. (*Compendio*, 3:403)

[He who composes tragicomedy takes from tragedy its great persons but not its great action, its verisimilar plot but not its true one, its movement of the feelings but not its disturbance of them, its pleasure but not its sadness, its danger but not its death; from comedy it takes laughter that is not excessive, modest amusement, feigned difficulty, happy reversal, and above all the comic order of which we shall speak in its place.][25]

Wrongly used as Guarini's definitive list of characteristics proper to tragicomedy, this cookbook-like formulation considers the components of tragedy and comedy as materials to be carefully combined in the composition of tragicomedy. For Guarini as for Shakespeare, because the style, tone, action, set, and social organization of pastoral could mediate between tragedy and comedy, pastoral structures and topoi could also constitute the material of tragicomedy. Such practical use of generic material demonstrates the central principle of theatrical production in early modern Italian drama: theater is produced from theater in the continual combination and transformation of theatrical moving parts.[26]

Guarini develops various analogies to illustrate the careful mixture of generic material practiced by the playwright of tragicomedy. The analogies all imply a high degree of artistic control and aim to distinguish the careful mixtures of late-Cinquecento drama from the "mungrell tragicomedy" of medieval drama or what Guarini (incorrectly) perceived to be the ad hoc generic combinations of the *commedia dell'arte*. The playwright mixes generic material as deliberately as the painter mixes colors from the palette (*II Verato*, 3:158–59). As music blends the diatonic with the chromatic, and the chromatic with the enharmonic, the playwright counterpoints various tonalities in the hybrid play (159). Perhaps the maker of tragicomedy may be compared to the metallurgist, firing bronze out of copper and tin (158). New kinds are constructed artifacts, like the new inventions changing European technology: tragicomedy is like gunpowder, a mixture of sulfur and niter (158).[27] Generic production is a kind of grafting: just as tragedy itself did not arise archetypally from a Platonic essence but was "grafted" onto the "trunk of the Dithyramb" (*I Verato*, 2:297), many other "new grafts," such as tragicomedy itself, have been added to the "trunk of poetry" since Aristotle's time (234). Or tragicomedy resembles the mixtures of the

Venetian republic, where oligarchical forms representing the power of the few paradoxically blend with democratic forms representing the power of the masses.

Although it is improbable that Shakespeare actually read any of Guarini's theory, his colleague John Fletcher did. As with the theoretical writings of Scaliger, Minturno, and Castelvetro, Guarini's ideas were well disseminated in England and the continent. The repressive effects of the Index and the Inquisition did not prevent late-humanist poet-theorists from generic experiments as innovative as the formal and stylistic explorations in late-Cinquecento music and painting.

4

Pastoral as Tragicomedic

PASTORAL PRACTICE AND THEORY

From the fifteenth century on, Italian humanists conceived of the pastoral play as a third kind supplementing tragedy and comedy. In theory, pastoral could become an entirely distinct third genre. In practice it became modally tragicomic whether or not it was a fully realized genre, combining modalities of the antecedent genres. For humanists, the absence of classical precedence (unless one counted the Greek satyr play) and the lack of theory regarding the pastoral mode was enabling as well as frustrating, because pastoral could then become an arena of experimentation, innovation, and debate, one that combined theory and practice as discussed in the previous chapter. Late-Renaissance playwrights like Guarini and Shakespeare inherited a very flexible and capacious mode.

The prominence of Tasso and Guarini has unfortunately eclipsed the rich and diverse body of Italian pastoral drama that extended from the fifteenth to the early-seventeenth centuries. The "origins" of pastoral drama in Italy and Europe, the subject of an important recent collection of essays, can always be antedated—even the dialogue form of Vergil's eclogues provided the suggestion that pastoral was intrinsically dramatic.[1] From Enrico Carrara's 1909 *La poesia pastorale* to Marzia Pieri's magisterial 1983 study of late-Quattrocento and Cinquecento pastoral drama, a picture emerges of an extremely diverse (and diversely labeled) form in respect to style, subject, social register, dramaturgy, and theatrical venue.[2] In the Quattrocento, especially from 1470 on, the pastoral eclogue was a capacious form capable of incorporating ancient and modern themes, courtly and popular tonalities, and tragic and comic registers. In the late-fifteenth century, a flowering of pastoral drama took place in the northern courts of Mantua, Milan, and

Ferrara. Between Poliziano's 1480 *Orfeo* and Castiglione's 1506 *Tirsi* there was a significant body of mythological pastoral drama, which despite the classicizing and tragedic dimensions of *Orfeo* remained insouciant in regard to its generic status. For example, the prologue to Niccolò da Correggio's 1487 *Cefalo* presents the play neither as comedy nor as tragedy, but "fabula o istoria, quale ella se sia" [tale or history, whatever it may be].[3] This fertile period of secular pastoral theater in Italy occurs in the context of early-humanist interest in the Greek satyr play, discussed below, and the most seminal nondramatic pastoral work of the Italian Renaissance, Sannazaro's *Arcadia* (1480–85).

A crucial difference between classical and medieval/Renaissance pastoral, as Pieri has argued, is that much of the latter is structured by a "double linguistic and social code," normally represented by the elegiac, Petrarchan *pastore* and the coarse, realistic *villano,* and sometimes also by a binary division of dance and musical styles integrated into the drama.[4] As early as the thirteenth-century Provençal *pastourelles* and the influential *Jeu de Robin et de Marion* of Adam de la Halle (1283), pastoral drama explored the relationship between the court and the country, and was implicitly tragicomedic in regard to social register. Contemporary with the courtly pastoral drama of the northern courts, and of longer duration, was a rustic, farcical, romantic line of pastoral (often hinged to the ecologue form) designed for a more heterogeneous, sometimes academic audience such as watched the rustic pastorals of the Sienese pre-Rozzi in the 1520s and the 1530s. In the ambience of the university centers Padua and Bologna, multidialectal and carnivalesque pastoral eclogues and plays were produced during carnival or May Day.[5] Exploiting the vogue of the pastoral mode, Ruzante's 1521 *La pastoral* plays on the incongruous, sometimes parodic juxtaposition of two antithetical character groups: the Petrarchan, amorous shepherds and the realistic, Paduan-speaking peasants.[6] But there was little or no impulse to reconcile the implicitly tragicomedic dimension of pastoral with the dramaturgical principles articulated in contemporary experiments in comedy and tragedy. As a result, to many after 1525 pastoral drama seemed to be old-fashioned compared with the increasingly classicized and theorized forms of tragedy and comedy.

The Italian Renaissance reception of the Greek satyr play, although neglected in most accounts of tragicomedy, is important in tracing the Ferraran line of mixed drama that culminates with Guarini, a line more potentially tragic than rustic pastoral or other courtly pastoral that eliminates or diminishes the satyr figure. With other Renaissance theorists, Guarini identified Euripides *Cyclops* and the Greek satyr play as important classical precedents for pastoral tragicomedy, along with Aristotle's tragedy with a double ending and Plautus's *Amphitryon* (*I Verato*, 2:265; *Compendio*, 3:398). Because Guarini perceived a link between his tragicomedy and the satyr play, he makes the surprising claim that Horace's brief description of the third classical dramatic form is the best ancient theoretical expression of the new genre he would like to establish (*I Verato*, 2:266).

In the pastoral plays of Guarini and his contemporaries, the palpable link between the ancient satyr play and modern pastoral drama becomes the rustic satyr: the figure, we remember, who with the shepherd flanks Tragicomedia in Jonson's Horatian illustration. If Guarinian tragicomedy tempers not only tragedy and comedy but also the extreme harshness of the satiric mode, the satyr character becomes a licensed satiric persona appropriate to the mode of pastoral, and not only because the satyr is a rustic figure at home in the post-Sannazaran pastoral landscape. For Renaissance pastoral tends to critique courtly vices in generalized and abstract terms, avoiding the barbs of Aristophanic comedy and the political dangers (courted by the English but never by the Italians) implicit in the tragedic critique of the tyrant.

At the service of the satiric satyr of pastoral drama was a venerable etymological confusion concerning the Latin word *satira*, a confusion extended to *satira* in Italian. The confusion had ancient origins, and was probably transmitted to the medieval and Renaissance periods through Diomedes' late-fourth-century A.D. report of the ancient grammarians. The *satira*, Diomedes writes, refers to the abusive but corrective poetry of Lucilius, Horace, and Persius, which is "composed in the style of the ancient comedy."[7] The word *satira*, in his view, derives either from the "satyr," a figure who says the kind of ridiculous and shameful things found in Latin satire; or (improbably) from the sword used in primitive sacrifices and called *satura* because it produced a satiety (*saturitas*) of communal benefits; or (correctly) from *satura*, meaning a mixture of dishes, and thus a mixed composition. Diomedes' approach to definition, one followed by Renaissance theorists, is itself a kind of "satura," syncretic rather than exclusive. Thus, from Diomedes one could conclude that Horatian satire followed a dramatic model (though probably that of Old Comedy rather than the satyr play), that the satyr is an intrinsically "satiric" figure, and perhaps that the *satira* was attached to some kind of ritual tradition. From Diomedes, the Latin and

Italian word *satira* referred to both the ancient satyr play (and modern imitations of it, such as that of Giraldi) and nondramatic satire, whose speaker could assume the persona of the scourging "satyr."

It was quite possible for Renaissance humanists to see both pastoral and tragicomedic elements in the Greek satyr play. The satyrs themselves, of course, are extraurban figures. In Euripides' *Cyclops*, they are shepherds of Polyphemus's flock, who in the *parodos* call the sheep back to the *locus amoenus*. And if the satyr play, both classical and Hellenistic, is situated in a rustic, removed place, it is a place of marvelous objects and occurrences, relatively less observant of verisimilitude than tragedy and New Comedy.[8] As such, it functions as a precedent for the marvelous registers more conducive to pastoral than to tragedy or to comedy. Furthermore, whereas the obscenity, hilarity, and happy endings of the satyr play are comic, the form contains most of the formal appurtenances of tragedy: its meter, chorus, and the structure of prologue, *parodos*, alternating episode and ode, and final *exodos*. Horace's commentary on the satyr play is crucial for Guarini because it provides a dramaturgical calibration of the intermediate form. Horace writes,

> The poet who in tragic song first competed for a paltry goat soon also brought on unclad the woodland Satyrs, and with no loss of dignity roughly essayed jesting, for only the lure and charm of novelty could hold the spectator, who, after observance of the rites, was well drunken and in lawless mood. But it will be fitting so to seek favour for your laughing, bantering Satyrs so to pass from grave to gay, that no god, no hero, who shall be brought upon the stage, and whom we have just beheld in royal gold and purple, shall shift with vulgar speech into dingy hovels, or, while shunning the ground, catch at clouds and emptiness. Tragedy, scorning to babble trivial verses, will, like a matron bidden to dance on festals days, take her place in the saucy Satyrs' circle with some little shame. Not mine shall it be, ye Pisos, if writing Satyric plays, to affect only the plain nouns and verbs of established use; nor shall I strive so to part company with tragic tone, that it matters not whether Davus be speaking with shameless Pythias, who has won a talent by bamboozling Simo, or Silenus, who guards and serves his divine charge.[9]

Horace's remarks that the satyr play was introduced in the City Dionysia to detain the drunken spectator who had performed the rituals are usually taken to support the view that the satyr play was modally comic, or "tragedy at play." But Horace actually sees in the satyr play a tonally *intermediate* register. Like "Tragicomoedia" in the Jonson title page, the

Horatian satyr play historically follows tragedy. When attempting the lighter form, however, the tragedic playwright must be careful not to shame a god or hero "in oscuras humili sermone tabernas" [with vulgar speech in dingy hovels]. Reframed in a new satyric decorum, the tragedic muse will behave like a matron asked to dance on festival days. Similarly, when the woodland characters of the satyr play are brought into the city, they are to refrain from the bawdy and shameless jokes of low city comedy. "Deducti silvis" [coming from the forests] rather than the city, Horace's satyrs retain a higher decorum than the urban denizens of comedy. Horace's satyr play, then, is carefully calibrated between tragic and comic registers.

Highly influential in codifying the dramatic *satira* was the dissemination of Vitruvius's *De architectura*, "rediscovered" in Montecassino in 1414.[10] It became a text that functioned like Aristotle's *Poetics*—generative of multiple interpretations and creative misinterpretations. Vitruvius distinguishes between tragedic, comedic, and "satyric" scene designs: the tragedic scene utilizes monumental, courtly structures; the comedic scene displays the private and commercial buildings of a city; and the satyric scene is adorned with "trees, caverns, mountains, and other rustic elements delineated in rustic style" (V.vi.9).[11] Pellegrino Prisciano, a librarian for Ercole I in Ferraro, was the first fifteenth-century humanist explicitly to link Vitruvius's tripartite division of scenic design with the genres of tragedy, comedy, and the "satyric" play. In the *Spectacula*, written between 1486 and 1500, he conceives of the latter in terms of pastoral *otium* and erotics: "la dolcezza et piacere de le campagne et ville, li amori, et inamoramenti de' pastori" [the sweetness and pleasure of the country, the loves and passions of shepherds].[12] But it was Poliziano, author of *Orfeo*, who provided the most insightful fifteenth-century account of the third genre. Poliziano identifies Euripides' *Cyclops* as the only extant satyr play, connects it with the Renaissance satyric play, and carefully distinguishes the form from both comedy and tragedy. In his *praelectio* on Persius of 1484/85, well known through J. Bade's 1510 edition, Poliziano writes: "Satyrica hilaritatem lachrymis admiscebat atque ab eiulatu in laetitiam desineabat" [The satirical poem mixes laughter with tears and from lament ends in happiness].[13] In other words the *satira* is tragicomedic, both mixing tragic and comic emotions and deflecting from a tragedic towards a comedic ending. And for Poliziano, the representative figure of the classically based satyric play is not the shepherd but the satyr: "satyrice vero a satyris vocata . . . idest a rusticis et humilibus personis" [the satyrical poetry is named from satyrs . . . that is from rustic and humble people].[14]

An important paradox arose in regard to the nature of the Vitruvian satyric scene. Differing from Horace in his 1521 commentary on Vitruvius, Bramante's student Cesare Cesariano places the satyric play below comedy in the generic hierarchy, because he conceives of satyrs as allegories of vice and the wild *scena satyrica* as an apt locale for "la gente vitiosa e rustica, aut senza intellecto" [vicious and rustic people without intelligence].[15] For Cesariano, who follows the incorrect conflation of the ancient satyr play and Latin satire, it is a wild and bestial place for those who have been excluded from the city because of their vices. The highly influential Sebastiano Serlio similarly views the satyric scene as the wild habitat of those, like satyrs, who live "licenziosamente" but goes on to praise the arts that have magnificently added to nature in productions of recent satyric plays.[16] The *scena satyrica*, in Italian drama as in *The Tempest*, could thus be a place of wildness, negatively defining "civilization," and could at the same time be gloriously adorned and consequently a display of civilized arts.

The theoretical revolution of the 1540s fundamentally altered assumptions about the pastoral play. Dramaturgy closely followed upon scenography. Serlio's 1545 codification of the *scena satyrica* as staging a wholly distinct and integral third genre—an innovative if perhaps unjustified extrapolation from Vitruvius—closely preceded the revolution of pastoral dramaturgy that took place in Ferrara, beginning with Giraldi and culminating with Tasso and Guarini. Although Agostino Beccari's 1554 *Il sacrificio* is often considered to be the Ferraran pastoral play that initiated the line leading to *Aminta* and *Il pastor fido*, Giraldi is more important for our purposes because of his marriage of theory and practice and because of the tragicity of his model. I dwell on Giraldi because I consider the satyr figure as central to a Renaissance pastoral mode that had tragicomedic possibilities.[17]

Giraldi deliberately intended to revive the Greek satyr play and chose the satyr rather than the shepherd as its chief protagonist, along with his fellow fauns, nymphs, sylvans, and pastoral superiors Silenus and Pan. In the play *Egle* (first performed in 1545, the same year as Serlio's treatise) and then in a theoretical defense of his satyric play or *satira* published in 1554, he offers a fairly coherent dramaturgy of the new genre.[18] His theoretical justification of his own play is necessary, he says, because of the complete absence of any classical theory of the genre, excepting Horace's brief but influential remarks. The *Lettera* provides a neo-Aristotelian justification of the *satira*, a form whose immediate antecedents in the Italian pastoral tradition might suggest it as primitive and beneath the dignity of comedy and tragedy. Giraldi's theory is at once neoclassical and innovative.

Taking a historical approach to genre (as did, in fact, Aristotle), Giraldi considers various theories regarding the primitive origins of the satyr play. He treats the satyr play as a distinctive kind of its own, not merely an "imperfect tragedy" waiting to evolve into its mature form or an *intermezzo* designed for comic relief in tragedy. From primitive and rustic beginnings may evolve a perfected and discrete form, more substantial than minor kinds like the epigram and fully capable of being staged, unlike the pastoral eclogues of Vergil and his Renaissance imitators. (Genres, then, are historically mutable and become adaptable to new mediums.) Giraldi's *satira* is tragicomedic not because it indiscriminately juxtaposes tragic and comic elements but because it carefully calibrates an intermediate generic register in the Horatian tradition. In palpably Aristotelian terms, Giraldi rationalizes the generically liminal quality of a form that had previously been tragicomic only by accident: "La satira è imitazione di azione perfetta di dicevole grandezza, composta al giocoso ed al grave con parlar soave . . . rappresentata a commovere gli animi a riso, ed a convenevole terrore e compassione" [The *satira* is an imitation of a complete action of a suitable grandeur, with the light and the heavy mixed with sweet speech, represented in order to move people to laughter and appropriate terror and pity].[19] The chief *action* of *Egle* depicts the struggle of the Olympian gods with the semidivine sylvans for the erotic attention of the nymphs, also semidivine. As a cosmic conflict that threatens universal order itself, the action is comparable to the chthonic-Olympian struggle of the *Oresteia*, but clearly reduced in magnitude from the heights of tragedy. *Stylistically*, satyric diction strikes "un certo convenevole mezzo tra la comedia e la tragedia" [a certain decorous mean between comedy and tragedy] in its frequent recourse to bittersweet Petrarchan poetics and in the use of tragedic meter instead of comedic prose.[20] *Emotionally*, the satyrs' pathos and the play's unhappy ending (which Giraldi alone of major Cinquecento playwrights ascribed to the pastoral play) elicits an attenuated, tragicomic register of "appropriate terror and pity," a controlled diminution of the affective intensity proper to tragedy. *Structurally*, Giraldi follows the ancient satyr play in placing jocose material in a tragedic structure: tragedic meter, a chorus, a prologue, and an alternation of episode and chorus ending in a final *exodos*. And as we shall see in the following chapter, the satyr is a tragicomedic figure, generically liminal in regard to *person*.

VERISIMILITUDE AND THE MARVELOUS

An inherent tension in neo-Aristotelian poetics arose from the promulgation of two apparently contradictory desiderata. On the one hand, the poem was supposed to be verisimilar, constructed from possible and not impossible or miraculous events. On the other hand, it was supposed to be marvelous and elicit wonder in the reader or audience. Castelvetro attempts to reconcile these principles when he says that the pleasure of the marvelous lies in seeing something happen that we had previously thought impossible.[21] Although Castelvetro is extreme among classical and Renaissance critics in his valorization of history and verisimilitude (even Aristotle tolerated impossible events if they rendered the poem more marvelous), he is typical in the way that he carefully *negotiates* the claims of the marvelous and verisimilitude. All literary mediums should hold to verisimilitude, according to neoclassicists like Castelvetro, but especially drama, less capable of fictional license because of its physical immediacy. Whereas narrative romance of the medieval and Renaissance periods was relatively unconcerned with verisimilitude, dramatic romance had to reckon with the problem.

Such a negotiation is central to the dramaturgy of Giraldi's *satira*. Based on the fantastic satyr, Giraldi's new form follows the ancient satyr play in treating mythological stories in a less verisimilar manner than in tragedy. *Egle* ends with a marvelous, Ovidian metamorphosis typical of many Italian plays that used pastoral as an licensed arena for supernatural phenomenon. But unlike earlier playwrights, Giraldi carefully reconciles the claims of verisimilitude and the marvelous. And so the Ovidian metamorphosis is not enacted onstage but is rationalized as narration. The increasingly sophisticated stage machinery developed by Ferrarese scenographers, may

> [fanno] nascere le maraviglie, come l'apparire degli dei, se la qualità della favola introdotta il chiede, il fare veder folgori, sentir tuoni, cader dal cielo grandine e pioggia, ed altre tali cose, le quali nondimeno arrecano bruttezza e sconvenevolezza, se non vi sono attamente, ed a tempo introdotte

[{cause} marvels to be born, like the appearance of gods, if the quality of the plot requires it, and make one see lightning, hear thunder,
make hail and rain fall out of the sky, and other such things. But
such displays bring ugliness and unseemliness, if they are not
handled properly and at the right time.][22]

The marvelous, an important element of late-Quattrocento and early-
Cinquecento pastoral drama, now becomes cautiously regulated. Certainly the meteorological marvels mentioned by Giraldi resemble
Prospero's dazzling stage effects in *The Tempest*, but an even more striking similarity between Giraldi's and Shakespeare's pastoral plays is the
continual negotiation between the verisimilar and the marvelous, the
supreme image for which is Prospero's intention to "drown" his magic
book (*The Tempest* 5.1.57).

Many late-Cinquecento pastoral playwrights were less constrained
by the claim of verisimilitude than Giraldi and his Ferraran successors
Tasso and Guarini, although because of Counter-Reformation proscriptions of pagan alternatives to Christian supernaturalism, magic was
presented in an ideologically neutral, vaguely pagan fashion. Luigi
Pasqualigo's 1581 *Gl'intricati* brings three *arte*-like buffoons into an enchanted Arcadian world inhabited by a *maga*, who guards a magic liquor
and book, and terrifies the buffoons with mysterious voices issuing from
the woods.[23] The plays of Pasqualigo, Pietro Cresci, Gieronimo Vida,
Camillo Della Valle, and others preserve the Ovidian metamorphoses
popular in earlier Cinquecento pastoral: male and female magicians,
nymphs and shepherds transformed into fountains, plants, and trees;
and clowns changed into animals and back into human form.[24] Giovanni Battista Leoni's 1595 *Roselmina, favola tragisatiricomica* imports
supernatural devices from *Orlando Furioso*: a magic, Astolfan horn that
puts people to flight and an enchanted ring that renders one's inter-
locutor mute.[25] And supernaturalism also survived in the pastoral tragicomedies of the *commedia dell'arte*. The *commedia mago* wields all manner
of fantastic power, if he sometimes also recalls Prospero by throwing
away his magic rod and book.[26] And as reflected in the title of one scenario, *Arcadia incantata*, the entire island of the *arte* plays is, as Caliban
might put it, "full of noises, / sounds, and sweet airs, that give delight,
and hurt not" (*The Tempest* 3.2.133–34). If, in comedies from Bruno's
Candelaio to Jonson's *Alchemist*, the agent of supernatural change is exposed as a fraud, the pastoral mode can partially suspend the imperative of comedic verisimilitude, rendering the *mago* a figure to be taken
seriously.

In the cases of the more strictly Aristotelian *Aminta* and *Il pastor fido*, metamorphosis is only preserved in marginal or vestigial form. *Aminta* relegates Proteo, the god of transformation, to an *intermezzo*.[27] Guarini's play is also characterized by an alternation between the verisimilar action of the play and the mythological marvels of the *intermezzi*. After a farcical struggle, the Satiro of *Il pastor fido* thinks that Corisca has escaped by miraculously losing her head; in fact she has only left her wig in the Satiro's hands (2.6). Ultimately, metamorphosis may become no more than the psychological changes wrought by love and other forces, over which Tasso's Amore and Proteo declare their rule. The supreme virtuosic feat of the tragicomedic playwright, according to Guarini, is to elicit the marvelous without violating verisimilitude. The excellence of his own play lies in its capacity to "produrre la maraviglia, dov'ella è si malagevole da trovarsi, che s'alcuno Poema Eroico si ritrova, che habbia questa qualità del mirabile, non è da farsene maraviglia, potendo esso con le parole finger cose impossibili, e lontane dal verisimile" [produce the marvelous, which is difficult to do {in drama}, for if one finds this quality of the marvelous in an epic poem, one should not be surprised, because epic may depict impossible things far from verisimilar].[28] What is important here is Guarini's careful distinction between the ways in which the playwright and the epic poet treat the marvelous. Whereas the epic poet can elicit wonder by means of miracles, the dramatic poet has a greater challenge, for he must remain within the limits of verisimilitude. The playwright of pastoral drama has some advantage here, because the first shepherds in Guarini's view possessed the natural power of wonder that, according to Aristotle, leads men to philosophy (*Annotazioni* 1:7–8).[29]

Although Shakespearean pastoral, like *The Faithful Shepherdess* and *The Sad Shepherd*, is partial to marvelous supernaturalism (to which it in part owes its theatrical success), it continually negotiates the claims of verisimilitude and the marvelous after the manner of the Aristotelian Italians. The distance from *A Midsummer Night's Dream* to the late plays may be measured by the elevation of the claims of verisimilitude in relationship to the marvelous. In the final scene of *The Winter's Tale*, what appeared to be a supernatural, Ovidian metamorphosis is finally rationalized by Paulina, whereas the most crucial transformation turns out to be the change wrought in Leontes' heart: the psychological "unstoning" of Hermione. *The Winter's Tale* also displays an interesting vestige of pastoral supernaturalism; instead of actually staging gods (as Fletcher's "To the Reader" would allow), Perdita and Florizel are merely, if persistently, compared to divinities (1.4.1–34).*The Tempest*'s dramatization of the limitations of magic, best expressed in the epilogue, is at least as important as its dazzling marvels.

TASSO, GUARINI, AND THE TRAGICITY OF PASTORAL

One must look beyond Tasso and Guarini, to early-Cinquecento pastoral farces and eclogues, to the *commedia dell'arte* play, and to later courtly and academic pastoral plays, to find the full range of pastoral theatergrams and dramaturgical strategies available to Shakespeare. Still, *Aminta* and *Il pastor fido* do merit special consideration in a comparative study, if only because they were known by English playwrights as early as 1591 via Wolfe's edition. And Guarini's theory of tragicomedy, which in the *Verati* includes a discussion of the bridging function played by pastoral, illuminates both plays and supremely expresses the achievement of a dramaturgy for a form that in the late Quattrocento and early Cinquecento had been chiefly shaped by scenographic and mythological considerations and by the aristocratic, civic, and rural festival. Following their Ferraran predecessor Giraldi, Tasso and Guarini most fully explore the *calibration* of tragicomedic dramaturgy in regard to set, semiotics, style, and affective response. Finally, Guarini and Tasso's plays deserve special consideration because they are the most tragedic of Italian pastoral tragicomedies. Most of the courtly and academic pastorals contemporary with *Aminta* and *Il pastor fido* follow the intrigue structure of the *commedia erudita*, unlike *Aminta*, and lack anything like the Sophoclean weight of *Il pastor fido*. Character types and relationships common to New Comedy and *commedia erudita* populate these plays.[30] In regard to the tragicity of the pastoral mode, Shakespeare follows the famous Ferraran playwrights more than Daniel and Fletcher, who are more content with the traditional limits of pastoral.

Although Tasso, in *Delle differenze poetiche*, argues against the mixing of genres,[31] his *Aminta* is important for the way it accommodates higher generic registers than those traditionally allotted to pastoral and thus prepares for Guarini, who took *Aminta* as his prototype. In the persona of Tirsi, Tasso describes how, after having worked on *Gerusalemme Liberata*, he intends to graft epic elements onto a pastoral tree:[32]

> Ed in quel punto
> sentii me far di me stesso maggiore,

pien di nova virtù, pieno di nova
deitade, e cantai guerre ed eroi,
sdegnando pastoral ruvido carme.
E se ben poi (come altrui piacque) feci
ritorno a queste selve, io pur ritenni
parte di quello spirto: né già suona
la mia sampogna umil come soleva:
ma di voce più altera e più sonora
emula de le trombe, empie le selve.

(1.2.633–43)[33]

[Then, full of new power and new inspiration, I felt that I had made
something greater of myself, and I sang of wars and heroes, disdain-
ing rough pastoral song. And if later (as it pleased another) I returned
to these woods, still I retained something of that spirit; my pipe does
not sing humbly as before, but with a higher and more sonorous
voice; it emulates the trumpets, filling the woods.]

Tasso here proposes an alloy of pastoral and epic, a bucolic poetry whose
register has been raised in contact with epic. Tasso would elevate the
mode above the early-sixteenth-century rustic pastoral that privileges
the *villano* either alone or flanked by the sophisticated *pastore* or urban
dweller. Relative to the earlier pastoral, Tasso's new kind will engage
higher subjects, a higher style and diction, and characters of more elevated social station: courtiers disguised as shepherds. Instead of setting off the *villano* against the *pastore*, Tasso aims, in a kind of cultural
and theatrical metamorphosis that would displace supernatural Ovidian
metamorphosis, to transform the *villano* into the refined *pastore*: "Spirerò
nobil sensi a' rozzi petti, / raddolcirò de le lor lingue il suono" [I will
inspire noble sensibilities in rustic hearts, I will sweeten their speech]
(prologo 80–81). Proteus, the god of metamorphosis himself, presides
not over the changes that would violate Aristotelian verisimilitude but
over theatrical transformations, both the spectacular scenography of
which scenic artists working at the Ferraran court were supremely capable ("Trovai l'arte onde notturna scena / cangia l'aspetto" [I have
discovered the art by which the nocturnal scene changes its appear-
ance]) and the amatory metamorphoses that, effectively, transform the
genre of pastoral drama itself: "Quinci Amore istesso / trasforma in
tante guise i vaghi amanti" [And from this place Love himself transforms in many guises desirous lovers] (intermedio primo).

In opposition to the early *commedia erudita*'s cynical and farcical

handling of eros, *Aminta* along with other late-Cinquecento drama elevates eros, which can generate tragicomic, even tragic, experience.
Against Denores, who argues that tragedy is an exclusively political
genre that treats the fall of tyrants, Guarini points to the many domestic tragedies in the ancient Greek canon that concern love (*I Verato*, 2:242).
Tasso's *Aminta* casts love as a potentially tragic experience of harsher
registers than those that obtain in Petrarchan poetics; in Tasso it is productive of suicidal falls that only in perspective turn out to be fortunate. To a large degree, what moves *Aminta* from a static pastoral eclogue
to a play is the possibility of tragedy. The threat of tragedic violence is
displaced from the courtier to the satyr, whose attempted rape of Silvia
finally spurs Aminta to action, transforming the play from eclogue to
drama, *contra* Denores. "Disposto di morire" [ready to die], Aminta later
creates a tragedic horizon of expectation for the play's internal, if not
its external, audience: Tirsi speaks for other spectators of Aminta's tragic
passion when he says, "presago è il mio cor di qualche male" [my heart
forebodes some evil] (3.1.1310). To announce Aminta's apparent death,
a tragedic *nuncio* practically quotes from Aristotle's *Poetics*:

> Io ho sì pieno il petto di *pietate*
> d sì pieno d'*orror*, che non rimiro
> né odo alcuna cosa, ond'io mi volga,
> la qual non me spaventi e non m'affanni
> (5.2.1634–37, emphases mine)

[My heart is so full of *pity* and *horror* that, wherever I turn, I see or
hear nothing that does not terrify and distress me.]

Just before Aminta leaps to his ultimately fortunate fall, he casts himself as a tragedic actor. In a "pazzo furor " [mad fury] he utters "scongiuri
orribili" [horrible oaths], calling upon both local pastoral gods and the
hellish powers appropriate for tragedy (5.2.1684–86). From below, Elpino
describes the "sudden spectacle" of Aminta's fall in Aristotelian terms:
"Noi muti di *pietate* e di *stupore* / restammo a lo spettacolo improvviso"
[We remained dumb with pity and amazement at the unexpected spec-
tacle] (5.1.1919–20; emphases mine). The theoretical tags serve the practical purpose of forging an alloy of pastoral and tragedy.[34]
    Mostly excised from Guarini's *Compendio* is an extensive argument
for the generic capaciousness of the pastoral mode. Guarini defends
the comedic range of pastoral against Denores, who claims that the

rural pastoral form is incapable of expressing comic urbanity and wit. For Guarini, pastoral dwellers are not paragons of virtue living in pre-lapsarian states of grace, but are certainly capable of the moral turpitude that provided the matter of most Renaissance comedy. But Guarini is mostly interested in establishing the tragedic potentialities of pastoral, in a way that illuminates the "unwritten poetics" of Shakespearean drama from *King Lear* to *The Tempest*. In humanist fashion, Guarini locates classical precedents for an extended notion of pastoral that accommodates tragedic form and tragic experience: "Le pastorali sono capaci della grandezza Tragica, e . . . d'loro soggetti si possano formare buone Tragedie" [Pastorals are capable of tragedic grandeur, and good tragedies can be made out of pastoral subjects] (*I Verato*, 2:291). Even the paradigmatic tragedy *Oedipus the King* contains significant pastoral elements: Oedipus is raised by a shepherd who, in the denouement of the play, clinches Oedipus's self-recognition. In fact, if recognition becomes a standard element of neo-Aristotelian tragedy, pastoral stories can easily produce the requisite device because shepherds often travel from one country to another (288). In the pastoral-tragedic play, then, the *cognitio* typical of the pastoral romance story could be brought into accordance with neo-Aristotelian dramaturgy. And shepherds, Guarini continues, can themselves be tragedic protagonists, not merely ancillary to an Oedipus: "La nobiltà, e i casi orribili de'pastori non sono cose abborrenti dal verisimile del poeta" [The nobility of shepherds and the horrifying events that befall them do not violate poetic verisimilitude] (*II Verato*, 3:252). In pointing out that tragic atrocities such as blindness and hanging have befallen literary shepherds, Guarini's scheme in its widest interpretation would allow for blind Gloucester on the heath.

The capacity of pastoral to assimilate a tragedic apparatus is tested in *Il pastor fido*. Tasso's tragicomedic, pathetic plot of unrequited love, wound, and conversion is relegated to Guarini's subplot, the Silvio-Dorinda story. Guarini does also reprise the general contours of Tasso's Aminta-Silvia plot in the tragedic *antefatto* of the play, the story of Aminta and Lucrina narrated by Ergasto in act 1, scene 2, but in Guarini's case the "danger not the death" is turned into actual suicide. Like Tasso's Silvia, Lucrina spurns Aminta's love, but since Aminta is a priest of Diana's temple, the results are more public and more grave than in Tasso's play. Aminta beseeches Diana to revenge his broken faith, and she answers by imposing a Sophoclean blight on the country of Arcadia. The pastoral landscape, therefore, is literally transformed into a tragedic one. Only the sacrifice of Lucrina or a substitute will abate Diana's fury, and so Lucrina "fu con pompa solenne al sacro altare / vittima lagrime-vole condotta" [was lead in solemn pomp to the sacred altar, a pitiful victim] (1.2). Seemingly about to perform the tragedic act of vengeance himself, apparently incensed with tragic fury, Aminta suddenly turns the sword onto himself, "vittima e sacerdote in un" [at once victim and priest], whereupon Lucrina follows suit. Not even this double suicide, however, removes the blight; it is not lifted until a long recognition scene based on the ending of *Oedipus the King* sanctions the natural erotic link between Amarilli and Mirtillo. The dramaturgy of *Il pastor fido*—tragedic *antefatto* leading to tragicomedic resolution—thus reca-pitulates the historical transformation of tragedy into tragicomedy that took place in the late Cinquecento.

As with *Aminta*, the codes of tragedy are particularly evident, but now Sophoclean as well as Aristotelian. For example, the account of ominous, terrifying signs and sounds from the temple is lifted from Tiresias's speech in Sophocles' *Antigone*.[35] As he recognizes the identity of his son in a dialogue structure lifted from *Oedipus the King*, Montano becomes another Oedipus: "Oh qual me sento orror vagar per l'ossa!" [Oh, how I feel horror moving through my bones!] (5.5). *Il pastor fido* should be seen as a companion to the *Verati*, theorizing the tragicity of pastoral.

Both *Aminta* and *Il pastor fido* oppose "soft" or escapist pastoral to a tougher and more capacious version capable of negotiating with trag-edy. Versions of the pastoral pleasance, mythologized as the golden age and fantasized as escape from the court or city, are proposed only to be tested against the harsher realities of nature or the intrusion of court and city into the pastoral space. Aminta's childhood friendship with Silvia—"conforme era l'etate, / ma 'l pensier più conforme" [they were equal in age, but even more in thought] (*Aminta* 1.2.416–17)—bears comparison with that between Polixenes and Leontes ("twinn'd lambs that did frisk i' th' sun" [*The Winter's Tale* 1.2.67]) for a pastoral idyllism suddenly unable to accommodate the "stronger blood" of sexu-ality, which, in both cases, nearly generates tragedy. In *Il pastor fido*, the idyllic pastoral fantasized by Amarilli ("Felice pastorella . . ." [2.5]) with its corresponding vision of altogether benign and nonviolent love, is not Guarini's pastoral, which admits within its borders city sharpers like Corisca, beasts even more dangerous than the wolf typical to pas-toral, and love in its tragicomic, even violent, dimensions.

THE *SCENA SATYRICA*

Serlio's Vitruvian extrapolation codified the comedic scene in a urban locale, the tragedic scene in a courtly setting, and the *scena satyrica* as a outdoor, forested place.[37] The *scena satyrica* accommodated greater possibilities for scenographic imagination and experimentation than the two established kinds, incorporating elements of the tragedic and comedic decors. Because of its flexibility and the occasions it offered for dazzling metamorphoses and theatrical effects, pastoral became the preferred genre for scenographers in northern Italian courts by the end of the sixteenth century. In the prologue to *Il pastor fido*, Alfeo's aqueous peregrinations represent the flexibility and transportability of the pastoral mode itself: he came from Arcadia, the legendary home of pastoral, fled to Sicily in pursuit of Arethusa, and arrived in Turin for the production of Guarini's pastoral play (one that, in fact, never took place). Alfeo establishes a new Arcadia by deictic fiat: "*Questa* la chiostra è pur, *questo* quell'antro / dell'antica Ericina; / e *quel*, che colà sorge, è pur il tempio / a la gran Cintia sacro" [*Here* is the enclosure, *here* is the cave of ancient Ericina, and *here*, where it rises, is the temple sacred to Diana] (prologo; emphases mine). Guarini's pastoral is defined not by physical walls but by modal outlook: "Cingea popolo inerme / un muro d'innocenza e di virtute" [A wall of innocence surrounded an unarmed people] (prologo).[37]

In the two *Verati*, Guarini proposes for the third kind a generically flexible set capable of depicting experience of a greater range than that normally associated with the pleasance of the pastoral greensward. The pastoral set described by Serlio and realized in many late-Cinquecento pastorals could include not only pleasant meadows and woods, but mountains, caves, rocks, deserts, seashores, and dark, labyrinthine woods reminiscent of the landscapes of Dante and Ariosto.[38] For Leoni's heroine Roselmina wandering through Ireland, it is the confusion and discomfort of the *selva* (forest) and not the pleasance of the *prato* (meadow) that marks the landscape: "queste strane habitazioni di fiere e di gente selvaggia" [these strange dwellings of beasts and savage people] (1.1). The Sophoclean blight upon Arcadia at the beginning of *Il pastor fido*, replete with a land-ravaging boar, renders Guarini's pastoral landscape a place of hardship. The sea, sometimes tempestuous as in the *arte* scenarios, can also constitute the pastoral locus. In *Alceo*, Ongaro transposes *Aminta* to a maritime setting, and even inland pastorals like *Roselmina* can open out to the sea, where the glutton lives and where Roselmina takes her equestrian recreation.[39] The generically liminal, maritime pastoral set of *The Winter's Tale* 3.3, the stark, stormy Bohemian seacoast in which men are mauled by bears and "things new born" are discovered, is then very like the late-Cinquecento pastoral set in the polyvalence of its generic codes and in its atmospheric range.

The *scena satyrica* as described by Serlio adds to its natural elements temples and statues that, as Guarini points out, appropriate the classical sculpture of the court-based tragedic set (*Il Verato*, 3:269–70). Almost every Italian pastoral set features a temple, and the shepherds in Pasqualigo's *Gl'intricati* are said to render homage to a statue of Athena.[40] Anticipating the expected objection of Denores that the inclusion of such architecture constitutes a monstrous pastiche of different genres, Guarini defends such scenic latitude. Whereas the royal palaces and sumptuous edifices of tragedy signal the splendor and ambition of courtly life, pastoral transforms classical magnificence into a religious decorum—in Guarini's imagination, shepherds built temples not for ostentation, but for primarily religious reasons. Like several other pastoral plays, the action of Pasqualigo's *Gl'intricati* converges on the temple, with the lovers beseeching the goddess Athena for delivery from their complex erotic misalignments. The most significant counterpoint to Leontes' court tragedy of acts 1 to 3—the description by Cleomenes and Dion in act 3, scene 1, of the solemn temple and reverent religious ceremony they had witnessed on the "fertile" and "sweet" isle of "Delphos"—can then be understood in terms of the communicative power of place codes in tragicomedic dramaturgy. The account of the temple lends a religious, reverent cast to the high decorum and prefigures the play's movement from tragedy to pastoral to what the Italians would call *commedia grave*.

"HARD" AND "SOFT" PASTORAL IN SHAKESPEARE'S LATE PLAYS

A brief look at Daniel's *Queenes Arcadia* will demonstrate that interest in pastoral-tragic modalities extended from Italy to England. Daniel explicitly raises the issue of pastoral boundaries: the relationship of pastoral with other experiences and genres. The imposing physical boundaries of Daniel's Arcadia—the mountains and the rocks that bound the set as described by the corrupt foreigner Lincus (3.1.1026)—seem to represent the utter separation of the pastoral locus from the outside world: the Arcadians have "no intertrading with the rest / Of men" (3.1.1027–28).[41] In its definition by negatives ("no purchasings, no contracts, no commerse, / No politique commands, no services") (3.1.986–87), Lincus's account anticipates Gonzalo's utopian vision of Prospero's island in *The Tempest*. Daniel had worked and would continue to work in the explicitly political kinds of tragedy and verse chronicle, but the prologue to the *Queenes Arcadia* explicitly shuns politics. Pastoral tragicomedy is a "claustrall exercise / Where men shut out retyr'd, and sequestred / From publike fashion, seeme to sympathize / With innocent and plaine simplicity" (prologue 14–17). It is difficult to say whether this abjuration of politics covers bitterness or relief for someone who had been called into the Privy Council because of controversy aroused by his tragedy *Philotas*. For Daniel, it is the idea of generic decorum that insures that pastoral tragicomedy does not overreach itself into the dangerous realm of politics. One should "dare not enterprize to show / In lower stile the hidden mysteries, / And arts of Thrones" (prologue 21–23).

Even Daniel's professedly humble pastoral, however, does not remain within these self-declared bounds. The dramatic interest of the play precisely consists in the negotiation of pastoral with comedic and tragedic elements. Contested boundaries signify that all is not well in Arcadia:

> MELIBAEUS. And we that never were accustomed
> To quarrel for our bounds, how do we see
> Montanus and Acrysius interstrive
> How farre their severall Sheep-walks should extend.
>   (1.1.35–38)

As we have seen, the play tests the world of Arcadia against the satirically coded, corrupt urban world, represented by Colax the traveler, Techne the "subtle wench," the charlatan Alcon, and the conniving lawyer Lincus. And transgressions of pastoral decorum are conceived in tragedic terms as well. Like the pastoral place of *Il pastor fido*, Daniel's Arcadia suffers from a blight evocative of the beginning of Sophocles' paradigmatic tragedy; "our very aire is chang'd / Our wholesome climate growne more maladive" with "new infirmities, / New Fevers" complains Ergastus (1.1.25–26, 31–32)—evocative plague references for a 1605 London audience. According to Melibaeus, the "infection" has been brought across the boundaries of Arcadia by Colax the corrupted traveler, whose "will" is "Without all bounds" (1.4.317). The initial postulate of the play is the tragically coded "distemperature" (1.4.312) and passionate "extremities" (2.4.907) of the lovers, referred to once as "A sullen subject for a Tragedy" (4.4.1832), which will be tempered by tragicomedic dramaturgy in the manner of Guarini. Here dramaturgy and plot coalesce. The realignment of eros moderates potentially tragic passions.

From a cameo appearance in *King Henry VI, Part III*, to the green worlds of early comedies such as *Two Gentlemen of Verona*, to the magic forest of *A Midsummer Night's Dream*, to the ferocious antipastoral of *King Lear*, to the late plays, the pastoral mode continually appealed to Shakespeare's imagination. The general tendency, in Shakespeare's career, for pastoral to become increasingly capacious and increasingly tragicomedic culminates in the late plays in ways that fulfill the promise of Cinquecento theory.

In the early history play, the hapless Henry VI fantasizes a pastoral escape from the cares of government in a time of war (*King Henry VI, Part 3* 2.5.21–54).[42] The otiose vision of the shepherd's life, in which the fullness of time is achieved by honest and simple pastoral labor, could not be more opposed to the tragic world of "Care, Mistrust, and Treason" hurtling the king to his catastrophe. Not experientially but allusively the pastoral arena of *A Midsummer Night's Dream* (its supernaturalism anticipating the charmed island of *The Tempest*) begins to bridge tragedy and comedy, providing a space for the mechanicals to rehearse their tragicomic production ("lamentable comedy"; "tragical mirth") (1.2.11; 5.1.57) of the Pyramus and Thisbe story, of near tragedic consequence in Tasso's *Aminta* and of tragedic issue in the contemporary *Romeo and Juliet*. But it is *As You Like It*—a play G. K. Hunter sees as influenced by Guarini not only in its "faithful shepherd" reference (5.2.80)—in which Shakespeare most fully "rehearses" the tragicomedic possibilities of the pastoral mode, thus anticipating the late plays.[43] The idyllism implicit in secondary accounts of Duke Senior's voluntary exile—Charles the wrestler has heard that he and his men "fleet the time carelessly as they did in the golden world" (1.1.118–19)—is belied by Duke Senior's stoic acceptance of the "icy fang / and churlish chiding of the winter's wind" (2.1.6–7), the snake and lioness that bloody the green world red (4.3.98–156), and the satirist Jacques' recognition of pain and violence in the usually innocuous pastoral sport of hunting (2.1.25–66). The fraternal enmity that would provide the matter of *Hamlet* and *King Lear* continually locates tragedy, in an abbreviated form, at the margins of the pastoral space. But just as Duke Senior translates the stubbornness of (tragedic) fortune into a "quiet" and "sweet" pastoral style (2.1.19–20), pastoral transforms potential tragedy into a different generic register. Duke Frederick, a humorous tyrant in his court, is conjured away from his fratricidal project, not by any psychologically developed conversion but apparently by genre, by the magic circle of the pastoral space (5.4.153–64). (That it only seems like magic, and is given the verisimilar and orthodox explanation of a religious conversion, echoes a similarly Italianate negotiation of pastoral supernaturalism and verisimilitude in the disguised Rosalind's odd reference to her magician tutor, whom she insists is not "damnable" [5.2.62] despite his "desperate studies" [5.4.32]). Orlando at first misreads the pastoral landscape as he charges the Duke's men with his sword drawn, but he enters a nontragic world in which "gentleness" may become his "strong enforcement" (2.7.118). It is not a tragic place of horror but a tragicomic locus of pity and pathos, a community of men and women who know "what 'tis to pity and be pitied" (2.7.117), where the "big, round tears" (2.1.38) of the stricken hart may even induce compassion. The "wide and universal" pastoral theater (2.7.137) and its community of fellow sufferers transforms tragic particularity (one suffers alone) to comic generality. Pastoral serves as a stage for Jacques's famous metatheatrical observation that thus tempers tragedy—and may also refer to four of the *commedia dell'arte* comedic types: the lover, the braggart soldier, the doctor, and Pantalone.[44]

Relative to the late plays, the tragicomedic potentiality of the pastoral mode is realized less fully in *As You Like It*. In the prominent persona of the "satyrist" Jacques, who "rail[s] against our mistress the world" (3.2.273), satire is given a higher thematic and dramatic profile than it has in the late plays—and it is worth noting that the play was written just before dramatic satire emerged on the English Renaissance stage. Many of the pastoral transformations of tragedic matter are narrated, as in Jacques De Boys's anticlimactic account that ends the play proper, giving way to the principally dilatory and verbal nature of a play. The pastoral mode in *As You Like It* most importantly functions as the scaffold for dilation and debate in the exchanges between Rosalind and Orlando, Touchstone and Corin, and in the expostulations of Jacques.

The boundaries of pastoral in Shakespeare's tragical-pastoral-comical late plays are even more porous than those of *As You Like It*, allowing the mode to negotiate with comedy and especially tragedy. Each of Shakespeare's late plays posits a version of soft pastoral only to extend the pastoral mode's range, whether by moving to the mountainous, hard life of Belarius and his sons, traveling to the strange Bohemian "seacoast" plagued by violent storms and terrifying bears, or by admitting the Antonios and Sebastians not taken into account by Gonzalo's republic.

The first explicit version of pastoral in *Cymbeline* is static, escapist, and soft, recalling Henry VI's vision of timeless pastoral *otium*. Beset by the oppressive court, Imogen fantasizes a pastoral retreat in which she and Posthumus would play at being shepherds:

> Would I were
> A neat-herd's daughter, and my Leonatus
> Our neighbor-shepherd's son!
>
> (1.2.79–81)[45]

Invoking the theatergram of the presexual, innocent childhood friendship in a pastoral retreat that characterizes the *antefatti* of *Aminta* and Bonarelli's *Filli de Sciro*, Imogen would return to her apparently nonsexual relationship with her "playfellow" (1.2.76) Posthumus. Such pastoral defines itself in absolute opposition to court and city. It is a pure, enclosed kind, such as pastoral was understood by Denores, and not capable of communication with other kinds.

The dichotomized opposition of the oppressive court and Imogen's soft pastoral fantasy follows an overall scheme of moral polarization that characterizes the beginning of the play. To a greater degree than in *The Winter's Tale* and *The Tempest*, this moral polarization is expressed in the modalities of romance, with stock romance characters such as the evil stepmother. (We may remember, however, Jameson's linking of the pastoral and romance modes.)[46] Although Imogen's later mistaking of Cloten's body for that of Posthumus may symbolically suggest that Posthumus's violent misogyny has reduced him to Cloten's moral level, the First Gentleman conceives Posthumus as absolutely good:

> FIRST GENT. He that hath miss'd the princess is a thing
> Too bad for bad report: and he that hath her
> (I mean, that married her, alack good man,
> And therefore banish'd) is a creature such
> As, to seek through the regions of the earth
> For one his like; *there would be something failing*
> *In him that should compare.* I do not think
> So fair an outward, and such stuff within

Endows a man, but he.
SEC. GENT. You speak him far.
FIRST GENT. I do extend him, sir, within himself
                                    (1.1.16–25, emphases mine)

The speech polarizes good and evil so that neither can be compared or
measured against each other or against the world. Posthumus is a tau-
tology, only capable of being "extend[ed] . . . within himself." Organic,
soft pastoral metaphors of effortless growth characterize the account of
the young Posthumus's formation in Cymbeline's court: he receives
instruction "as we do air, fast as 'twas minister'd, / And in's spring
became a harvest" (1.1.45–46). *Cymbeline* begins, then, with an absolute
moral dualism that Shakespeare's rich tragicomic sense of life as a
"mingled yarn, good and ill together" (*All's Well That Ends Well* 4.3.70–
73) will submit to critical scrutiny.[47]

The version of pastoral enacted by the play is tougher and of more
porous boundaries than that fantasized by Imogen or described in the
play's exposition. Although no shepherds inhabit the Wales of *Cymbeline*,
Rosalie L. Colie and Michael Taylor have rightly identified in the
Belarius-Arviragus-Guiderius scenes an example of hard pastoral: a life
of hard work in the face of hostile weather and a forbidding landscape,
but, qua pastoral, a selected, separated space created and maintained
as an alternative to the court or city.[48] The set, featuring a cave (site of
important action here as well as in *Il pastor fido*) and mountains, extracts the roughest aspects of the *scena satyrica*, with the rough weather
of which the boys complain practically removing any traces of the pleasance. *Otium* takes the form of vigorous, athletic games (3.3.75).

At first, what seems to be most significant about the pastoral space
Belarius has created is precisely its boundedness, its complete isolation
from the court. From the boys' point of view, the boundedness of
Belarius' pastoral is oppressive, denying them the comparative perspective available to their exiled father:

> GUID. Haply this life is best
> (If quiet life be best) sweeter to you
> That have a sharper known, well corresponding
> With your stiff age; but unto us it is
> A cell of ignorance, travelling a-bed,
> A prison, or a debtor that not dares
> To stride a limit.
>   (3.3.29–35)

The boundaries of Wales, however, turn out to be much more porous than those of soft pastoral or of Belarius's professed moral pastoral. Belarius begins a series of audience asides that indicate to us the true, princely nature of the boys and suggest that they will not remain forever in Belarius's cave. Crude devices in the opinion of some critics, these asides indicate the provisional nature and modal flexibility of Belarius's (and Shakespeare's) pastoral. So Belarius:

> How hard it is to hide the sparks of Nature!
> These boys know little they are sons to th'king,
> Nor Cymbeline dreams that they are alive.
> They think they are mine, and though train'd up thus meanly,
> I' th' cave wherein they bow, their thoughts do hit
> The roofs of palaces, and Nature prompts them
> In simple and low things to prince it, much
> Beyond the trick of others. This Polydore,
> The heir of Cymbeline and Britain, who
> The king his father call'd Guiderius,—Jove!
> When on my three-foot stool I sit, and tell
> The warlike feats I have done, his spirits fly out
> Into my story: say 'Thus mine enemy fell,
> And thus I set my foot on's neck,' even then
> The princely blood flows in his cheek, he sweats,
> Strains his young nerves, and puts himself in posture
> That acts my words.
>
> (3.3.79–95)

Although they are bounded in a pastoral nutshell, Guiderius and Arviragus are kings of infinite space. If telling stories is an appropriately pastoral activity, Belarius's stories test and almost push beyond the cave's—and pastoral's—boundaries. It is as if the pastoral is an artificial but serious theater in which the boys can rehearse deeds to be performed in the real world of history. In language that strikingly evokes the physical work of the actor, Guiderius "sweats, / Strains his young nerves, and puts himself in posture / That acts my words." Likewise, Arviragus "strikes life into [Belarius's] speech." Belarius reads the script and the boys enact it in a theatrical space that stops just short of actualization. Belarius's fiction remembers, reprises, and rehearses the engaged events of his worldly past, but it preserves itself as distinct fiction only so long as it stops short of fully engaged heroism and engagement with history.

Belarius recognizes that the arrival and killing of Cloten spell the beginning of the end of his protected, pastoral theater and initiate the move back into history: Cloten's body "hath a tail / More perilous than the head" (4.2.143–44). The killing of Cloten initiates a more active interplay between pastoral and history than that effected by Belarius's cave stories. Violence inappropriate to the pastoral decorum invades its boundaries—although the displacement of violence offstage adjusts the levels of violence in a manner appropriate to a tragicomedic decorum. And Belarius realizes that as an uncanny messenger, Cloten is an earnest of further negotiations with the court. As "pastoral-historical," *Cymbeline* aims to join the "lopp'd branches" to the "old stock" of the "stately cedar": to graft the pastoral denizens Guiderius and Belarius back onto the British dynastic tree.

Comparable to the transportability of Guarini's Alfeo is the modal flexibility of pastoral in *The Winter's Tale*, in which Shakespeare moves pastoral from Sicily (as the legendary home of pastoral) to Bohemia back to Sicily, insofar as the newly gentled shepherds are transported to Leontes' kingdom. The notorious geographical errors for the two important places alternative to the Sicilian court—the "isle" of Delphos (with the temple common to the pastoral landscape) and the "seacoast" of Bohemia—might be thought to reflect less Shakespeare's carelessness than their status as places of the imagination: "landscapes of the mind" that transform the original tragedy for both the internal and external audience.

Like *Cymbeline*, *The Winter's Tale* explores the range of pastoral by opposing soft pastoral and a more realistic version of the mode. The purity and isolation of something like Denorian pastoral is invoked by Polixenes shortly before Leontes initiates the tragedy; it is far less capacious and variegated than the pastoral actually enacted later on:

> We were, fair queen,
> Two lads that thought there was no more behind,
> But such a day to-morrow as to-day,
> And to be boy eternal.
> .   .   .   .
> We were as twinn'd lambs that did frisk i'th' sun,
> And bleat the one at th'other: what we chang'd
> Was innocence for innocence: we knew not
> The doctrine of ill-doing, nor dream'd
> That any did. Had we pursu'd that life,
> And our weak spirits ne'er been higher rear'd
> With stronger blood, we should have answer'd heaven

Boldly 'not guilty', the imposition clear'd
Hereditary ours.

(1.2.62–65, 67–75)

With Denores and against Guarini, Polixenes remembers a pastoral of complete innocence, altogether bounded from the world of city and court and unable to converse with the potentially tragic consequences of sexuality. *The Winter's Tale* moves to center stage the pastoral theatergram of an innocent childhood friendship that suddenly is imperiled by sexuality. It is a world undifferentiated regarding time ("such a day to-morrow as to-day"), individual identity ("twinn'd lambs"), and sexual gender: "stronger blood" has not yet, in a bawdy pun, "higher rear'd" the boys' innocent selves to an acknowledgment of sexual difference and the concomitant sense of guilt that pervade Shakespeare's tragedies. The timelessness and *otium* of the speech link it with Polixenes' earlier pastoral account of his time in Sicilia—"Nine changes of the watery star hath been / The shepherd's note since we have left our throne / Without a burden" (1.2.1-3). The nine-month period suggests both an abandonment of political responsibility that has bred fears of "sneaping winds at home" (1.2.13) and a time that is "fill'd up" with Leontes' suspicions that Polixenes has fathered Hermione's child. Continuing to polarize absolute good and evil in the manner of romance and soft pastoral, Polixenes later contrasts the "varying childness" of his son with "thoughts that thick my blood" (1.2.171). It would appear that the "pure" version of soft pastoral yields, as its unmediated opposite, the pure tragedy that Leontes (Polixenes' "twin") attempts to project onto Polixenes, Hermione, Camillo and the court.

Like *Cymbeline*, *The Winter's Tale* dramatizes a pastoral much more capable of dialogy with tragedy than the soft pastoral fantasized or memorialized at the beginning of the play. With the harshness of its desert shore, savage bears, and tempests, the maritime pastoral of act 3, scene 3, resembles the hard pastoral of *Cymbeline*'s Wales; it is both a place of "things dying" and of "things new born." Placed in the middle of the play, it negotiates, as soft pastoral cannot do, the turn from tragedy to the comic denouement. The pastoral mode, then, is a crucial dramaturgical instrument of the tragicomedic genre. Whereas Leontes as "twinned lamb" suddenly become adult is unequipped to recognized sexuality in terms other than guilt and illegitimacy, the old shepherd is not shocked at the sight of what he takes to be illicit sexual behavior. Autolycus's frank and accepting attitude toward sexuality, establishing a context for the sexual play between Perdita and Florizel, further differentiates the enacted pastoral of *The Winter's Tale* from the presexual soft pastoral *antefatti* of Italian and Shakespearean tragicomedy. The greensward outside the shepherd's cottage incorporates the pastoral pleasance, but the old shepherd's admonishment to Perdita that she must labor as his late wife did complicates the pleasance with an element of georgic.

The pastoral section of *The Winter's Tale* reprises prior tragedy in order to revise it. In both the tragic and pastoral sections of the play, kings violently disrupt a placid situation and break or threaten a male-female bond. Leontes opposes the mixing of Polixenes and Hermione ("To mingle friendship far, is mingling bloods" [1.2.109]), and Polixenes, despite his official position in the debate, opposes the mixing of the "gentler scion" and the "wilder stock." Realizing Perdita's fears as expressed to Florizel (4.4.17–24, 39–40), Polixenes does transgress the pastoral boundaries and becomes the new tyrant, reprising aspects of Leontes' earlier actions: threatening to hang the shepherd, deface Perdita, and bar Florizel from succession. Both Paulina and Perdita undermine the tyrannical kings, at least in word ("The selfsame sun that shines upon his court / . . . / Looks on all alike" [4.4.445–47]). And in both sections Camillo "serves his master's highest interest by betraying him."[49]

In general the pastoral episode proves sufficiently capacious to address important issues of the tragic section of the play: sexuality and tyranny. Like the London theater itself, the pastoral place of *The Winter's Tale* is marginally positioned in relation to the tragedic court, neither one with it nor absolutely isolated from it in the manner of soft pastoral.[50] It is a place of measured liberty and license for the Bohemian courtiers: both Autolycus, who formerly served Prince Florizel, and the prince himself. The pastoral is also marginally positioned in relation to the Sicilian court, as the extracivilized place consigned Perdita by Leontes. The pastoral locus becomes a "theater" capable of playing with problems that had had catastrophic issue in the first part of the play. As with *Il pastor fido*, tragicomedic dramaturgy provides a distilled version of a historical process: in the pastoral reformation of tragedy, Shakespeare also refashions the historically prior *Othello*.

Consideration of the pastoral inflections of *The Tempest* need not oppose the now predominant approach to the play from new world and colonialist perspectives, since Europeans continually projected conceptions shaped by literary pastoral (especially the myth of the golden age) onto the new world.[51] Because the nature of the pastoral landscape in *The Tempest* is a function of imaginative projection, a "landscape of the mind," the opposition of soft and hard (or realistic) pastoral is dramatized in the form of debates between different points of view. Soft pastoral is critically invoked both in Gonzalo's visionary discourse and in the wedding masque. If soft pastoral is often formed as an escapist reaction to the court, the court party scene of act 2, scene 1, dramatizes both the formation of the utopian vision and the critique of the vision by the cynical court realists Sebastian and Antonio. Whereas Gonzalo and Adrian see the pleasance ("The air breathes upon us here most sweetly"; "How lush and lusty the grass looks! how green!"), Sebastian and Antonio see bad air and parched earth. The famous Montaigne passage describing the new world that is lifted for Gonzalo's speech (2.1.143–52, 155–60, 163–64) itself resonates with literary pastoral, and Gonzalo's "golden age" tag links the speech with the well-known choruses from Tasso and Guarini's pastoral tragicomedies, and with Renaissance pastoral at large. Gonzalo's ideal society allows no *negotium* or financial exchange, no political or social hierarchy, no labor, no violence, and no impure sexuality ("all men idle, all; / And women too, but innocent and pure").

The slave Caliban's labor on which Prospero depends and the love-trial labor of log-bearing undergone by Ferdinand introduce not only the georgic element present in the actualized pastoral of the two other plays but the socioeconomic differentiation that belies Gonzalo's egalitarianism. (Guarini's contention, seconded by Fletcher, that there are social distinctions between shepherds is reflected in the sharp sense of political and social hierarchy in Shakespeare's shepherd-less pastoral.) Prospero's violence and the nearly violent actions of Caliban and the two groups of conspirators sharply contrast with Gonzalo's pacifism. The libido of the satyr Caliban, Stephano's lust for Miranda, and Prospero's obsession with sexuality (an element, in fact, found in the *mago* of the *arte* scenarios) all contrast the vision of presexual pastoral that characterizes Italian and Shakespearean soft pastoral. Unlike the *Queenes Arcadia*, *The Tempest* does not emphasize the comedically coded problem of "traffic" or the perceived corruption of *negotium* in Arcadia, although we may see in the corrupting influence of Stephano's liquor a parallel to Alcon's tobacco. In fact, Prospero's pastoral island negotiates in many and complex ways with the world of the tragedic court and, to a lesser extent, the comedic city.

From the reports of the court party and Caliban, the actual landscape of *The Tempest* is much rougher than Gonzalo and Adrian imply, if ultimately not as bleak as the satirists' account. Gonzalo himself later complains that the island is not as idyllic as it originally appeared: "a maze trod, indeed, / Through forth-rights and meanders" (3.3.2–3). The pastoral "maze" described by Gonzalo should be seen in the context of Italian pastoral drama, in which the labyrinthine *selva* carries Dantesque and Ariostan resonances of a place of spiritual bewilderment or madness, a place that demonstrates the need for providential direction.[52] In *The Tempest*, the maze exhausts the bedraggled court party as well as the hapless buffoons, opposing both to the omnipotent and providentially prescient magician, who is capable both of magnificent displays of art and of thwarting their conspiracies. In Italian pastoral entertainment, James J. Yoch has argued, the magnificence, power, and order of the *intermezzi* respond to the disorder and confusion of the labyrinthine pastoral *selva*, in order to show "how neatly and awesomely prince and art controlled [disorder] within their greater powers."[53]

That the "vanity of his art," the pastoral masque produced by Prospero for Ferdinand and Miranda's wedding, falls short of absolute power is most obviously registered in Prospero's famous acknowledgment of its ephemerality, but is also suggested by the content of the masque itself, a version of pastoral that is cognate not only with contemporary Jacobean masques such as Daniel's *Tethys Festival* and Jonson's *Oberon* but also with Italian pastorals and *intermezzi*. Unlike Gonzalo's golden-age vision, Prospero's utopian pastoral recognizes the civilizing need for both labor (e.g., "poll-clipped vineyard") and sexual repression. As Stephen Orgel has argued, the masque recapitulates issues central to the play: the fear of rape and the power of virginity, as well as the conjunction of marriage and royal power.[54] But like Gonzalo's pastoral, the masque leaves no place for eros outside of marriage, with its "cold nymphs," "dismissed bachelor," and banishment and unsexing of Venus and Cupid. Similarly, as Orgel has pointed out, Prospero's pastoral elides "winter and rough weather" (winter mythologically originating from the rape of Proserpine), as Shakespearean pastoral normally does not do. Ceres' wish to the royal couple is that "Spring come to you at the farthest, / In the very end of harvest!"— that spring follow directly upon winter. Here is the timelessness, in other words, that also characterizes the soft pastoral fantasies of Henry VI, Imogen, and Polixenes. It is a fragile and delicate world, and it is not surprising that the mere recollection of the buffoons' conspiracy interrupts it.

The pastoral of *The Tempest* itself, however, is much more capacious; it is a place where tragedy is remembered and replayed in the manner of Guarinian tragicomedy. *Il pastor fido* recollects past literary tragedy in the form of *Oedipus the King* and begins by narrating a tragically coded *antefatto*. *The Tempest* both reprises past Shakespearean tragedy (the introspective ruler, violent sibling rivalry, physical and metaphorical tempests) and begins with Prospero remembering his own tragic past, as Belarius does in *Cymbeline*. From Vergil to Sannazaro, pastoral is a site of memory where one remembers the painful events of the past: political usurpation and amatory loss. Prospero also jogs and reshapes the memories of Miranda, Caliban, Ariel, and especially his Italian enemies. In a pastoral arena, he stages a kind of theater of memory in order to remind Antonio and Alonso of their earlier actions and to move them toward repentance. The chaos of the tempest, which "cares not for the name of king," reprises the earlier tragic breakdown of authority. The theatrical spectacle of the banquet and Ariel's harpy speech recall to the "three men of sin" their past crimes. In *The Tempest* and *The Winter's Tale*, and to a lesser extent in *Cymbeline* , tragedy is replayed and revised in a kind of pastoral theater, after the idea of Italian tragicomedy. In these plays, Shakespeare pursues something very similar to Guarinian tragicomedy in creating a variegated, capacious pastoral arena capable of incorporating tragic modalities.

The dramaturgical strategy, central to Renaissance tragicomedy, of negotiating pastoral with tragic claims is theorized by the Italians, and is taken to more tragic intensity by the English playwrights, especially Shakespeare. Neither *The Queenes Arcadia*, *The Faithful Shepherdess*, nor *The Sad Shepherd* deploy the codes and actions of tragedy in any sustained manner. Although English tragicomedy of the "public," "private," and even court stage produced in the center of a nation refers much more directly to politics than does the court-based Italian tragicomedy produced in an age of Counter-Reformation absolutism, the Italian hybrids of Tasso and Guarini provide a model for the offsetting and/or fusion of tragedy and pastoral that could take a more political and more unstable form on English soil.[55]

5

The Tragicomedic Satyr

CALIBAN

In the third act of Shakespeare's *Tempest*, the buffoons Stephano, Trinculo, and their new ally Caliban drink, argue, and slouch towards conspiracy, planning to seize Prospero's magic books, murder him, and possess his daughter and his kingdom. The invisible Ariel baffles them with taunts and a mysterious tune. To the terrified buffoons, Caliban says,

> Be not afeard; the isle is full of noises,
> Sounds, and sweet airs, that give delight, and hurt not.
> Sometimes a thousand twangling instruments
> Will hum about mine ears; and sometime voices,
> That, if I then had wak'd after long sleep,
> Will make me sleep again: and then, in dreaming,
> The clouds methought would open, and show riches
> Ready to drop upon me; that when I wak'd,
> I cried to dream again.
>
> (3.2.133–41)

This is an extraordinary speech for a creature variously called a "slave," "salvage," "beast," "earth," "filth," "misshapen knave," "bastard," "fish," "hag-seed," "mooncalf," and a "monster." If, according to Miranda, Caliban once "gabble[d] like a thing most brutish" (1.2.358–59), his poetic, musical, and imaginative faculties seem extremely developed. Caliban, in fact, is a figure of profound power and ambivalence, eliciting a wide range of responses in audiences. On the one hand, in accusing Prospero of betraying his first loyalty and keeping him in oppressed servitude, he delivers a speech of great anguish and pathos (1.1.333–46). And recent accounts of the imperial/colonial subtexts informing the play have shown how Caliban may evoke the tragic conquest of indigenous American peoples.[1] Colonialist accounts of the play usually ignore, however, the sheer comic business performed by the slave and his fellow conspirators, and the pleasures that Renaissance audiences might have taken in the drunken Caliban, played by the clown Robert Armin as the grotesque "natural fool" that contrasts the artificial folly of the court jester Trinculo. Tragicomedic in regard to his social status as well, Caliban is utterly degraded as a "salvage and deformed slave" and is treated as bestial and subhuman by those around him. At the same time, as the son of a witch and a devil, he is demonically divine. His central function in the play's pastoral treatment of nature, art, and civilization is also paradoxical. He is a natural man who satirically measures, like Montaigne's cannibals, the corruption of the civilized courtiers. If his linguistic instruction has bereft him of his innocence, it has taught him enough to reject, cursingly, Prospero's wrought world.[2]

As the antihero of a pastoral play, Caliban invites comparison to the pastoral satyr, especially to those of the tragedic plays of Giraldi, Tasso, and Guarini. The satyr of Italian pastoral drama embodies the paradoxical and tragicomic oppositions noted above in Caliban, as a figure of laughter and pathos, roughness and musical skill, bestiality and divinity, stupidity and occult wisdom. Thus, the satyr merits its alignment on the Jonson title page as a central character of the genre tragicomedy. The satyrs of Euripides' *Cyclops* (the only complete extant Greek satyr play), Cinquecento Ferraran pastoral drama, and Shakespeare's *Tempest* all sharpen the opposition of civilized, urban arts and savage, rustic nature. As such, they paradoxically elicit both envy and reproach, representing both hidden desire and negative exemplum. They are grotesque, but remain on the human side of monstrosity, standing for a form of "species corruption" not so exotic that it is without human, civic implication.[3]

Caliban, of course, has been considered as a figure for various objects of colonial exploitation: an American Indian, a Caribbean, an African, etc.[4] But because European explorers, as has amply been demonstrated, viewed the American native through the prisms of literary pastoral, it is fair to examine Caliban's literary ancestry as a supplement to and not as a negation of recent historicist inquiries. Literary and mythological investigations of Caliban's precursors have emphasized the wild man, because the figure appears in sixteenth-century English festivals and drama, but have given scant attention to the satyr. This is a serious oversight, because the wild man typically took the form of the satyr in

Renaissance pastoral. The revival of pastoral at the time of *The Tempest* also saw the return of the satyr in English drama: that of *The Faithful Shepherdess*, the antimasque in Ben Jonson's 1611 *Oberon*, and the dance of the twelve satyrs in the pastoral episode of *The Winter's Tale*.[5]

CLASSICAL BACKGROUND

Represented in many different ways throughout recorded antiquity, the satyr of the classical period seems to derive from a sixth-century combination of the equine, Attic-Ionian *silen* and the Peloponnesian satyr.[6] In the famous Pronomos vase, which depicts the cast of a satyr play from around 400 B.C., the satyr is depicted as a horse-man, wearing a horse's tail and a loincloth of animal skin with phallus, and a mask of a balding, bearded man, with a snub nose and pointed ears.[7] In almost any representation or account of the classical satyr, the figure is a complex and paradoxical blend of animality, humanity, and divinity. If satyrs are coarse, hedonistic, and at times comically stupid, their portion of divinity renders them potentially wiser than humans. In a fragment from a satyr play possibly by Sophocles, the satyrs thus describe themselves: "We are children of the nymphs, devotees of Bacchus, and neighbours of the gods. . . . In us you will find musical song, knowledgeable prophecy with no fakery, discriminating knowledge of medicine, measuring of the heavens, dancing, lore of the underworld . . . ."[8] At the same time when the *silen* and satyr were combined, records indicate the conjunction of the satyr with the seriocomic worship of Dionysos in both public festivals and religious rituals. For example, on the second day of the Anthesteria, the ancient Attic spring festival, men dressed up as satyrs probably accompanied a figure representing Dionysos to his fictive marriage with the wife of the Archon Basileus. And Plato mentions the participation of satyrs in mystic ritual (*Laws* 815c). As Richard Seaborg has argued, the satyrs are οὐ πολιτικόν (not of the polis) and thus nostalgically represent to the urban public an ancient community based on kinship and mystic ritual.[9] As such, they restore a primitive, extraurban, and Dionysian element to the Athenian festival.

In the satyr of Euripides' *Cyclops*, Cinquecento writers could have seen an ambivalent and tragicomic figure. Euripides' play treats of Odysseus's grim encounter with the cyclops Polyphemus, a story well known from the ninth book of Homer's *Odyssey*. Like Renaissance pastoral drama and *The Tempest* itself, the play explores relationships between nature and civilization. Euripides departs from Homer in making Polyphemus the master of Silenus and a small band of satyrs who tend his sheep. David Konstan has argued that the satyrs of Euripides' play provide much more than a token gesture to the formal requirements of the satyr play, as some classicists have maintained.[10] Konstan argues that Euripides replaces Homer's dyadic structure (the Greeks versus Polyphemus) with a triadic structure consisting of the Greeks, the satyrs, and Polyphemus and his brethren. Categorized as a "monster" both because of his physical appearance and his enmity toward Greek civilization, the individualistic Polyphemus knows neither the *polis* nor the festive *komos*, the bases of the annual spring theater festival in Athens. He represents mere appetite untempered by the civilized reciprocity expressed in the gift-giving relationships between host and guest. On the other end of the spectrum, Odysseus engages in the civilized practice of commerce (he wants to trade gold and wine for goods) and conducts his relationships according to the principle of *philia,* loosely translated as "friendship," an unsentimental term designating a network of contracted, mutual social responsibilities.

The satyrs, according to Konstan, represent a third term intermediate between the cyclops Polyphemus and the Greeks. Like Caliban, the satyrs of Euripides' *Cyclops* and many other of his satyr plays (judging from titles and extant fragments) are in captivity in a remote and savage place. In *Cyclops* they have been shipwrecked upon Sicily while sailing in search of their lord Dionysos. Like the race of cyclopes they are god-descended beasts, a monstrous mixture incapable of the relationships of reciprocity and exchange demanded by the *polis*. When they are not slaves to Polyphemus, they are slaves to their other master Dionysos. Although they may be associated with cannibalism via their master Polyphemus, they actually do not consume human flesh, only wine (for Caliban, the association is produced by his name and by the Montaigne allusion). Unlike the solitary Polyphemus, their Bacchic revelry aligns them with the festive *komos*, a less-civilized practice than Odysseus's *philia* but still an important ingredient of the political-festive City Dionysia, and of ancient Greek society in general. Also unlike Polyphemus, they worship more than their belly, approaching something like an Odyssean exchange relationship with Bacchus, who rewards their honor with nourishment. Their rescue by Odysseus and journey with him back to Athens represents, for Konstan, the integration of the rural *komos* into Athens and the City Dionysia. Odysseus reconciles different orders of being, negotiating with gods, humans, and beasts. In his grand synthesis of city and country, *civitas* and festivity, seriousness and lightness, Cinquecento theorists could have seen, in Odysseus, the figure of the synthesizing tragicomedic playwright.

GIRALDI

It is the human but animal-like wild man, rather than the satyr, who dominates the medieval imagination, first as an antisocial and violent figure of loathing and disgust roaming the wilderness. But in the fourteenth and fifteenth centuries, Richard Bernheimer has shown, the wild man's libidinous and violent vices were gradually redeemed as virtues, as indications of a freedom and an innocence untainted by corrupt civilization but at the same time capable of positive transformation by the best aspects of civilized humanity.[11] When Renaissance humanists begin to revive the satyr, he was conflated with the wild man, and thus acquired a greater moral complexity than belonged to his classical forebears. Increasingly aware of Euripides' *Cyclops* as a classical precedent for the *satira*, humanists like Poliziano accorded the satyr a dramaturgical complexity as well.

For Giraldi, Euripides' *Cyclops* functions as the classical paradigm for the *satira*. As he argues in the *Lettera*, the satyr play derives from Dionysian, dithyrambic ritual in Greece as well as Roman purification and fertility rituals. Giraldi's legendary satyrs are devotees of Bacchus, singing dithyrambs and performing the goat sacrifice that Renaissance theorists held to lie at the origins of tragedy (*Egle* 2.4). Giraldi tends to domesticate Dionysian religion as Renaissance pastoral *otium*. Still, Giraldi astutely sees that the *satira* does not serve a paratragic, parodic function but reminds urban dwellers of Dionysian religion and the origins of tragedy itself.

In the *Lettera*, Giraldi explains why the satyr himself is not merely a formal requirement, but occupies a dramaturgically central role, rendering the *satira* a specifically *tragicomedic* form. On one hand, the satyr provides an acceptable, decorous locus for the *festevole* (festive) and *lascivo* (lascivious) elements that humanists could not ignore in the satyr play and in Old Comedy, but had difficulty reconciling with neoclassical aesthetics and Counter-Reformation ethics.[12] The satyr of Italian pastoral drama, says Richard Cody, is the Renaissance "courtier under a partial aspect of his inner life—the Bacchic" pursuing the claims of Venus and Bacchus without the civilized inhibitions necessary for the courtier.[13] At the same time, Giraldi's satyr is a deeply ambivalent figure, justifying a form midway between tragic and comic registers. Whereas a chorus, according to Giraldi, does not belong in comedy because of the "lowness of its action," it is appropriate to the *satira* because the choric satyrs "tengono così nondimeno del divino, e perciò portano con loro maggiore considerazione che le persone popolaresche" [still approach something of the divine, and thus carry greater weight than popular characters].[14] The notion that satyrs are semidivine is merely an ancient superstition, says Giraldi, but it is immensely useful in dramaturgical terms because it allows a higher style, a greater action, and more serious emotions to be granted to the satyrs than could be given to simple shepherds or to the denizens of comedy. If genre is largely constituted by the status of its principal characters, the fantastic, mythological satyr provides an appropriately multivalent register— at once bestial and human and divine—for the tragicomedic *satira*.

The satyr even contributes a formal characteristic of the Giraldian *satira*: its use of tragedic meter rather than prose, the medium of Cinquecento comedy by the mid Cinquecento. Giraldi bases the idea that the satyrs are naturally metrical on Vergil's sixth eclogue, in which two boys and the naiad Egle bind the drunken Silenus and constrain him to sing them long-promised songs telling of the world's creation.[15] Overjoyed to finally hear their master's song, the fauns and satyrs register their delight in a predominantly dactylic meter that suggests their light mobility:

> Tum vero in numerum Faunosque Ferasque videres
> Ludere, tum rigidas motare cacumina quercus
>
> *(Eclogues* 6.27–28)[16]

[Then indeed you might have seen fauns and beasts sport in measured time, then stiff oaks nod their heads.]

The classical tradition of the dancing and musical satyr, who deftly coordinates voice and dance, renders the satyric chorus more mobile than that of tragedy, which should be more stationary according to Giraldi.[17]

Lacking the complicated intrigue structure of many later Italian pastoral plays, Giraldi's otiose play has plenty of time to dilate on the Dionysian underpinnings appropriate to its central figure. As Egle tells it, the Vergilian song delivered by the wise drunkard Silenus offers a kind of cosmic philosophy of pleasure:

Più volte, e più m'ha detto il mio Sileno
Narrandomi i principii de le cose,
Che 'l piacere introdotto fu nel mondo,
Perché 'l mondo per lui si conservasse . . .

(2.1)

[In telling me of the beginnings of things my Silenus has often said
that pleasure was given in order to conserve the world.]

Pleasure is the final, Aristotelian end, one perpetually enjoyed by the
gods. As for Rabelais and other Renaissance writers, Silenus is a richly
ambivalent figure who mixes sense and nonsense (2.3), but his share of
wisdom legitimates pleasure for the decorum of the *satira*, as distinguished from that of comedy. Giraldi conceives of Dionysos more narrowly than did the ancient Greeks, as a god of wine, but wine is touted
as a marvelous *élan vital* and elixir of the gods: it makes mind and body
strong, is "vero maestro / D'ogni vertù, d'ogni scientia buona" [true
master of every virtue and knowledge] (3.1), and grants beauty and
happiness. Whereas most later Cinquecento pastoral plays limit their
conception of pleasure to the innocuous pastoral pleasance, the notion
of pleasure operative in *Egle* is frankly Bacchic, as befitting an imitation
of the Greek satyr play.

In their ontological status, their affective tonalities, and the quality
of their action, the satyrs and fauns of *Egle* are poised between tragedic
and comedic registers, like Caliban, and thereby perform a crucial
dramaturgical function in the tragicomedic *satira*. Like Euripides' satyrs,
they duly worship Bacchus, promising a goat sacrifice to him if Egle's
stratagem succeeds. They certainly are "ambulatory genitalia" eager to
enjoy the recalcitrant nymphs, who seem to prefer the Olympian gods.[18]
They express an intense physicality of which the typical pastoral shepherd is incapable: "gelar mi sento per le vene il sangue" [I feel the blood
freezing in my veins] (3.2), says the Satiro, the choral leader. Initially,
the Satiro distrusts the cunning plan laid by Egle and argues for *forza*
over *arte,* and a direct confrontation between the Olympians and the
sylvan gods. Behind the satyr of Egle and other sixteenth-century pastoral plays always lies the threat of rape, so that the physical violence
that might constitute the tragedic action of the pastoral protagonist is
always displaced onto the wild figure, safely outside the courtly boundaries.[19] And yet like Caliban, the paradoxical satyrs of Egle are imbued
with pathos—not the pathos of political subjection, as in *The Tempest,*

but the pathos of love. In contrast to the comic, buffoonish Silenus, for whom "tutto è festa" [everything is a festival] (1.3), their rejection by the nymphs fills them with anguish and torment, expressed in the terms of a Petrarchan lover, who reads in the allegorized pastoral landscape the signs of his own amatory woes. The central figure of the *satira*, then, is capable of expressing and perhaps eliciting levels of pity and terror appropriately adjusted to a tragicomedic decorum. Just as Silenus alternates between sublime wisdom and drunken nonsense, the sylvan deities are paradoxically wise and foolish in love, according to Egle:

> Così costor, naturalmente rozzi,
> Poi c'han sentito l'amoroso ardore;
> Si son svegliati in parte, e parte sono
> Rimasi ne la lor prima grossezza
>
> (2.3)

[And so those who are naturally crude when they have felt amorous desire are partly awakened and partly remain in their original coarseness.]

The satyrs are rough, undeveloped lovers who can never achieve the full civilizing benefits of Venus, but know enough to realize what they are missing.

To the satyrs' pathos are added supernatural powers befitting their semidivine status. Whereas Egle and the Faun joyously anticipate the fruits of their cunning plan (compared to the deceit of the Trojan horse), the satyr broods, correctly interpreting a series of tragedically coded auguries: a falcon descending to devour two doves, a raven's plaintive voice, a lovesick goat, and a sick bull whose miserable *mugiti* (bellows) arouse the trees themselves. His occult wisdom enables him to correctly read these signs, significantly altering the audience's generic horizon of expectations (normally comedic, in a pastoral play): "giungendo tutti questi segni / In un, non trovo onde sperar mi debba" [putting together all these signs I find no reason for hope] (3.3). Egle attempts to convince the nymphs that the satyrs are worthy lovers, arguing grotesquely that the composite physical attributes of the satyrs are all possessed by one god or another: Bacchus has the satyrs' horns, Apollo their fiery face, Neptune their terrible aspect, Hercules their stiff beard, Mars their bristly body, and Vulcan their goatish feet, bandy legs, and blackened skin (3.1). In according center stage to Silenus and the satyrs, Giraldi thus preserves a grotesquely tragicomedic register, one profoundly ambivalent in its conjunction of the bestial and the divine.

TASSO, GUARINI, AND THE *COMMEDIA DELL'ARTE*

No other Cinquecento pastoral play so purposefully imitates the Greek satyr play and so centrally features its chief personage, although the satyr becomes a standard figure of pastoral drama.[20] The satyr of Agostino Beccari's influential 1555 *Sacrificio* provides a rich object of comic *beffe*, anticipatory of Caliban's torment at the hands of Prospero, and establishes the comedic pattern that most pastoral dramatists would follow.[21] Playwrights continued to explore the satyr's ontological ambivalence. In Leone De'Sommi's *Hirfile, pastorale*, the satyr is acutely conscious of his hybrid nature:

> Se con le parte mie ferine il senso
> a la carnal imperfettion m'abbassa,
> non son io poi ne la supreme forma
> de l'essenza divina essempio intiero?
>
> (4.5)[22]

[If, with my bestial parts, sensuality lowers me to carnal imperfection, am I not ultimately an example of the divine essence?]

The neo-Aristotelian dictate of verisimilitude, well in place by the time of the famous pastorals of Tasso and Guarini, changed the nature and function of the satyr in the satyric play, but in ways still relevant to Caliban, because of Shakespeare's own impulse towards verisimilitude, which is preserved even in the marvelous "romances." Divested of his supernatural powers, Tasso's satyr is a rustic, plebeian figure—rejected by Silvia, he claims, because he is poor (2.1). If no less erudite than the other highly allusive characters in Tasso's *drame à clef*, he self-consciously patterns himself after the rustic Polyphemus—the antiurbane figure of Theocritean idyll, not the monstrous cannibal of Euripides' satyr play. As such, he and he alone in Tasso's play dimly preserves a residue of the strong plebeian element of earlier sixteenth-century Italian pastoral. In a play that negotiates pastoral and heroic strains by blending feminine and masculine registers, Tasso's nonsupernatural satyr is imbalanced in regard to gender: his grotesque body stands for a virility intended to shame the shepherd-lovers, whom he views as effeminate. Tasso's satyr replaces the *villano*'s comic inversion of pastoral Petrarchanism with an intense, almost tragic physicality that functions as an antidote for the high-amorous discourse typical of the play: "Ohimè, che tutte piaga e tutte sangue / son le viscere mie" [O, my guts are all blood and wounds]. As the "courtier under the aspect of the Bacchic," he is Silvia's other lover, as capable of Petrarchan conceits as Aminta. But he uses his one speech of the play to reject language, adapting the principle of *forza* from which Giraldi's Satiro was narrowly dissuaded by the crafty Egle:

> Ma perché in van mi lagno? Usa ciascuno
> quell'armi che gli ha date la natura
> per sua salute
>
> . . . . . .
>
> perché non per mia salute adopro
> la violenza, se mi fe' Natura
> atto a far violenza ed a rapire?
>
> (2.1)

[But why do I lament in vain? Let each one use those weapons that nature has given him for his good. . . . And why shouldn't I use violence, if Nature has made me fit for violence and rape?]

Correlatively, he also rejects the urbane, civilized notion of the golden-age topos, which reads civilized virtues into the country. For the Satiro, "le ville / seguon l'essempio de le gran cittadi; / e veramente il secol d'oro è questo, / poiché sol vince l'oro e regna l'oro" [the country follows the example of the big cities, and the golden age really means that only gold conquers and reigns]. Tasso's satyr, then, rejects "civilization" both in the form of Petrarchan language and the pastoral attitudes of disguised urbanites. But notwithstanding his important dramaturgical function in catalyzing the apparently tragedic plot, Tasso's satyr does remain marginal, because the play turns on the verisimilar psychological trans-formations wrought by love, not on *forza*, comic cunning, or supernatu-ral metamorphosis.

The satyr of *Il pastor fido* brings into even sharper focus the drama of a failed lover who rejects "civilization" as he knows it in the form of Petrarchan discourse. He confesses that "un tempo anch'io credei che, sospirando / e piagendo e pregando, in cor di donna / si potesse destar fiamma d'amore" [once even I believed that sighing and crying and begging would arose the flame of love in a woman's heart] (1.5), but now rejects such amatory discourse as effeminate. Inveighing against the art of love as practiced by "civilized" city slickers such as Corisca, the satyr becomes a "satyrist" and delivers a misogynist diatribe against makeup. The Tassan and Guarinian satyr, then, provides a vestigial outlet for satire. English playwrights, it is worth noting, similarly dramatized the satyre/satire confusion. In *The Malcontent*, Marston appropriates parts of Guarini's satyr's speech for Mendoza's diatribe against false female arts (1.6.91–93). And in the same satiric period of English Renaissance tragedy, Shakespeare's Hamlet misogynistically rants against female artifice: "God hath given you one face, and you make yourselves another" (*Hamlet* 3.1.145–46). More like Claudius than he would like to admit, Hamlet here is more wild "satyrist" than cool Hyperion (*Hamlet* 1.2.140).

The satyr of the Locatelli/Corsini scenarios, as we might expect, evokes several specific details of Shakespeare's Caliban. Certainly he shares Caliban's naïveté: just as Stephano convinces Caliban that he is a god, the *arte* travelers dress up as Jove, Mercury, and Cupid (a comically verisimilar treatment of mythology similar to the masque of *The Tempest*) and deceive the native shepherds and satyrs. Like Caliban, the satyrs repeatedly switch allegiances. At first the satyrs obey the magician, but then agree to abet the conspiracy of the rebel-buffoons. Finally, however, they recognize their error and obsequiously resign themselves to the magician. Inhabiting a strange and marvelous Arcadian environment, the *arte* satyr is both human and nonhuman. In *La pazzia di Filandro*, two of the Italian buffoons suddenly encounter the satyr, who is alone lamenting his hapless love. Astonished by this creature, they "have their tricks pretending that he is a "red-cap, a hooded lark, a boar, a big eagle, a little bat, a cuckoo, and a screech-owl." [23] For the ludicrous encounter of Trinculo with Caliban and then Stephano with the Caliban-Trinculo monster (2.2), Shakespeare may have conflated the above scene with two others: one in which a Zanni is belched from a whale (just as Stephano first believes Trinculo to be "vented" from the "moon-calf" Caliban [2.2.107–8]); and another scene in which Gratiano encounters Zanni but is unsure whether he is a man or beast (it has a head, he says, and legs, but so has an ass). Finally, although the *arte* satyr is principally an object of comic *beffe* as in Beccari and Guarini, he resembles Caliban in that he is a figure who elicits fear as well as laughter.

CONCLUSION

Notwithstanding the wild man's presence in the Kennilworth entertainments, Lord Mayor's Pageants, and the early plays *Gorboduc* and
Promos and Cassandra, there are reasons why Shakespeare may have
had the satyr especially in mind when he wrote *The Tempest*.[24] The satyrs of the antimasque to Ben Jonson's *Oberon* were played by professional actors, probably from the King's Men. Jonson's satyrs, led by
their "prefect" Silenus, cavort and make "antic action" in a satyric scene
of darkness and wildness. For Jonson, the satyr truly is the "courtier
under the aspect of the Bacchic" already realigning his impulses, for
the presence of Oberon so pervades the antimasque that the satyrs soon
wish to leave their usual master Dionysos for the radiant prince. From
the erudite Jonson, an intriguing reference to the blinding of the
Cyclops could plausibly be taken from Euripides' satyr play rather than
from the ninth book of *The Odyssey*.[25] This might suggest that Jonson
conceived the antimasque to function as a satyric complement to the
masque proper, somewhat in the manner of the Greek satyr play relative to tragedy. If, as has often been argued, *The Tempest* has many
masquelike features and the Caliban-Stephano-Trinculo subplot functions something like an antimasque, it is plausible to argue that the
recent *Oberon* suggested to Shakespeare the satyr as the pastoral antihero. In fact, in *The Winter's Tale*, Shakespeare's pastoral play immediately preceding *The Tempest* but probably postdating *Oberon*, a "dance
of twelve satyrs" animates the sheep-shearing episode, a scene whose
frank depiction of sexuality provides a salutary corrective to the pessi-
mistic, tragic view of sex depicted in the first part of the play. The chorus of satyrs, perhaps dancing to the same music as animated the satyrs of Jonson's antimasque, provides a faint but intriguing hint of the
classical tradition.[26] The representative pastoral figures of *The Winter's
Tale* are not satyrs but the shepherds and the trickster Autolycus. If the
composition of *The Tempest* was triggered by Shakespeare's exposure
to the Arcadian scenarios, the satyrs of these scenarios would have provided a third occasion for Shakespeare to think about the figure.

Considering Caliban in the context of the satyr tradition brings several moments into sharper focus. Like the satyr, especially those of the
verisimilar *Aminta* and *Il pastor fido*, he evokes monstrosity to those
around him: Stephano, Trinculo, and Prospero, who deems him "not
honour'd with a human shape" (1.2.283–84). At the same time he re-
mains largely human, thus functioning both as a projection of illicit

desire and as the negative definition of civility. Just as the Euripidean satyr is associated with but not identical to a monstrous cannibal, Caliban is a cannibal only in name and by virtue of Montaigne's subtext. If he attempts a rape of the nymphal, "semi-divine" (1.2.424–25) Miranda, he represents her uncivilized, rejected lover, the obverse side of Ferdinand. As a pastoral antihero, he represents both the uncivilized liberation of desire and the sharp punishments attending that liberation. Like the Italian satyr, he has now lost his innocence, and as "satyrist" curses civilization as he has met it. His Bacchic worship of "celestial liquor" as he follows the Silenic Stephano yields scenes similar in tone both to the ancient satyr play and to the satyric, Jonsonian antimasque. Like the satyr in many ancient satyric plays, he is captive in a savage place, where the arrival of newcomers brings the possibility of liberation. To his natural wisdom may be added the capacity to appreciate the supernatural charms of Ariel's music, a musical and poetic aptitude not evidenced by any of the courtiers. Finally, the more serious satyr plays of Euripides and Giraldi help place in context Caliban's tragicomic complexity, his capacity to elicit both grotesque laughter and tragic pathos.

6

"Gentleman-like Tears": Tragicomedy and Affective Response

A DRAMATURGY OF THE EMOTIONS

Cinquecento theorists and playwrights were interested in the affective as well as the cognitive and ethical dimensions of audience response. Guarini largely conceives tragicomedy in terms of the emotional responses elicited in the audience. He seeks a form that would mediate between the horror elicited by the atrocities of Senecan tragedy and the laughter of *commedia dell'arte*-style farce. Tragicomedy does not discard but sublimates the historically prior genre of tragedy, replacing the violent external actions of Senecan tragedy with various internal responses on the part of the "internal audience": characters within the plays who function as audience members to other characters and actions.[1]

The neo-Aristotelian tradition is usually associated with concerns of structure rather than those of audience response. Susan Bennett represents a common view when she contrasts the palpable presence of the audience in the City Dionysia with what she considers to be Aristotle's negligence of the audience: "In Aristotle's *Poetics* the audience is chiefly of interest in so far as they prove the power of good tragic texts/performances."[2] In fact, Aristotle places great importance on emotional, as well as cognitive and ethical, audience response. Whether or not the notorious catharsis passage refers to the emotional purgation of pity and fear in the theater audience or to the purgation of pitiable and fearful events in the action of the play itself—and not all classicists uphold Gerald F. Else's revisionist argument for the latter proposition[3]—other passages in the *Poetics* clearly claim that tragedy arouses pity and fear in the audience.[4] Despite the potential ambiguity in the catharsis passage, Renaissance commentators universally believed that Aristotle was referring to the catharsis of pity and fear in the theater audience and tended to psychologize the notion of catharsis.[5] The neo-Aristotelian tradition, then, could focus dramaturgical strategy on audience response even more than was perhaps warranted by the *Poetics*. The notion of catharsis became a flexible, general "Aristotelian" principle extracted from the *Poetics* that could be used to justify generic innovation and experimentation.

Guarini's theory of tragedic catharsis aptly demonstrates the interventionary relationship that he imagines obtaining between the playwright and the audience.[6] He challenges a strictly homeopathic theory of tragedic purgation, arguing that in many cases terror actually increases terror, and questions whether the commendable quality of compassion should be purged in the sense of "eradicated." In effect, Guarini combines allopathic and homeopathic approaches by dividing terror and pity each into two kinds: one that purges and one that is purged. The positive, "purging" terror of infamy and of the "death of the soul" drives out the ignoble, "purged" terror of merely bodily death. Pity for the protagonist's internal suffering expunges an inferior form of pity for merely corporeal suffering. The playwright, then, resembles a doctor, who does not remove an entire humor but "sol quella parte che trabboccando fuor dei termini naturali, corrompe la simetria degli umori" [only that part which, passing beyond natural limits, corrupts the symmetry of the humors] (*I Verato*, 2:250). The theory assumes a high level of control over audience response.

Similarly, Guarini defines comedy not by external characteristics or subject matter (as Julius Caesar Scaliger usually does, for example) but by the effect elicited in the theater audience.[7] All comedy relaxes, even the farce produced by the emerging *commedia dell'arte*, but Guarini attributes a more specific rhetorical function to his ideal form of comedy, in which melancholy is purged by means of laughter and delight. Because melancholy is an "affetto tanto nocivo, che bene spesso conduce l'uomo a darsi la morte" [emotion so harmful that it often leads men to kill themselves] (247), comedic purgation becomes a rather serious enterprise for Guarini, who was intent on countering the popular *commedia dell'arte* with a higher, more dignified form of comedy that actually approaches tragicomedy in many respects. In fact, Guarini identifies the practical end of tragicomedy with that of comedy as the purgation of melancholy.

Tragedy, comedy, and tragicomedy all operate according to the same system, one not based on literary structure but on audience reception and the dynamics of the theater experience. In distinguishing their audience functions, Guarini contrasts the psychological effect of comedy to that of tragedy, but the terms of description are the same for both genres and imply that dramaturgy is keyed to biophysical rhythms. Comedy works centrifugally, loosening the soul that has become constricted by serious concerns. Tragedy achieves a centripetal effect, reclaiming the overly relaxed soul. As Guarini puts it, "l'un [comedy] rilassa, e l'altro [tragedy] ristringe . . . l'uno va dal centro alla circonferenza, e l'altro cammina tutto all'opposito" [one {comedy} relaxes, and the other {tragedy} constricts . . . one goes from the center to the circumference, and the other moves in the opposite direction] (258). In reality, Guarini does not employ distinct, firmly bounded generic categories that are set in stone but rather assumes a fluid, flexible generic continuum with a hypothetically infinite number of kinds largely established by the kind of emotional effect elicited in the audience. The modalities of the "tragic" and the "comic" can be finely adjusted by the playwright, according to an almost infinitely variable spectrum: "Nella Tragedia il terrore più e meno temperato costitiusce i gradi del più, e meno Tragico; così il riso, più e meno dissoluta fa la favola più, e men Comica" [In tragedy, terror that is more and less tempered constitutes degrees of more and less tragic quality; similarly laughter that is more and less dissolute renders the play more and less comic] (260). Guarini extracts a doctrine from the *Poetics* that cannot be justified from Aristotle's treatise itself but that has implications for tragicomedic dramaturgy:

> Quanto una favola avrà più del terribile e del compassionevole sarà ella tanto più Tragica. Per la qual cosa se l'esser Tragico è alterabile qualità, che si può accrescere e sminuire, come dai detti d'Aristotile s'argomenta, sarà in man del Poeta di far la favola più e meno Tragica secondo che più e men di terrore e di compassione vi s'indurrà. (*I Verato*, 2:255)

> [When a story has more terror and pity it will be more tragic. Therefore, if the tragic state is a variable quality that one can increase and diminish, as can be argued from the precepts of Aristotle, the poet may render the story more and less tragic according as he includes more and less terror and compassion.]

Such a nuancing habit of thought permeates Guarini's theory. Dramatic style is conceived of as a musical continuum, as befits a genre that incorporated lyrical and madrigalesque strains. (*Aminta* and *Il pas-*

tor fido provided fertile sources of madrigals and operas.) Stylistic registers are not like bells, fixed with one tone, but like musical strings that
change pitch according to their tension: "Gli stili a uso non di campane,
ma di corde musicali, ricevano maggiori intensioni, e minori, e che il
magnifico può esser più, e meno magnifico, e il dimesso più, e meno
dimesso, nì però si rimangono di essere quel che sono, e che le forme si
confondono insieme come i colori" [Not like bells, but like musical
strings that receive greater and lesser tension, the magnificent style can
be more and less magnificent, and the low style more and less low, so
that the stylistic registers blend into one another like colors] (*Il Verato*,
3:226). Tragicomedy, in particular, blends together what Guarini calls
the *polito*, or polished style, and the *grave*, or solemn style. To blend
generic elements together in tragicomedy is like mixing together various colors of the palette, or like forming complex musical chords
(*Compendio*, 3:399–400).[8]

This is a sophisticated exploration of the gradations of theatrical
components, worth comparing with the reflections of the twentieth-
century Czech theorist, Jan Mukarovsky. Mukarovsky examines the
complexity of the theater, constituted not only by different arts (music,
sculpture, painting, literature) but by the "internal differentiation" of
its different components: "voice, facial expression, gestures, movement,
costume." But each of these components, according to Mukarovsky,
admit of further gradation:

> Thus the voice components are the articulation of speech sound ele-
> ments, the pitch of the voice and its changes, its tone, the intensity of
> expiration, and tempo. But we still have not come to the end. The
> individual vocal components can be broken down further. Take, for
> example, tone of voice: every person has a particular voice colora-
> tion comprising part of his physical personality. A speaker can be
> recognized by the coloration of his voice even if the listener does not
> see him. There are, however, also tones of voice corresponding to
> individual mental dispositions and their meaning is independent of
> the individual's personal vocal coloration ("angrily," "joyfully,"
> "ironically," etc.).[9]

Tragicomedy explores gradations of emotion intermediate between
the extremes of tragic terror and comic relaxation. If tragedy and comedy operate on the same centrifugal-centripetal system, and if there are
many generic registers between the furthest extremes of high tragedy and
low comedy, much of the middle territory is claimed by the playwright of

tragicomedy, who is especially adept at manipulating audience response by means of various interventionary techniques. These techniques include the pastoral tempering of tragic intensity, the modulation of terror, the interjection of fictional distance, the use of dreams in a tragicomic modality, the enactment of "the danger not the death," the deployment of tragedic rhetoric (rather than action), and the aestheticizing of tragedy. Some of these techniques are explained in Guarini's theory; others are developed in the self-consciously theoretical plays themselves of Tasso and especially Guarini; others are best demonstrated by Shakespeare's late plays, whatever the degree of his conscious knowledge of Italian dramaturgy.

TRAGICOMEDIC TECHNIQUES

Pastoral Pathos. According to Guarini, the emotional tonalities of pastoral temper the emotions of both tragic and comic extremes and generate a wide range of emotional registers. Pastoral tragicomedy reprises characters, themes, or events that have tragedic issue and places them in a new generic and emotional register. The sweet *(dolce)* style proper to the pastoral mode tempers tragic intensity: "il dolce . . . tempera quella grandezza, e sublimità, che è propria del puro Tragico" [the sweet style tempers that grandeur and sublimity which are proper to the pure tragic style] (*I Verato*, 2:274). If neoclassical tragedy and comedy tended to imitate the external actions and customs of, respectively, the court and the city, post-Tridentine pastoral turned its lens inward, to matters of the mind and especially the heart.[10] The passive suffering of pastoral speakers in the face of meteorological, occupational, political, and especially amatory misfortunes elicits the emotion of pity without extreme terror—what might be called "pathos": a passive, plaintive, elegiac register of grief. With a diminished strength relative to his world compared with the protagonists of epic or tragedy, the pastoral figure (not necessarily a shepherd in Shakespeare's capacious understanding of the mode) tends to suffer more than act. Pathos bespoke a certain dignity and prestige in an age when the *commedia* was under attack for its perceived licentiousness; it functioned, in fact, as the emotional register of choice for leading divas such as Isabella Andreini of the Gelosi, who often performed pastoral roles with her husband Francesco and even wrote a pastoral play herself.[11]

The pathos of Imogen (in the Wales wilderness), Hermione (especially at the trial scene), and several characters in *The Tempest* (including Prospero himself, when he abandons his "noble anger") are all central to the emotional tonalities of Shakespeare's late plays. This intermediate register, often related to a pastoral modality, achieves a nuanced, tragicomedic blend of contrapuntal emotions nicely evoked in the pastoral speakers' descriptions of the androgynous Fidele:

> ARV. Nobly he yokes
> A smiling with a sigh; as if the sigh
> Was that it was, for not being such a smile;
> The smile mocking the sigh, that it would fly
> From so divine a temple, to commix
> With winds that sailors rail at.
> GUI. I do note
> That grief and patience, rooted in them both,
> Mingle their spurs together.
>
> (*Cymbeline* 4.2.52–58)

Sighing is mixed with smiling, as opposed to the rough laughter elicited by the farcical characters of Shakespeare's late plays: Cloten, Autolycus, and Caliban. Grief, as opposed to tragic anger, mingles with patience. Shakespeare certainly does not reject the pleasures of coarse laughter in his late plays, but the more genteel and sophisticated audience of the Blackfriars seems to tip the hand slightly in favor of pathos. As the shepherds of *The Winter's Tale* are raised to gentlemanly status, they also seem elevated to new emotional registers: "and so we wept; and there was the first gentleman-like tears that ever we shed" (5.2.144–45). Autolycus, who before has provided much of the theatrical pleasure with his *arte*-like *lazzi*, becomes subdued and overshadowed in the new context of pastoral pathos.

Simulacra of Terror; Fictionality. Whereas, in the *Compendio*, Guarini takes pains to proscribe any form of terror for his hybrid play, in the *Verati* he explores ways by which the tragicomedic playwright may modulate terror. Guarini contests Denores's claim that terror admits of no gradation, arguing thus:

> E siccome ogni cosa terribile non purga il terrore (ciò si pruova nelle viste delle pitture quantunque orribili, e spaventose, e nelle cose della medesima qualità narrate semplicemente, e senz'arte alcuna dramatica) così ogni rassomiglianza del terribile non produce Tragedia, s'ella non vien condotta con l'altre necessarie parti, che ci concorrono. (*I Verato*, 2:259)

[And just as every terrible thing does not purge terror (this is proven by the sights of horrible and frightening paintings, and with the same kind of subjects narrated simply, without any dramatic art), so every likeness of the terrible does not produce tragedy, if it is not accompanied by the other necessary and converging parts.]

Guarini distinguishes between three gradations of terror: actual, tragic, and tragicomic. Actual terror experienced in real life disturbs us emotionally and even physically—creating a *batticuore*, or palpitation (*Il Verato*, 3:192). The fully purgative terror of tragedy seems to take a physical form, as it is "imprinted" or "impressed" upon the soul with "force," but it also entails a rational operation: the fear of the sickness or death of the soul causes one to believe that it is better to die than to live with dishonor. But there are other forms of terror or fear (*spavento*) that are less forcefully pressed onto the soul because they are mediated in various ways—and these can be exploited by the dramatist of tragicomedy. In general, tragicomedy seems to be based on constructing "rassomiglianze del terribile": simulacra of terror that yield less than the full tragedic catharsis.

As in Aristotle's *Poetics*, the cognitive faculties of the audience moderate emotional response for Guarini. This is true for the terror of tragedy, but even more so with that of tragicomedy. Those who are spectators of the fictive terror of someone else ("spettatori dello altrui finto pericolo") rather than fully participating in actual terror ("con le proprie loro persone parteciparon del vero") experience terror of a specifically tragicomic register (*Il Verato*, 3:191). The awareness of fictionality (as with a painting) or the indirect mediation of a terrifying event (as with narration) both diminish what might otherwise be full tragic terror. Tragicomedy, then, often makes the theater audience aware of the fictionality of events that might be perceived as real by the characters within the plays. Fictionality, in fact, is especially the province of Guarinian tragicomedy, as compared with tragedy: "Dunque la verità, che aiuta al verisimile, s'appartiene al poema Tragico, se noi crediamo ad Aristotile, e non al Tragicomico, che non ha bisogno di storia, per formar la sua favola, ma se la finge esso a suo modo, e talora con nomi noti, e talora con finti, secondo che più gli piace" [Therefore truth, which contributes to the verisimilar, belongs to the tragedic poem, if we believe Aristotle, and not to the tragicomedic poem, which has no need of history to formulate its story but rather fabricates its story in its own way, sometimes with familiar names and sometimes with fictional names, according to its pleasure] (189). Differing with Castelvetro here, Guarini claims for tragicomedy a version of verisimilitude unconstrained by historical exactitude.

With the exception of *The Winter's Tale*, the theater audience is aware that most of the "deaths" in Shakespeare's late plays are fictional. Prospero, along with the *mago* of the *arte* scenarios, may be seen as the archetypal playwright of tragicomedy, as he manipulates the internal audience (the Milanese-Neapolitan court party) with the terror of an illusory storm, a "simulacrum of terror" whose emotional power is finally diminished for Miranda as Prospero reveals to her its illusory quality.

The Rhetoric of Tragedy. Tragicomedy also modulates terror by deploying the rhetoric and not the actions of tragedy. Its fictional deaths are usually meant to transform the internal audience of the play, and are announced in tragedically coded rhetoric. *Aminta* is a paradigmatic case. "La falsa morte" [false death] (4.2) is crucial to the play, which tempers terror by means of aesthetic distance and a rhetorical (as opposed to actual) deployment of tragedy. Tragedy enters the play via the narrations of the nuncios and not by direct enactment. The attention of the theater audience is given more to the reception of the tragedic narration than to the substance of the story itself—to first Aminta's, then Silvia's, emotional responses of terror and pity at the false reports of the other's death. By moving its internal audience (if probably not its external audience) to pity and terror, the microtragedy moves the play towards an eventually comedic denouement. What might in tragedy proper be an external action of revenge is in *Aminta* conceived of rhetorically. The narration of a terrifying and pitiable event, distilled into the rhetoric of tragedy, is compared to "coltei pungenti / che costui porta ne la lingua" [piercing knives that he holds in his tongue] (4.2.1654–55) that will purge Silvia and prepare her for the comedic end. The point is not the external action (which may or may not be true) but her internal transformation. She vows to bury the supposedly dead Aminta and perform offices of grief, just as Leontes does in *The Winter's Tale* after hearing Paulina as a kind of tragedic *nuncio* deliver a false, but transformative account of Hermione's death (*The Winter's Tale* 3.2.172–214).

Tragicomedic Dreams. Dreams, frequently deployed in Italian and Shakespearean pastoral, focus attention on inner experience, which is especially the province of the pastoral mode. They allow a verisimilar framing of the fantastic or marvelous. And they provide another

simulacrum of terror. Denores points to the real terror produced by
dreams as evidence that terror admits of no degree. For Guarini, the
terror of dreams constitutes a unique, diminished emotion appropriate
for the new genre. In tragicomedy, dreams may temper grief or provoke generically ambivalent, nuanced emotional registers. In *Il pastor
fido*, the shepherd Montano recounts to Titiro the painful memory of
the terrifying flood that deprived him of his son: the Arcadians were
"sepolti / nel *terror*, ne le tenebre e nel sonno" [buried in *terror*, darkness, and sleep] (1.4; emphasis mine). But Montano soon modulates
generic registers. He recounts a dream of tragicomic tonality that reprises the storm only to temper its terror. In a fluvial *locus amoenus*, an
old man rises from a river holding an infant and warns Montano not to
kill his son. The original trauma, the deadly storm that had carried his
child away, begins to repeat itself in the dream only to give way to a
comforting oracle. In fact, the "l'imagine gentil di questo sogno" [gentle
image of the dream] later prevents him from ritually sacrificing his son
Mirtillo, as Montano himself later explains in act 5, scene 5. If sacrifice
constitutes one of the principal explicit or implicit actions of Greek tragedy, according to René Girard,[12] the deflection of sacrifice provides
Guarini a resonant tragicomedic theatergram. The tragicomedic dream
may seem deceitful ("ingannevole") but constitutes an internal "action"
that prevents the tragedic action of sacrifice. Tragicomedic dreams are
oracular: riddlingly ambivalent but truthful. For Montano, tragic horror modulates into a tragicomic register. The "improvviso orrore" that
is really a form of piety ("insolita pietate") becomes benign, deflecting
the sacrificial sword at the last moment.

In Shakespeare's *Winter's Tale*, a dream of tragicomic tonality also
prevents the enactment of a tragedic sacrifice. The dream Antigonus
describes in act 3, scene 3, tells him that he should deposit the baby in
Bohemia, where, we soon discover, shepherds will save it from what
would have been certain death. The dream's significance lies not only
as an internal "action" that prevents tragedic action but as an exploration of gradated tonalities. Antigonus recounts the dream as part of the
generically liminal scene in the "desert shore of Bohemia." The scene is
crucial in altering generic "horizons of expectation." If the mortal bear
and the Clown's homespun account of Antigonus's death provide a
grotesque tragicomic register, the dream explores gradated tragicomic
tonalities in a manner akin to Guarinian dramaturgy. The dream evokes
pity and fear only to temper or modulate them. Antigonus is "affrighted
much" by the dream but adds that he "did in time collect [himself]"

(3.3.37–38). Various devices achieve this controlled diminution of tragic intensity. The Senecan-style ghost, a figure of significant tragic power in *Hamlet*, does not take the stage but is mediated through a narrated dream: the apparition of Hermione's spirit to Antigonus. With a kind of mannerist exaggeration, Antigonus emphasizes the dream's pathos much more than its terror: Hermione is a "vessel of . . . sorrow," whose eyes become "two spouts" as she struggles to speak. But as terror is modulated, so is extreme grief: her fury becomes "spent." Also tempering tragic terror is the ritualistic patterning of Hermione's movements, which lends the dream a solemn, not terrifying, tone: she holds her head on one side, then another and bows before him three times.

The subject, characters, tone, and diction of Posthumus's dream in *Cymbeline* similarly befit a tragicomedic decorum. As in *Il pastor fido*, the dream provides riddling comfort to assuage the grief of familial loss. Under the false belief that Imogen is dead, Posthumus expresses the pathos and penitence typical of tragicomedy in his open-air "prison." "Death," or really the felicitously false belief in Imogen's death, serves him as a "physician" (5.4.7). The plaintive, "poor ghosts" of the dream, which Posthumus later takes to be fairies, mark a falling-off in tonality and power from the terrifying Senecan ghosts of tragedy. Sicilius Leonatus, Posthumus's father, begins the dream by banishing the horrible prospect of tragedy, modally revising *King Lear*: "No more thou thunder-master show / thy spite on mortal flies" (5.4.30–31).[13] Posthumus's family express pathos for him—"A thing of pity!"—and protest the events that have befallen him in a register of post-tragic regret: "Why did you suffer Iachimo, / slight thing of Italy, / To taint his nobler heart and brain / with needless jealousy; / And to become the geck and scorn / o' th' other's villainy?" (5.4.63–68). Iachimo is reduced to a "slight thing," inflicting "needless" jealousy on a Posthumus rendered as much a comic ("geck") as a tragic victim. As in *Il pastor fido*, the dream yields an ultimately benign but riddling oracle, leaving the dreamer to question the truth-status of his oneiric vision. Still, the dream is a grandsire to Posthumus, conforming to the pastoral pattern of healing dreams experienced while sleeping in the open air.

AFFECTIVE RESPONSE IN *AMINTA* AND *IL PASTOR FIDO*

The entire premise of Tasso's *Aminta* is rhetorical and revolves around internal response and transformation, beginning with Dafne's opening persuasion to the chaste, repressed Silvia to acknowledge the pleasures of love. As blocking element, the internal resistance and repression of Silvia (really a female version of Euripides' Hippolytus) replaces the external *senex* figure typical of New Comedy. *Aminta* proposes a religion of love whose priest is Amore. In the prologue, Amore announces the internal, rhetorical project of the play: "che la pietà mollisca / quel duro gelo" [that pity may soften that hard frost {around Silvia's heart}] (prologo 63–64). The plaintive, elegiac registers of Petrarchan pathos replace the haphazard mixtures of high and low styles that characterized late-Quattrocento and early-Cinquecento pastoral drama. And the pathetic fallacy common to pastoral poetry renders the landscape itself an expression of the new style.[14] Incapable of active heroism, the passive Petrarchan figure fantasizes a distant day when the sight of his pastoral grave finally extracts pity from the cruel Silvia (1.2.383–98). The sweet pastoral style, in a community of fellow sufferers, tempers the extremity of pain: the "wise" Elpino knows how to "raddolcir gli amarissimi martiri / al dolce suon de la sampogna chiara" [allay bitter torments with the sweet sound of my pipe] (3.1.1319–20). The grotesque stylistic conjunctions of the earlier, folkloric pastoral cede to the pathetic style.

The passivity of the lyric, Petrarchan registers that dominate the first half of the play leave the play, however, in dramatic stasis. *Aminta* requires the higher registers of tragedic rhetoric infused by the *nunci* who announce the false deaths of Silvia and then Aminta. The rhetoric of tragedy both registers and generates tragedically coded internal responses on the parts of Aminta and Silvia. Said to be "tramortito . . . d'affanno" [frightened to death], Aminta declares "io sento / che mi s'agghiaccia il core e mi si chiude lo spirto" [I feel my heart freezing and my spirit closing up] (1374–75). At the sight of the supposedly dead Aminta, Silvia is described as a mad Bacchante (5.1.1940–42).

The extremity of these tragic responses, however, is tempered by various techniques. The tragic Bacchante modulates into tragicomic pathos: falling on Aminta's body, Silvia revives him with her tears, eliciting a "doloroso ohimè" [painful sigh] from his "petto interno" [inner heart] (5.1.1952–53). The doctor Alfesibeo, paired with the poet as recipient of the Apollonian arts (5.1.1928–30), has been sent for to heal the wounded Aminta. Whereas in many Italian pastorals the doctor heals with magical, secret herbs, the verisimilar and post-Tridentine *Aminta* translates pastoral healing into rhetorical and psychological terms, so that Silvia supplants Alfesibeo and her tears take on healing, "magical" properties. Tragedy is also tempered by the high degree of aesthetic distance placed between the speaker and the theater audience; the latter is ironically detached from the passions of adolescent sexuality that are staged in a self-consciously theatrical manner. Aminta's suicidal leap (later described as a literally "fortunate fall" [5.1.1876]) is patently theatrical, staged for the witness Ergasto: "Fa che tu conti / a le ninfe e a i pastor ciò che vedrai" [Be sure to tell the nymphs and the shepherds what you see] (1696–97). As a "spettacolo improvviso" [sudden spectacle] (5.1.1920), the fall elicits "pietate e stupore" [pity and astonishment] in Elpino as he watches at the foot of a precipice. The sight of Aminta's death is revealed as a "rassomiglianza del terribile," in Guarini's terms, or in Tasso's words, "una dolente imagine di morte" [a painful image of death] that brings "vita e gioia" [life and joy] to the lovers. The solemn *intermezzi* modulate "orrore" [horror] into a register of solemnity and awe, not tragic terror: "Ne la notte serena, / Ne l'amico silenzio e ne l'orrore, / sacro marin pastore / vi mostra questo coro e questa pompa" [In the still night, in the friendly silence and the awesome stillness, the sacred water shepherd shows you this chorus and this ceremony] (intermedio primo).

Largely modeled on *Aminta*, *Il pastor fido* shares many of the stylistic/emotional blends of Tasso's pastoral: the pathetic fallacy; the tragicomedic, pathetic treatment of eros infused by Petrarchan rhetoric; and the concern to separate such tragicomic blends from the low-comic registers allotted to the satyr and Corisca. And the main action of the play, despite its Sophoclean apparatus, also calibrates tragicomedic response. Since the news of Amarilli's apparent infidelity seems to jeopardize the oracle and require the tragedic action of human sacrifice, the play's tonalities are conventionally tragic, as we have seen. But later, obscurely aware of the felicitous outcome, the priest Tirenio (the Tiresias figure) describes the modulation of tragic into tragicomic tonalities:

> Cessâr tutti i mostrüosi segni:
> non stilla piú dal simulacro eterno
> sudor di sangue, e piú non trema il suolo,
> né strepitosa piú, né piú putente
> è la caverna sacra; anzi da lei
> vien sí dolce armonia, sí grato odore,
> che non l'avrebbe piú soave il cielo,
> se voce o spirto aver potesse il cielo.
>
> (5.6)

[The monstrous signs have stopped. The sweat of blood oozes no more from the eternal likeness, the ground trembles no more, the sacred cavern is no longer noisy or putrid. From it instead comes such a sweet harmony, such a pleasant odor, that the heavens itself could not be sweeter, if the heavens had a voice or a spirit.]

The tragically coded signs emitted in the temple are shifted as though along a musical scale, in keeping with Guarini's notion of a continuum of emotional responses that resemble "musical chords" (*Il Verato*, 3:226). Terror is modulated and aestheticized. Tirenio himself responds in kind, feeling a "non so che d'insolito e confuso / tra speranza e timor" [something strange and mixed with hope and fear] (5.6). The priest Montano, a kind of Prospero figure, is raised to high, tragedic anger by Amarilli's supposed crime and later by Carino's interruption of the sacrifice, but Carino enjoins him to temper his fury with "un fiato sol di generoso affetto" [just one breath of generous feeling] (5.5). Spectator to Mirtillo's impending death as well as his would-be executioner, Montano responds with pathos, the tragicomic *pietà* that actually prevents him from killing his son. Here, then, is the internal response that prevents the tragedic action of sacrifice: "quell insolita pietate, quell'improvviso orrore" [that strange pity, that unexpected horror]. If genres are largely defined by affective response, the transformation of high anger to pathos constitutes a generic transformation.

"Gentleman-Like Tears" in Shakespeare's Late Plays

In regard to affective response, the tragicomedies of Beaumont and Fletcher are comparable to Shakespeare's late plays. *Philaster* and *A King and No King* center more upon virtuosic rhetorical demonstrations and displays of emotion than on the imitation of decisive dramatic actions.[15] Contemporaries especially admired Beaumont and Fletcher for the liveliness and range of emotions depicted in their plays. So Thomas Stanley in the 1647 Folio:

> He to a Sympathie those soules betrai'd
> Whom Love or Beauty never could perswade;
> And in each mov'd spectatour could beget
> A reall passion by a Counterfeit:
> When first *Bellario* bled, what Lady there
> Did not for every drop let fall a teare?

And when *Aspasia* wept, not any eye
But seem'd to weare the same sad livery;
. . . .
Thus he Affections could, or raise or lay;
Love, Griefe and Mirth thus did his Charmes obey:
He Nature taught her passions to out-doe,
How to refine the old, and create new;
Which such a happy likenesse seem'd to beare,
As if that Nature Art, Art Nature were.[16]

Beaumont and Fletcher's capacity to "refine" old passions and to "create" new ones follows the general lines of Guarinian dramaturgy, which focuses less on the dramatic action per se than on the emotions experienced by the internal audience and elicited in the "gentle," refined theater audience, be those emotions "counterfeit" or "real." Stanley's praise for emotional virtuosity entails a new awareness of the participatory role of the theater audience and recalls Italian contemporaries' admiration for the emotional virtuosity of new *commedia dell'arte* divas such as Vicenza Armani and Isabella Andreini.

Although it is not now thought that *Philaster* preceded and significantly influenced *Cymbeline*, the two plays do share a common dramaturgy of the emotions.[17] In *Cymbeline* as well as in *Philaster*, the characters' passions change rapidly and sometimes improbably according to the situation. Posthumus's "character," mystically venerated by the first gentleman, proves suddenly unsubstantial, protean, and vulnerable to the vagaries of situations, which generate sudden and volatile shifts in emotion. Still, the emotional peripeteias of Shakespeare's protagonists are less passionate than those of Beaumont and Fletcher. Like the violent, irrational forces that destroy the protagonists of Greek tragedy, Fletcherian passion is an unholy power. In *A King and No King*, Arbaces complains that "Each sudden passion throws me as it lists, / And overwhelms all that oppose my will" (4.469–70). The king's vagrant moods continually provoke comment, for they are the center of dramatic interest. Mardonius says of Arbaces that he is "vainglorious and humble, and angry and patient, and merry and dull, and joyful and sorrowful, in extremities, in an hour" (1.1.188–90) and that the king's "passion eclipses [his] virtues" (1.1.340). In *Philaster*, pastoral pathos makes a striking cameo appearance but is not at all central to the play's dramaturgy. In lacrimose and pathetic terms, Philaster describes his first sight of the androgynous Bellario next to a fountain (*Philaster* 1.2.115–42). Allegedly the son of "gentle" parents, Bellario exudes appropriately gentle emotions as he tearfully distributes flowers from a "mystic" garland. The tonally intermediate affective register here mirrors the intermediate and ambivalent gender status of Bellario, whose masculinity is not revealed until the final act of the play. That Bellario's pathos is narrated rather than enacted, however, suggests its marginal status in the play, whose pivotal moments turn on less nuanced and more histrionic exhibitions of emotion.

In general, it is fair to distinguish between Fletcherian *passion* and Shakespearean *pathos* in plays written between 1608 and 1613. In Shakespeare's late plays, emotional response follows more closely the Guarinian pattern of tragicomedic "tempering": the exploration of generically intermediate registers of diminished terror, pathos, and wonder. At the same time, in the late plays registers of popular farce, censored by Fletcher in "To the Reader," dramatically counterpoint the new genteel emotions.

In *Cymbeline*, the prolonged, curiously aestheticized "death" and funeral of Fidele (4.2) provides a fine example of tragicomedic gradation under the aegis of pastoral. The scene explores and adjusts various levels of aesthetic and emotional response. As in the plays of Tasso and Guarini, tragicomedy replaces the imitation of a confirmed tragedic action with an exploration of cognitive, aesthetic, and emotional responses to supposed tragedic events. The funeral the boys perform for Fidele itself is also resumptive, employing the same music and language used for the rites regularly performed for their dead "mother" Euriphile. As a repeated mourning ritual, it resembles an elegiac pastoral complaint rather than a decisive tragedic transition ritual. The sentimentality of the scene should not be criticized as a decadent falling-off from tragic intensity but should be explored in the terms of Guarinian dramaturgy.

From the first solemn note of Belarius's strange musical instrument, the pastoral speakers display a curious concern with decorum, with the tonalities of their response to Fidele's death. To the solemn music played by Arviragus, Guiderius asks,

> What does he mean? Since death of my dear'st mother
> It did not speak before. All solemn things
> Should answer solemn accidents. The matter?
> Triumphs for nothing, and lamenting toys,
> Is jollity for apes, and grief for boys.

(4.2.190–94)

This sounds like Sidney's censor of the mixing of "hornpipes and funerals." In a neoclassical manner, Guiderius criticizes "mungrell" stylistic mixtures and the inappropriate matching of subject and emotional expression. But when Arviragus enters with Imogen dead in his arms, Belarius confirms that the subject, or the "occasion," matches the expression. The scene here begins to shift to a solemn, elegiac decorum, and all three speakers are concerned to strike the proper notes. The solemn music suggests a new genre about to appear on the horizon, but it is as if the boys must debate and work out its particular techniques—tone, diction, subject, meter, character—for themselves. Should flowers be strewn? Should there be singing or not? In what tone should one sing? In what direction should the deceased's head be lain?[18] "Grief for boys" describes both the subject and the generic challenge of the scene: how to find gradated tonalities adequate to the generically intermediate subject of the boys' grief for the false death of Fidele.

Arviragus's plaintive litany of allegorized flowers that will be strewn over Fidele's grave constitutes a pastoral theatergram, deployed by Bellario in *Philaster* (1.2.132–37), by Marina for Thaisa's grave in *Pericles*, by the "nymph" Ophelia before she meets her watery death in *Hamlet*, and, more festively, by Perdita in *The Winter's Tale*.[19] Arviragus thus casts himself in a female, elegiac role, attempting to "sweeten [the] sad grave" of Fidele. Of course, merely as a boy actor often playing the roles of women, the actor playing Arviragus is a gender-ambivalent figure, and he calls attention both to this ambivalence and to the corresponding liminality in vocal tonality: "though now our voices have got the mannish crack, sing him to th'ground" (4.2.235–36). The less-feminized and more-heroic Guiderius contests the decorum of his brother's response: it is too delicate, too "wench-like," inappropriate to the seriousness of the event, which is, after all, death. His brother, however, convinces him that singing is acceptable.

The rhetoric of all three pastoral speakers tempers, softens, and attenuates the sting of death. Belarius concludes that Fidele died, not of violent causes, but of melancholy, an emotion appropriate for a pastoral key. Arviragus imagines Fidele laughing—not even at "death's dart," but at sleep. Guiderius imagines the grave as a bed, frequented with only benign, female fairies, unvisited by worms (for Hamlet, a powerful image of the grim physicality of death).[20] As a pastoral ritual, the funeral dirge ritually wards off various materials of tragedy: the lightning and thunder of the tempest, sign of political, moral, and cosmic

chaos; the disfavor or oppression of the tyrant, the typical protagonist
of tragedy; and the typical supernatural agents of tragic horror:

> Guɪ. No exorciser harm thee!
> Arv. Nor no witchcraft charm thee!
> Guɪ. Ghost unlaid forbear thee!
>
> (4.2.276–78)

As we have seen in our discussion of Antigonus's dream in *The
Winter's Tale*, the transitional scene in the Bohemian "desert shore" is
tonally liminal. Atmospherically, it is a place of death without terror
and comic savagery, tonally well calibrated to effect a change from
"things dying" to "things newborn." The bear provides the most notorious example of tonal ambivalence, the mitigation of terror by laughter.[21] The popular, homespun style of the pastoral speakers differs from
Guarini's bucolic sweet style, but it achieves a similar effect by tempering the stylistic and emotional registers of tragedy.

> O, the most piteous cry of the poor souls! sometimes to see 'em, and
> not to see 'em: now the ship boring the moon with her main-mast,
> and anon swallowed with yest and froth, as you'd thrust a cork into
> a hogs-head. And then for the land-service, to see how the bear tore
> out his shoulder-bone, how he cried to me for help and said his name
> was Antigonus, a nobleman. But to make an end of the ship, to see
> how the sea flap-dragoned it: but first, how the poor souls roared,
> and the sea mocked them: and how the poor gentleman roared, and
> the bear mocked him, both roaring louder than the sea or weather.
> (3.3.90–101)

The young clown describes a terrifying event, registering his own response
of pity for a person of high social station, he is careful twice to note. But
the low diction ("hogs-head," "land-service," "flap-dragoned"), and the
grotesqueness of his account severely "contaminate," in a generically
productive sense, tragedic decorum.

From Leontes' initial accusation on, Hermione is a tragicomic figure
of pathos, eliciting pity without terror, as we have seen in our account
of Antigonus's dream. In the trial scene, she stops short of tragedic rhetoric, although insistently recalling her high station. Her father, the Em-
peror of Russia, is invoked as a model spectator of tragicomedy: "O
that he were alive, and here beholding / His daughter's trial! that he
did but see / The flatness of my misery, yet with eyes / Of *pity*, not

revenge!" (3.2.120–23; emphases mine). Even as narratively evoked by Paulina as a "sainted spirit" (5.1.56–67), Hermione functions not as a tragedic ghost with the power of Hamlet's father but as an oddly tempered and aestheticized presence, her Hamlet-like shriek "Remember mine" diminished in power by virtue of its narrated status and the shrewish quality of the speaker.

The three gentlemen's extended narration of *The Winter's Tale*'s first recognition is often considered an example of the dramaturgical naïveté of the late plays, or as Shakespeare's way of saving his best for the second recognition scene. Actually, the scene reveals now-familiar techniques of tragicomedic dramaturgy. In a curious way, third-party narration allows an extremely nuanced, detailed account of audience response. Autolycus's secondary, diminished role in the scene anticipates the comeuppance he will receive at the hands of the newly gentled shepherds. Wonder and "gentleman-like tears" pervade the narration, even experienced by the now-gentle shepherd, who is said to stand "like a weather-bitten conduit of many kings' reigns" (5.2.56–57). Unlike the grotesque, ambivalent coincidence of emotion evoked by the bear, the deliberate, baroque mixture of emotion described by the gentlemen follows something like Guarini's idea of tragicomedy, as the response of Paulina is described as an equipoise of tragic and comic registers: "O, the noble combat that 'twixt joy and sorrow was fought in Paulina! She had one eye declined for the loss of her husband, another elevated that the oracle was fulfilled" (5.2.72–76). The third gentleman carefully describes Perdita's emotional response to the false news of her mother's death; in tragicomedy, response is at least as important as the truth of its object.

The second, enacted recognition scene presents a tragicomedic theatergram of "resurrection," with due adjustments for verisimilitude. Proscriptions of superstition and witchcraft (5.3.43,89–91) preserve the verisimilitude of Guarinian tragicomedy even as they recall the *maga* figure of fantastic Ovidian pastoral drama. A tone of ritual solemnity similar to the endings of Italian *commedia grave* replaces the festive, if complex, endings of Shakespearean comedy. Wonder and pathos are again the major keys. As a tragicomedic physician, Leontes' purgatorial "comfort," Paulina administers bittersweet "affliction" (5.3.76). As theatrical director, Paulina is intensely focused on Leontes' internal response, in the manner of tragicomedy. She continually gauges his responses and prepares him for each stage of the spectacle. Paulina's "dramaturgy" is keyed to the spectator, who is an active participant in the theatrical process.

The obvious "theatricality" of *The Tempest* includes Prospero's function as a playwright. Prospero still irresistibly evokes Shakespeare himself but he also resembles the playwright of tragicomedy according to the general practices of Guarinian dramaturgy. As recommended by Guarini, he continually enacts the illusions, not the reality of tragedy: false deaths and "rassomiglianze del terrible." Like the playwright of tragicomedy, Prospero is intensely concerned with audience response, exploring tonalities intermediate between generic extremes. Revenge is not consummated in the tragedic, external action of murder but rather takes the form of internal pathos. As Malevole (also an exiled duke who forgoes tragedic revenge at the last minute) declares in *The Malcontent*:

> The heart's disquiet is revenge most deep.
> He that gets blood, the life of flesh but spills,
> But he that breaks heart's peace, the dear soul kills.
>
> (1.3.158–60)

The Tempest continually veers away from the imitation of external, tragedic action—political conspiracy, murder, revenge—towards the exploration and reformulation of inner states. As playwright/rhetorician, Prospero intends to "persuade toward an attitude," that of contrition and repentance.[22] The entire action of the play turns on audience response: the emotional and ethical reactions of the court party to Prospero's mnemonic spectacles. And registers of pathos without terror appropriate to a pastoral decorum dominate the emotional landscape of the play.

Prospero elicits the tragic extremes of fury, passion, and terror in his subjects only to temper or modulate those responses into tragicomic registers. In her terror ("the cry did knock against my very heart") (1.2.9–10), pity ("O, I have suffered / With those that I saw suffer!") (1.2.5–6), and wonder Miranda experiences the affective responses of Aristotelian tragedy.[23] Prospero soon modulates this affective response by pointing out the fictionality of the apparently tragic event. The "amazement" caused by terror modulates into the "wonder" elicited by Prospero's art. Prospero tempers the extremity of Miranda's terror and pity by thus enjoining her: "Be collected: / No more amazement: tell your piteous heart / There's no harm done" (1.2.13–15). Ferdinand experiences the false illusion of his father's death, and responds in tragic kind by weeping, fury, and passion. Ariel's song modulates these extreme responses into tragicomic tonalities, "allaying" the "fury" and "passion" of the waters (and, implicitly, Ferdinand's heart) with its "sweet air" (1.2.395–96). This resembles the "sweet style" appropriate to the madrigalesque set pieces of Tasso and Guarini, often actually set to music in late-Cinquecento tragicomedy. In the song itself, death does not take the form of the grimly physical, tragedic body but of the aestheticized object: "Of his bones are coral made; / Those are pearls that were his eyes: / Nothing of him that doth fade, / But doth suffer a sea-change / Into something rich and strange" (1.2.400–404). The thunder and lightning, the sudden disappearance of the marvelous banquet, and the harsh speech of Ariel, as harpy and "minister of fate"— all suggest a tragic register, and the purpose of this spectacle is to recall to the court party the tragedic act of usurpation twelve years past. The tragedically coded terror elicited in Alonso, however, is curiously aestheticized and musically modulated into a tragicomic register: "The winds did sing it to me; and the thunder, / That deep and dreadful organ-pipe, pronounc'd / The name of Prosper: it did bass my trespass" (3.3.97–99). Gonzalo constitutes, in many ways, the perfect spectator of tragicomedy: responding with wonder to the "danger not the death" of the shipwreck and to Prospero's other spectacles. As Ariel reports to Prospero, Gonzalo reacts to the plight of the court party with tragicomic pathos "brimful of sorrow and dismay" (5.1.16–17).

The neoclassicism of *The Tempest* does not stop with the notorious observance of the unities (duly observed by Gonzalo at 5.1.205–13) but includes a distinctively Aristotelian reversal: the moment when Prospero decides to forgo revengeful action on Alonso, Sebastian, and Antonio. As befits tragicomedy, the reversal consists of an internal "action," an emotional response to a theatrically deployed event. Curiously, the playwright Prospero finally becomes the pathetic audience in the last of an extended series of emotional responses. To Prospero's inquiry about Alonso and the court party, Ariel responds:

> The King,
> His brother, and yours, abide all three distracted,
> And the remainder mourning over them,
> Brimful of sorrow and dismay; but chiefly
> Him that you termed, sir, the good old Lord Gonzalo,
> His tears runs down his beard like winter drops
> From eaves of reeds. Your charm so strongly works 'em
> That if you now beheld them, your affections
> Would become tender.
> PROS. Dost thou think so, spirit?

ARIEL. Mine would, sir, were I human.
PROS. And mine shall.
Hast thou, which art but air, a touch, a feeling
Of their afflictions, and shall not myself,
One of their kind, that relish all as sharply
Passion as they, be kindlier moved than thou art?
Though with their high wrongs I am struck to th'quick,
Yet with my nobler reason 'gainst my fury
Do I take part: the rarer action is
In virtue than in vengeance: they being penitent,
The sole drift of my purpose doth extend
Not a frown further.

(5.1.6–30)

I have quoted at length in order to emphasize the sustained tonality of pathos that infuses one of the pivotal moments of the play. The
action of the play, it may fairly be said, turns on emotional response, as
opposed to any tragedic action. The vectors of spectacle and audience
response, moreover, are extremely complicated. Prospero's pathetic reversal responds to Ariel's emotional response to Gonzalo's tears at the
sight of Alonso's contrite response to a spectacle (the harpy banquet)
that referred to a past tragedic action: four orders of emotional responses
to an original event.[24] Action, then, is heavily mediated and modulated
through internal registers. Tragic fury gives way to the affective, intermediate registers of tragicomedy, as vengeance modulates into forgiveness. Prospero's affections, at least with those who have responded
correctly to his spectacles, "become tender." If not with Caliban, Antonio,
and Sebastian, with Alonso and Gonzalo Prospero is capable of an affective kindness ("kindlier moved") occasioned by the recognition that
he is "one of their kind."

Prospero, of course, admits no more than a grudging or patroniz-
ing "kindness" with Antonio, Sebastian, and especially Caliban ("This
thing of darkness I acknowledge mine"), who manifestly do not provide the right emotional responses to Prospero's spectacles. The play
acknowledges the limitations of both pathos and generic mixture, which
makes the fragile achievements of "kindness" (in both the affective and
generic senses) the more compelling. This experiential honesty bestows
on the late plays more dramatic power relative to Italian tragicomedy.
Still, the dramatization of tragicomic tonalities as theorized by the Italians in the Horatian tradition of a calibrated third genre constitutes a
crucial dramaturgical practice of the late plays, one that places Shakespeare in the context of international Renaissance dramaturgy.

7

Place, Genre, and
"Horizons of Expectation"

In Renaissance tragicomedy, genre signals provide important cognitive signals for the audience. As suggested in the Jonson title page, tragicomedy deploys, for relatively sophisticated theatergoers, complex mixtures of codes from historically antecedent genres. The belated and capacious genre of tragicomedy is constructed from the materials of other genres. The precise nature of "metatheatricality" in Renaissance tragicomedy takes the form, not so much of "presentational" and "representational" stylistic oscillations (in twentieth-century terms), but of an increased deployment, relative to "purer" genres, of generic codes. One might say that Renaissance tragicomedy is *metageneric*. The generic multiplicity of the form offered, for the Renaissance theatergoer, not merely the pleasures of arch self-consciousness but a complex combination and negotiation of the various perspectives and attitudes provided by each of the four kinds standing below the figure of "Tragicomoedia" in the Jonson title page. Paradoxically, the analytical notion of Horatian decorum as quoted on the frieze lays the groundwork for the comparison and even synthesis of kinds or modes in Renaissance tragicomedy. Again, a neoclassical principle turns out to have innovative possibilities.

The role that the pastoral mode plays in this combinatory practice of tragicomedy may be seen in two ways. Pastoral is a highly expressive and symbolically resonant mode in its own right, which alters tragedic "horizons of expectations" in the reader/audience. But as we have seen in our discussion of the *scena satyrica*, it can also be said that pastoral provides a generically capacious arena that can admit tragedic, comedic, and satiric codes. Like the costume of Jonson's "Tragicomoedia," the pastoral costume could ingeniously combine generic indicators; Leoni's *tragisatiricomica*, for example, features the eponymous heroine Roselmina dressed as a Bradamantine warrior from the waist up and as a shepherdess from the waist down. Originally a sophisticated, historically belated Alexandrian form given to allusiveness and literary self-consciousness, pastoral became for innovators like Tasso and Guarini a vehicle for generic as well as in-group, courtly allusiveness. *Aminta* points to genre as conspicuously as it gestures, as a *drame à clef*, to members of the Ferraran court. The pastoral play became, for Italian courtly and academic writers, an arena of literary, specifically generic, theory.

The dramaturgical practice, common to Italian and English tragicomedy, of multiplying generic perspectives derives from homologies in the respective theatrical settings. The academic and courtly arenas significantly overlapped in Italy, so that court productions provided opportunities for humanistic, avant-garde experimentation. The courtly audiences of late-sixteenth-century Italian pastoral could easily recognize the allusions to genre in plays like *Aminta*. The private-theater audiences inherited in 1608 by the King's Men were used to self-conscious forms like Marstonian paratragedy, which wittily and parodically manipulated the codes of various genres. With many of its theatergoers coming from the Inns of Court, it was the most academic and learned of audiences available to the professional players. And the increasingly important theatrical venue of the court, deemed by Jonson sophisticated enough to decode the "more removed mysteries" of the masque, also provided a fit audience for tragicomedy. A prologue written for Middleton and Rowley's strange 1620 masque/play *A World Tost at Tennis* indicates that the Stuart court could consider its taste for generic awareness and multiplicity a sign of its avant-garde sophistication:

> This our device we do not call a play,
> Because we break the stage's laws to-day
> Of acts and scenes; sometimes a comic strain
> hath hit delight home in the master-vein,
> Thalia's prize; Melpomene's sad style
> Hath shook the tragic hand another while;
> The Muse of history hath caught your eyes,
> And she [that] chaunts the pastoral psalteries:
> We now lay claim to none, yet all present . . .[1]

That one did not have to wait until 1620 for this sort of generic awareness is, of course, indicated by the learned court theatergoer Polonius
in his knowing appreciation of the Elsinore players' "tragical-comical-
historical-pastoral" entertainment (*Hamlet* 2.2.394–95).[2]

GENERIC "WORLDS" AND PERSPECTIVES

The spatial metaphor in the Horace quote ("Let each particular variety hold the *place* properly allotted to it" [emphasis mine]) is telling. If
genre theorists have profitably enlisted various analogies in their understanding of literary genres—genre as an evolving biological species,
genre as an institution, genre as a speech act, and genre as a family[3]—
Renaissance genres may well be considered as analogous to places,
"habitats," or "worlds."[4] Genres tentatively erect boundaries, establishing an arena with certain attitudes, properties, and perspectives. Writers, of course, continually transgress generic boundaries, establishing
for the reader new territory that mixes features of the old and the new.
If genres establish horizons of expectation, readers "traveling" from
one genre to another experience shifting horizons. The salient Shake-
spearian image for this becomes the disguised Imogen traveling across
Britain from, in effect, tragedy to tragicomedy.

In the Renaissance, the resemblance of genres to "worlds" is largely
the result of the Horatian notion of decorum: a habit of mind of all
Renaissance writers whether honored in the breach or in the observance.
Decorum proposes that the parts of a given genre fit together in some
kind of discernible whole. Scaliger gives this a quasi-philosophical basis by arguing that because *verba* (words) depend on *res* (things), then
style must relate to subject matter.[5] By virtue of decorum, the various
components of kind—subject matter, action, person, style, topoi, emotional register, and sometimes place itself—constitute a kind of
subworld. Genre, then, is a principle of "fittedness" that may be most
powerful when used to dramatize the clash or inappropriateness of a
given generic tag, as with the pastoral *topoi* in *King Lear*.

To use Kenneth Burke's dramatistic vocabulary, in a literary work
in which the generic landscape figures heavily, Scene tends to prevail
over Act and Agency, and place becomes more important than character.[6]
What Frederic Jameson says of the romance world could be said of the
"worlds" of all Renaissance genres and is especially true of Renaissance
pastoral: the generic place tends to absorb many of the act-generating

functions of agent.[7] Jameson considers the use of "world" in phenomenology as the "ultimate frame or *gestalt*, the overall organizational category or ultimate perceptual horizon, within which empirical, inner-worldly objects and phenomena are perceived and inner-worldly experience takes place."[8] As opposed to the indefinite extension of objects in conventional narrative realism, as presented in film, in Jameson's romance "inner-worldly objects such as landscape or village, forest or mansion . . . are somehow transformed into folds in space, into discontinuous pockets of homogeneous time and of heightened symbolic closure, such that they become tangible analoga or perceptual vehicles for world in its larger, phenomenological sense."[9] Genre links particular objects in its world with a cognitive horizon or frame.

Cinquecento innovations in scenic theory and practice rendered the similarity of a dramatic genre to a "world" especially clear. The Vitruvian/Serlian tripartite codification of the tragedic court, the comedic city, and the pastoral *scena satyrica* nicely aligned place and genre, so that elements of a place could metonymically evoke the entire genre. Says Vitruvius, "Tragedic scenes are delineated with columns, pediments, statues, and other objects suited to kings; comedic scenes exhibit private dwellings with balconies and views representing rows of windows after the manner of ordinary dwellings; satyric scenes are decorated with trees, caverns, mountains, and other rustic objects delineated in landscape style" (5.6.9). [10] The temple in the pastoral set, as we have seen, evokes the world of tragedy. Ariostan comedy theorized its new perspective settings (constructed by professional artists like Pellegrino da San Daniele) with an Renaissance notion of a fictional, self-enclosed world governed by its own peculiar laws. As we have seen in our analysis of the *scena satyrica*, the objects of the scenic/generic world came to acquire highly symbolic resonance—the satyrs in Cesariano's scheme, for example, functioning as "perceptual vehicles" for vice and depravity.

The Italian fidelity to the unity of place—dictated as much by the imperatives of the set designers as by neoclassical theory—certainly did limit the semiotic flexibility and range of scene design. But the growing popularity of the *intermezzi* encouraged faster and more effective ways of changing scene settings. Whereas early-Cinquecento *intermezzi* were performed with pageant wagons or portable set pieces, by midcentury artists were experimenting with *periaktoi* and the manipulation of angled and flat wings (the latter requiring developments in perspective drawing to work successfully). *Periaktoi* (imported from Italy to England by Inigo Jones in the 1606 *Hymenaei*) were rotating columns

with two to six sides, each painted with a different scenic decor. Renaissance designers followed Vitruvius's brief, obscure discussion of
three-sided *periaktoi* with tragedic, comedic, and satyric genre scenes.
Although, by the seventeenth century, *periaktoi* were not the most sophisticated device available for changing scenes, they provided a striking
emblem (in both Italy and England) for tragical-comical-pastoral varia-
tions in set semiotics.

Certainly Italian courtly plays, with their prologues, *intermezzi*, and
choruses, provided a complex set of different and rapidly changing
perspectives, or "worlds." The Proteus *intermezzo* from *Aminta* associates the dazzling set changes made available by the new technology
with the marvelous psychological transformations wrought by love:

> Proteo son io, che trasmutar sembianti
> e forme soglio variar sì spesso;
> e trovai l'arte onde notturna scena
> cangia l'aspetto: e quinci Amore istesso
> trasforma in tante guise i vaghi amanti . . .
>
> (Intermezzo Primo)

[I am Proteus, who always changes forms and shapes. And I've discovered the art of nocturnal scene changes, where Love himself transforms longing lovers into many guises.]

The scenic decors of *Aminta* then constitute a continually changing perceptual horizon that lends its objects symbolic resonance. The focus
turns from Act or Agency to Scene as the originator of "action," which
now amounts to psychological transformation. The opening prologue
delivered by Amore, a framing structure that ultimately derives from
the *sacra rappresentazione*, guides the viewer of apparently tragedic action with an overall horizon of comedic and providential expectations:
tormented eros, death wishes, and near suicides are all to be viewed
sub specie comoediae. Within the overall frame, however, the *Poetics* tags
and solemn rhetoric suggest a tragedic horizon of expectations. In turn,
tragedic horizons are foreshortened by bathetic, comically incongruous moments like Aminta's "fortunate fall" into a life-saving bush.[11]
Taken together, the various generic frames of the play provide a complex perspectivism. For James J. Yoch, the stunning *intermezzi* in *Aminta*
and other pastoral plays provided a powerful frame to the disorder
enacted in the pastoral *selva*, a frame as ordered and substantial as the
proscenium arch.[12] And whereas Guarini sometimes speaks as if every

scene of a tragicomedy should be a finely blended puree of tragedy and comedy, in practice he conceives many scenes as either entirely tragic or entirely comic, as the *Annotazioni* shows. *Il pastor fido*, then, provides alternating comic and tragic perspectives guided by the appropriate generic tags, as was possible with the modally flexible pastoral set.

GENERIC "WORLDS" IN SHAKESPEARE

Professional English Renaissance drama, of course, was unconstrained by the unity of place. But even when continually altered in the multiple plot, generically coded places or "worlds" were still symbolically resonant devices for English playwrights. This was the case largely because they inherited a Horatian notion of decorum, although they were willing to violate it more often than the Italians. Although English plays did not always conform to the Vitruvian codification, English audiences would not have been unfamiliar with the associations of genre and place. Comedies like *Much Ado About Nothing* draw tragicomedic capital from the court setting, because Shakespeare's audience would have associated the court with tragedy, if less strictly than Italian audiences. In the relatively minimalist English stage, in which scenic constituents were often evoked by language and the imagination of the audience, generically significant places could be changed and even mixed to a much greater extent than on the Italian stage.

Polonius's famous litany of dramatic hybrids suggests that Shakespeare was no less aware of generic codes than the learned Jonson or than private-theater playwrights like Marston and Chapman. The tripartite, tragical-comical-pastoral arrangement of *The Winter's Tale*, by which Shakespeare separates Greene's romance story into the constituent dramatic kinds of Italian pastoral tragicomedy as codified by the *periaktoi*, is only the most obvious example of an implicit focus on kind characteristic of the late plays. Such generic awareness, of course, characterizes many other Shakespearean plays but is particularly pronounced in the generically recapitulatory and inclusive late plays. Multiple generic signals, worlds, and frames combine to provide complicated and shifting "horizons of expectations."

Designed with tightly woven single plots, the tragicomedies of Beaumont and Fletcher are much less "metageneric" than Shakespeare's late plays. They deploy generic codes less conspicuously and do not stage alternative, generically coded worlds, as we have seen in our discussion of pastoral. Because of their cultivation of surprise rather than wonder, they do not play with generic and perspectival frames in the manner of Italian tragicomedy and Shakespeare's late plays. In *A King and No King*, the machinations of the controller figure Gobrius (a far lesser figure than Prospero) are not revealed until the final act.

It has often been noticed that most of the characters of Shakespeare's late plays are less individually drawn than those of the tragedies; in fact, they often seem schematic versions of tragedic predecessors. Among the late plays, the dramatis personae of *Cymbeline* most obviously correspond to stock character types: the evil stepmother, the foolish and grotesque courtier, and the sophisticated and cynical Italian. And in the next two plays, Leontes abbreviates Othello, Prospero telescopes Lear, and Antonio and Sebastian encapsulate Macbeth in their conspiratorial language (*The Tempest* 2.1.193–292). In fact, characters within the late plays tend to view one another typologically, in ways that roughly correspond to generic outlooks. In *Cymbeline*, Imogen surveys the terrain: "A father cruel, and a step dam false, / A foolish suitor to a wedded lady" (1.7.1–2). Pisanio correctly typologizes Imogen's enemy as a "false Italian" (3.2.4). In Wales, Cloten expects to be recognized by his clothes as a type of a certain place: the court. The pure tragedy of conspiracy and revenge that Leontes projects onto the court, a dark countermode to Polixenes' retrospective idyllic pastoral, is filled with generically appropriate characters: the adulterous wife, the evil king, the "false villain" Camillo. For Leontes, these types constitute a tragedic "world": a claustrophobic court of intrigue and conspiracy. Paulina, for her part, rightfully views Leontes as a tyrant, a figure typical of Renaissance tragedy. In the *antefatto* narrated to Miranda at the beginning of *The Tempest*, Prospero casts Antonio as the political usurper who frequents Italianate tragedy. Later in the play, Prospero becomes the blocking father of New Comedy in his bridling of Ferdinand, even as Ariel has been seen to partly derive from the servant of Roman comedy.[13]

In Shakespeare's late plays, characters are so closely related to generically coded places that it can be said that Scene—and genre—prevail over Agent. If characters undergo transformation, it is rarely explained in psychologically realistic ways. Change is more frequently the result of a particular place working on a character: Posthumus's prison, the place where Leontes says he will make daily "offices of grief," and Prospero's marvelous island. Shakespeare's late plays structure themselves according to various places. The place shifts of *Cymbeline* and *The Winter's Tale* are clear enough. And whereas *The Tempest* outwardly follows the unity of place, it deploys the full variety of pastoral landscapes, often expressed as the projection of inner attitudes, in the manner of *As You Like It*. Even if each locale does not exactly correspond to a recognizable kind, it usually constitutes a subculture or habitat with distinctive subjects, attitudes, and tonalities. And the most important, most transformative place is that of pastoral.

The many shifts of place in *Cymbeline* should not be seen as the unfortunate effects of a dramaturgically undisciplined, sprawling romance, but as structuring the generic multiplicity by which the play provides its complicated perspectivism. The important moving parts of *Cymbeline* are not individual characters but larger "habitats" with distinctive attitudes, atmospheres, and subjects, each defined in comparison with one another. Shakespeare actually less resembles the First Gentleman, who claims that Posthumus is ideally and essentially good and thus cannot be compared with anyone (1.1.21–22), than he is like Iachimo, who argues for a comparison of (female) virtue (1.5.67) and bets that circumstances can change character. In the company of court familiars, Cloten sticks and whines. Confronted with Caius Lucius, Cloten's boasting approaches heroic defiance. Posthumus is removed from a romance world of ideal stasis, placed in a situation of cynicism and intrigue, and becomes a character seeking tragedic revenge. Isolated in Britain, receiving a sign of Imogen's apparent death, Posthumus repents. Characters behave the way they do not because of an invisible essence but according to the situation—often genre-coded—in which they have been placed.

Sharply opposed to the ideal, comparison-defying worlds described or imagined at the beginning of the play, Iachimo's Italianate Renaissance Rome provides a skeptical, comparative, and crudely materialistic "habitat." Iachimo devalues Imogen from Posthumus's ideal, superlative "jewel" to a material, exchangeable object. In his confession at the end of the play, Iachimo tellingly sees the contest between him and Posthumus as a generic conflict: "mine Italian brain / Gan in your duller Britain operate" (5.5.196–97). The generic fruits of Iachimo's world are mostly tragedic in nature, although mitigated by the overall tragicomedic frame of the play. As symbolic action, Iachimo employs the rhetoric of tragedy with Imogen and later Posthumus. With Imogen, Iachimo begins with the lurid and debased account of sexuality typical of Jacobean tragedy: "The cloyed will— / That satiate yet unsatisfied desire, that tub / Both fill'd and running—ravening first the lamb, / Longs after for the garbage" (1.7.47–50). Attempting to convince Imogen that she is a figure worthy of a tragedic deed, Iachimo claims that her supposed plight elicits "wonder" and "pity" (1.7.81–82). Furthermore, Imogen merits the tragedic paradigm because she is a figure of "great stock," or high social station (1.7.126–28). The rhetoric of Iachimo's speech, before he disavows it, means to persuade Imogen to the conventionally tragedic action of revenge.

Cloten, on the other hand, evokes the world of court-based, comical satire that dominated the private theaters before 1605. He embodies blood without breeding and a degenerate court that only values external signs such as his clothing. His plan of gaining admittance to Imogen's chamber by "lining the hands" of her servants recalls the corrupt stratagems of Marston's courtiers, as do his bawdy puns ("if you can penetrate her with your fingering") (2.2.13–14). As opposed to the relative social fluidity of pastoral, Cloten and his mother represent a rigid adherence to rank. That Guiderius does not recognize him by the external signification of his clothes measures the distance between the two habitats of the corrupt court and pastoral Wales.[14] Belarius, however, the only character who knows both worlds, correctly views Cloten in a generic manner, as representing a world larger than himself (4.2.144–45).

The most important habitat in *Cymbeline* is the pastoral world, liminally and pivotally introduced at the play's midpoint. Belarius reads the pastoral place in a moral fashion, drawing sermons in stones from the allegorized, semiotically rich landscape. As in romance for Jameson, the objects in Wales become "perceptual vehicles for world in its larger, phenomenological sense." The emblematic or symbolic resonance of place assumes a greater importance than individual characters: "this gate / Instructs you how t'adore the heavens; and bows you / To a morning's holy office" (3.3.2–4). Place, here, defines the physical and moral posture of character. Belarius has constructed the virtues of his pastoral habitat in contrast to the court (3.3.21–22) and Guiderius recognizes the comparative genesis of Belarius's pastoral mode: "Haply this life is best / (If quiet life be best) sweeter to you / That have a sharper known" (3.3.29–31). When the boys transgress their bounded pastoral space, they begin to move into a heroic, historical arena that shifts their horizons of expectation.

In *The Winter's Tale*, Shakespeare analyzes Robert Greene's *Pandosto* into the same constituent kinds of Italian pastoral tragicomedy. The tripartite, tragical-pastoral-comical arrangement focuses attention on three different kinds, or "habitats," and the relationships between them. If Renaissance kinds could provide interpretive perspectives on the world, the multiple generic network of *The Winter's Tale* invites its audience to consider, for example, tragic problems of state and sexuality from a pastoral point of view. As in *Cymbeline*, the several changes of place do not merely bespeak the expansiveness typical of romance, but also stage different generically inflected attitudes. The play begins in a court that soon becomes claustrophobically tragedic, narratively evokes the serene, beneficent "isle" of Delphos in tonal opposition to Leontes' tragedy, moves to the generically liminal and pivotal "seacoast" of Bohemia, shifts to the less terrifying but not escapist greensward next to the shepherd's cottage for the long pastoral scene, and ends in a Sicilia transformed into comedy less festive than *grave*, solemnized in Paulina's chapel.

Leontes remakes a court first characterized by witty and sophisticated verbal exchange into a place of tragedy. He effectively forces the initial place of the play, then, into the Vitruvian/Serlian codification, whereby the adulterous and conspiratorial court represents the site of tragedy. Acts 1 to 3 of *The Winter's Tale* encapsulate tragedy in a schematic or telescoped manner as a resonant world, although Leontes' attempt to impose a pure tragedy is countered, dialogically, by comic and satiric modes (as we shall see in the next chapter). But if place, symbolically and generically understood, is viewed as a central dramaturgical tool of the last plays, the short exchange between Cleomenes and Dion assumes a more important function than it may appear to have at first glance. The scene entirely subordinates character to a place with rich atmospheric and symbolic resonance. Altogether indistinguishable as characters, Cleomenes and Dion evoke a pastorally coded "habitat" that pointedly contrasts the increasingly claustrophobic, tragedic court of Leontes. Like a Renaissance kind, the isle of Delphos expresses an atmosphere and a point of view:

> CLEO. The climate's delicate, the air most sweet,
> Fertile the isle, the temple much surpassing
> The common praise it bears.
> DION. I shall report,
> For most it caught me, the celestial habits
> (Methinks I so should term them), and the reverence

Of the grave wearers. O, the sacrifice!
How ceremonious, solemn, and unearthly
It was i'th'offering!

(3.1.1–8)

For the theater audience, the evocation of Delphos counterpoints the oppressive court, contrasting the free air and fertile landscape of the island to the constriction and sterility of Leontes' Sicily. We may recall Guarini's theory that tragedy exerts a centripetal effect on the soul, comedy a centrifugal force. Here is the pagan temple central to Italian pastorals: the source of oracles, the site of fertility rituals, and often the converging point of the characters as they emerge from the disorienting *selva*. As a place of solemnity and ceremony, the temple anticipates the daily offices of grief that Leontes promises to observe.

The pastoral section of *The Winter's Tale* is the most clearly delineated place/kind of the play, where a place shift very clearly indicates a changed point of view. In the generically liminal scene on the hard pastoral Bohemian "seacoast," the shepherds reframe tragedic material ("Heavy matters! heavy matters!") (3.3.111) into a pastoral frame. The infant Perdita signifies illicit sexuality for the old shepherd, just as she did for Leontes, but the plain talk and attitude of the pastoral speaker reinterpret what had been a tragic experience for the Sicilian king into the generalizing frame of comedy: "Though I am not bookish, yet I can read waiting-gentlewoman in the scape. Tis has been some stair-work, some trunk-work, some behind-door-work: they were warmer that got this than the poor thing is here" (3.3.72–76).[15] The young clown also addresses "heavy matters"—the storm, the shipwreck, and the mauling of Antigonus—but frames the material in a new generic decorum. Instead of depicting something like the psychological transformation of Leontes, the play works impersonally and mythically by moving to a new generic "habitat," one with a significantly different climate and point of view. It is a generically coded change of place, anticipated in the earlier, brief evocation of the beneficent atmosphere of Delphos, that transforms the audience's "horizon of expectation" and might even be said to transform Leontes as well—as if he had dreamed the episode. In opposition to Leontes' attempt to cordon off the Sicilian court as the fixed place of tragedy, the play itself provides geographical and generic multiplicity. The play moves its characters and the external theater audience through different places/kinds, continually altering their horizons of expectation.

The spatially unified *Tempest* evokes genre less by place changes (although the fullest range of the generically capacious pastoral set is explored) than by Prospero's deft control of the arts of kind. As with the sophisticated Italian tragicomedies, tragedy in *The Tempest* is not fully enacted, but presented telescopically by shorthand codes of kind, probably more quickly decipherable by a courtly or Blackfriars clientele than by a Globe audience. The storm scene recalls the relationship, raised by *King Lear*, between natural forces and political authority.[16] As I have suggested in the previous chapter, the terms used by Miranda and later Prospero to describe her response to the storm strikingly recall Aristotle's account of the tragic effect: terror, pity, and wonder. And just as the young clown oddly specifies the social station of the victim Antigonus in his account of the storm, Miranda curiously assumes that the victims of the shipwreck are of a station adequate for tragedy: the "brave vessel" carries "noble creatures" in her (1.2.6–7). Prospero, a bitter victim of a tragedic past who remembers past injustice in pastoral exile along the lines of Sannazaro's *Arcadia*, must make others remember the prior tragedy as well. Certainly this is the purpose of the thunderous, incriminating speech Ariel delivers to the court party in the guise of a harpy. And the retrospective tale that Prospero tells Miranda amounts to an encapsulated tragedy. The story is set in an Italian court, involves characters of high station, and concerns conspiracy, political usurpation, and the fall of a powerful ruler. The narrative raises questions appropriate to Renaissance tragedy concerning good and bad rule, and presents the tragedic topos of the fall from heights of power. It creates tragedic horizons of expectation in both the internal audience and the external audience. Miranda represents both when she wonders why the tragedic end, the political murder, did not occur: "Wherefore did they not that hour destroy us?" (1.2.138–39).

Prospero's overall project is tragicomedic, comprising both tragedic and comedic actions, as well as pastoral and satiric modes. Insofar as he controls most of the action (like the *mago* of the *arte* scenarios who governs the theatrical action), he is indeed something like a playwright of a tragicomedic play. If he is curiously conscious of the unities of place, time, and action, and if his plot is informed by the Terentian structure of protasis, epitasis, and catastrophe, he also is a generic virtuoso.[17] He remembers tragedic events of the past, recalls them to the court party in a kind of theater of memory, and plans to exact revenge and punish his enemies.[18] He makes a father and a son both believe that the other has died, but finally is more interested in bringing his enemies to repentance than in completing the tragedic action. In the manner of Italian tragicomedy, tragedic Fortune, which had brought his enemies under his sway (1.2.178–84), modulates to tragicomedic providence, at least according to the choral speech given by Gonzalo at the end of the play (5.1.201–4).[19] This modulation repeats the movement from tragedic action to "providence divine" in the Milan story as recounted by Prospero. As Guarini advises, the comedic actions of the play are not merely juxtaposed to tragedy but are structurally integrated into it. The dynastic marriage of Ferdinand and Miranda may be considered structurally tragicomedic, rather than strictly comedic, because it is meant to solve the problems caused by Antonio's tragic usurpation.

In *The Tempest*, generic codes are largely but not entirely in the control of Prospero. Rather than actually changing places, the play dramatizes an arena onto which different inner "worlds" are projected—those of pastoral/utopian visions, colonialist exploitation (in both the tragic vein of Prospero and the comic vein of Stephano), tragic conspiracy, satiric undermining, and marvelous enchantment. The perspectival frames manipulated by Prospero further complicate the play's horizons of expectation. Shakespeare's places do not as neatly conform to generic codifications as those of the Italians dramatists, but they exploit a similar genre system and a similar dramaturgy of place in which Scene prevails over Agent. It is impossible to understand the multiple perspectivism of the late plays without attending to their generic multiplicity. In this regard, the historical context of continental tragicomedy serves us better than romance criticism.

8

Modal Dialogues

The Jonson title page allegorizes and animates genres and modes, suggesting that they have rhetorical functions. If we read "Tragi-comoedia" as comprising the other modes in the engraving (the tragic and comic modes deriving from the tragedic and comedic genres), it then has the most complex modal system and is capable of dramatizing a multitude of "debates" between different modal points of view. In the last chapter, we considered Renaissance kinds more as genres than as modes, studying them as "places" or "worlds" that adjust audience anticipations or "horizons of expectations." My analysis of the Renaissance term "kind" into "genre and "mode" is largely heuristic, because Renaissance kinds behaved like both genres and modes, and neither theorists nor writers of the period worried about naming the different types of behavior proper to kinds. But whereas the generic "worldness" of kind, supported by realized or verbally invoked scenic decors, enabled us to clarify the shifting perspectivism of Renaissance tragicomedy, the modal "dialogy" of kind will help us understand the interaction and contestation between different kind-coded points of view. Guarini is willing to defend the principle of modal interaction and debate against Denores (for whom the kinds were stable essences, unchanged by one another), because he could point to a well-unified end product that satisfied neoclassical conditions. As we might expect, English playwrights from Marston to Shakespeare took the generic practice of modal dialogism much further than did the Italians.

The pastoral mode again comes to the service of a tragicomedic practice, because of the dialogic nature of pastoral poetry from its Theocritan and Vergilian beginnings. The dual singing contest could easily be transformed into discursive debate. The emergence of pastoral drama, in the late-fifteenth and early-sixteenth centuries, coincided with the pronounced revival of dialogue as a form, and philosophical dialogue could easily be incorporated into the pastoral play. And much early-Cinquecento pastoral drama was in the dialogic form of the eclogue. Shakespeare's *As You Like It*, as we have seen, is largely a play of debate, allowing a forum for Touchstone and Corin to debate the relative merits of court and city, and for Orlando and the disguised Rosalind to dilate on love. Less committed than tragedy or comedy to any particular generic codifications, the capacious pastoral of Italian tragicomedy and Shakespeare's late plays may function as an arena of modal debate and interaction. In the late plays, the pastoral debate is more inflected by generic codes than in *As You Like It*.

If tragicomedy explores various relationships between kinds, then it must have as its background condition a complex genre system. Guarini and fellow Cinquecento commentators again provide the theory for a generic practice. No genre system can be justified in either Plato or Aristotle,[1] and it was left to the Italian Cinquecento theorists to provide a system of kinds, or rather competing and continually contested systems.[2] Aristotle's predilection for imitation, and in particular the imitation of action, tended to circumscribe the canon, eliminating the discursive and philosophic kinds of which the humanists were enamored. Without altogether discarding Aristotle, Cinquecento theorists like Mazzoni expanded the canon by extending the purview of the objects of imitation to include thoughts and feelings.[3] The late Renaissance is marked both by an increased complexity in systems of kind, and by the theorizing of that complexity.

For Guarini, it is necessary "arrichire il tesoro delle muse, e non d'impovirirlo" [to enrich the treasure of the muses, and not to impoverish it] (*I Verato*, 2:233). Much of the first *Verato*, then, devotes itself to the critical enterprise of expanding both classical and contemporary genre systems, in opposition to Denores's narrow, ternary genre system.[4] Near the beginning of the first *Verato* Guarini makes a case for the dithyramb as a distinctive kind with specific forms and functions. Whereas Denores restricts tragedy to public, political events revolving around the tyrant figure, Guarini argues for the subkind of domestic tragedy as exemplified in the *Medea, Hippolytus*, and *Alcestis* of Euripides. In fact, this critical discussion of domestic tragedy prepares for the kind of negotiation between private and public spheres that occurs in tragicomedy (*I Verato*, 2:242).

A more extensive genre system increases comparative, dialogic, and

contestatory possibilities. For Renaissance kinds did not signify in isolation but in relationship with other kinds. In this respect, the kinds
were like elements in a linguistic system, signifying in differential relationship with other elements in the network. Especially in a multigeneric
form like tragicomedy, such differential signification may occur within
a single play. Ralph Cohen's remarks on genres are highly relevant for
the relationships between kinds in Renaissance tragicomedy:

> A genre does not exist independently; it arises to compete or to con-
> trast with other genres, to complement, augment, interrelate with
> other genres. Genres do not exist by themselves; they are named and
> placed within hierarchies or systems of genres, and each is defined
> by reference to the system and its members. A genre, therefore, is to
> be understood in relation to other genres, so that its aims and pur-
> poses at a particular time are defined by its interrelation with and
> differentiation from others.[5]

Like ancient genres according to Francis Cairns, Renaissance kinds arose
to "contrast, complement, and define each other's aims."[6] Especially in
times of literary consciousness and experimentation, modes give rise
to countermodes, as Guillén's account of the generation of picaresque
from pastoral demonstrates.[7] And Colie discusses the mutual exchange
between the sonnet and the epigram in Renaissance lyric, by which the
epigram's status is "raised" by conjunction with the sonnet and the sonnet's sweetness is "counterpointed by the epigram's salt and vinegar."[8]
    Even for Denores, the three central kinds provoke political com-
parisons, based as they are on different forms of government (*Discorso*,
2:155–57). But unlike Denores's fixed-genre system, Guarini's more extensive genre system allows points of contact between the various kinds:
genres "non abbiano a contenersi ne' loro termini" [do not have to contain themselves in their boundaries] (*Compendio*, 3:402). He examines
the relationships and interactive possibilities between tragedy, comedy, pastoral, and satire, all of which will provide dramatic material for
his new genre. Comedy and pastoral are heightened by their association with tragedy; the emotional excesses of tragedy are checked in
dialogue with comedy. Whereas Guarini eventually wishes to unite tragedy and comedy under a new structuring form, in practice tragicomedic
dramaturgy is more like a debate than a stable blend. In the first *Verato*,
the kinds are likened to the elements—hot and cold, wet and dry—
which "con le loro opposite differenze una tal guerra si fanno" [in their
differences wage a great war against each other] (*I Verato*, 2:243) and

yet achieve peace. What emerges is less a stable recipe than a process of modal interaction.[9]

MODAL DIALOGUES

That the rhetorical animation of genres and modes as figured in the Jonson title page was an international "habit of thought" is confirmed by the presence, in both Italian and English Renaissance drama, of prologues depicting allegorical representations of tragedy and comedy debating one another. As we would expect, the Italian dialogues move toward negotiation and reconciliation, whereas the English analogues remain more contestatory and acrimonious.

The muses of "Tragedia" and "Comedia" introduce *L'Ortensio*, a comedy written by the Sienese Accademia degli Intronati and first performed in 1561.[10] The debate turns on three points: the ritual context of performance, the affective responses elicited by genre, and the audiences proper to tragedy and comedy. In response to Comedia's charge that she disrupts a festive context, Tragedia argues that her imitations elicit delight and benefit the general citizenry. Comedia claims for herself a wider audience than that of Tragedia (those of middle station), but Tragedia argues that her lessons and sententious wisdom apply to those of all social levels. Soon, however, their antagonism turns to reconciliation as they join in flattering Siena. And Comedia's final remarks are something of a retreat, as she classes herself, not as a political or social genre, but as a jocose, festive form produced for the delight of a female audience.

Somewhat more contestatory is a similar genre debate that begins the 1570 *Prigione d'amore*, written by the Neapolitan playwright Sforza Oddi.[11] Defensive and nostalgic, Oddi's Tragedia defends generic purity and defines herself by her traditional emotional effects: tragic sighs and shattered hearts. Comedia does not appeal as expected to laughter, but competitively promises to bring to the stage a new form of emotional and aesthetic pleasure, the more sentimental pleasures of *commedia grave* as well as of tragicomedy: "nuovo piacere e . . . non piú inteso modo di piacevolezza" [a new sort of pleasure and a charm never known until now]. Comedia offers the appeal of various emotional concoctions: "di lagrime e di riso una vaghissima mescolanza" [a pleasant mixture of tears and laughter]. Striving to beat Comedia at her own game, Tragedia claims that she too can move the audience to tears. They debate their place in the generic hierarchy: Comedia contests Tragedia's confining of her to the narrow Aristotelian purview of the ridiculous and the grotesque. Whereas Tragedia argues that the recent invasion of Italy by foreign powers renders its monitory lessons particularly important, Comedia claims to save desperate lovers from despair and suicide and, in a curious logical leap, to liberate the state from desperate conspirators like Spartacus and Catiline. (We are reminded of Guarini's roundabout ascription of a political function to comedy, by dint of its capacity to relieve political leaders of melancholy.) More animated and competitive than the *L'Ortensio* prologue, this debate dramatizes each kind's appropriation of practices proper to the other form. Here Comedy wins, although the prologue ends with the conventional compliment to the court and a reconciliation between the two kinds.

Much more charged than the Italian prologues is the exchange between Comedy and "Envy" (Tragedy) that begins and ends the extremely popular English pastoral play *Mucedorus*, probably written sometime in the early 1590s, printed in 1598, 1606, and 1610 (with the addition of the prologue, epilogue, and several scenes) and revived by the King's Men around 1609.[12] Adding to the contestatory tone of the debate is the gender difference between Comedy (female) and Tragedy (male). Envy interrupts Comedy's introduction in martial and violent mien, threatening to "mix" Comedy's music with the strains of tragedy—an aesthetic mixture in the manner of the Italians, but as discordant as the "vilest out-of-tune music" that creates the mood for the opening of *The Malcontent*. Instead of the negotiated settlement that ends the Italian prologue, the *Mucedorus* prologue closes with each kind threatening to subvert the other. Envy will turn Comedy's "mirth into a deadly dole" and darken the pastoral scene with tragic gloom: "I'll thunder music shall appall the nymphs . . . Flying for succor to their dankish caves." But Comedy vows that even if Envy interferes with her subjects she will reappropriate his intrusion and change it "from tragic stuff to be a pleasant comedy." Despite Envy's acknowledgment of Comedy's apparent victory in the epilogue, he threatens her with revenge. To the confident Comedy's taunts, Envy threatens to subvert her genre with violent and bilious satire, "whose high abuse shall more torment than blows"—a plausible threat, given the vigorous tradition of satire on the English stage and the "tragical-satirical" melds of Webster emerging at the time. The final peace between the two kinds, as they bow before the power and authority of King James, only thinly covers a tension far greater than in the Italian exchanges—a tension only resolvable by royal fiat. The relationship between Comedy and Envy is one, not of reconciliation or competition as in the Italian prologues, but reciprocal subversion, and points to a sharper and less resolved tension between modes in English tragicomedy. The constituent modes such as satire are less "tempered" than in the Italian plays. Still, English playwrights could have found in the Italian model a paradigm for modal interaction.

Debate and "Tempering" in Italian Tragicomedy

The very action of *Aminta* may be considered a move from monologue to dialogue.[13] Surprised in a moment of absorbed self-reflection, Silvia explicitly recalls Narcissus (*Aminta* 2.2.854ff.). Aminta is also solipsistic, trapped in lyric or madrigalesque stasis by the repetitive Petrarchan plaint. Bittersweet pathos does provide a tragicomic register, but does not complete the play. The trajectory from solipsism to exchange in the erotic realm is paralleled by a shift from lyric stasis to a dialogue of kinds. The threat of tragedic violence is displaced from the courtier to the satyr, whose attempted rape of Silvia finally spurs Aminta to action, transforming the play from ecologue to drama, *contra* Denores. Tragic, satiric, and comic modalities interact with the predominant pastoral modality. Tragic modalities infiltrate and contaminate pastoral, raising the actions and rhetoric of the traditionally humble mode.

Whereas Guarini's dramaturgical theory often stresses the homogeneous blending of tragedy and comedy under the aegis of pastoral, in practice *Il pastor fido* enacts a contestatory dialectic between kinds of contrasting perspectives. Guarini's play is even more dialogic than Tasso's. The scenes of bittersweet, pastoral erotics featuring madrigalesque plaints by Dorinda, Mirtillo, and Amarilli follow the registers of *Aminta* and do constitute a generic blend. But Guarini adds many scenes that are either almost completely tragic or comic. The effect of the play, then, is that of an alternating dialogue between kinds.

Guarini conceives of kinds almost as dramatic protagonists; not far beneath the surface of the dramatis personae can one detect debates of kind resembling those examined above. A solipsistic *contemptor amoris* figure like his female namesake in Tasso's play, Guarini's Silvio begins the play by quoting Seneca's *Phaedra*, heroically challenging the tragedically coded boar and the Sophoclean plague that has smitten Arcadia. He vows to confirm his heroic ancestry (he descends from Hercules) by ridding the land of the "terror of the shepherds." In effect, he aims to defy decorum and create a heroic space in a pastoral arena: "picciol giro, / ma largo campo al valor nostro" [a small ring, but a large field for our valor]. Linco counters the intended tragic heroism of Silvio with a more modest comic perspective, conspicuously quoting from Terence: "Uomo sono, e mi pregio d'esser umano" [I am a man, and value human things]. Silvio, according to his servant, ignores decorum: it is right for a young man to love and it is indecorous to be first surprised by eros in old age. The pastoral landscape, for Linco, is not a place of heroic, external actions but stands as an allegory of the inner life, inviting one to love. Here it is the modal ambivalence of the *scena satyrica* that spurs debate. If Scene determines Agent, Linco argues that Silvio does not know where he is.

As with the gendering of the *Mucedorus* exchange, the debate turns on gender as well. In fact, Guarini argues that tragicomedy is like the hermaphrodite. The new hybrid "si può paragonare al favoloso Ermafrodito, il quale di uomo, e di donna formava un terzo partecipante dell'una, e dell'altra natura, sì fattamente misto, che separare nè quel da questa, nè questa da quello non si potea" [can be compared to the legendary hermaphrodite, which formed a third creature from man and woman partaking of both their natures, so completely mixed that the man from the woman and the woman from the man could not be separated] (*Compendio*, 3:395–96). Unlike the mere embrace of a man and a woman, the hermaphrodite alters male and female forms in the production of a genuinely third nature. The hermaphrodite represents the mutual interaction, or negotiation of male and female, each mixing together and changing its proper form.

As a Hippolytus figure who wants to insulate himself with his male band, Silvio decries the "pensieri effeminati e molli" [soft and feminine thoughts] of pastoral eros. Claiming the purity of both genre and gender, Silvio refers to his heroic, masculine ancestor Hercules. Linco appeals to the tragicomic, generically flexible possibilities of the Hercules myth. Instead of only imitating the tragic Hercules Furens, "che nel proprio furor . . . si rompe" [who burst in his own fury], Silvio should also remember the comic, amorous Hercules, who dresses as a woman and spins at the distaff because of his love for Omphale. And Mirtillo, as "pastor fido" the authentic hero of the pastoral play, does enact this version of Hercules. On two occasions Mirtillo cross-dresses and transgresses a female ritual space in pursuit of Amarilli: once in the highly erotic "kissing game" and once in the game of blindman's buff. In *Il pastor fido*, then, the tragic-heroic mode is coded as "masculine" and the comic-pastoral as "feminine."

In terms of both gender and genre, Silvio and Mirtillo must be "tempered." Guarinian tragicomedy, at least in theory, is not a stable, "tempered" product (as critics have often seen it) but a process or practice of tempering.[14] And "tempering" may indicate the strengthening, in the metallurgical sense, as well as the diminishing of intensity, as in Linco's argument to Silvio that tempered iron is refined to greater strength.[15] Just as the tragic-heroic Silvio needs to be tempered by the force of love, the pastoral Mirtillo must be strengthened by a kind of heroism approaching violence that is impossible within the circumscribed decorum of pastoral strictly defined by Denores. Guarini deploys a potentially tragedic theatergram originally deriving from Ariosto's Ginevra story and used in *Much Ado About Nothing* and Della Porta's *Gli duoi fratelli rivali*.[16] Corisca stages for Mirtillo the false image of Amarilli's infidelity and so propels him into a higher generic decorum. Mirtillo vows: "Ceda il dolore a la vendetta . . . ceda la pietate a lo sdegno" [Let pain give way to revenge . . . let pity give way to disdain] (3.8), rejecting pastoral pathos for tragic vengeance. Guarini approaches violence without fully releasing it: Mirtillo plans to kill Amarilli, her putative lover, and finally himself. When discovered in the cave, he almost kills Nicandro. Drawing back from the extreme of tragedic action, he later offers to substitute himself for Amarilli as victim (thus reiterating Guarini's Aminta's prior sacrifice). To be such a heroic but pathetic victim befits a tragicomic register, and it is the very offer of self-sacrifice that fulfills the oracle and provides the felicitous ending of the play. Nor is Mirtillo ever tainted, for the theater audience, by the crimes of tragedy. He is only made to appear a rapist to the Arcadian community by means of the displacement of tragedic action onto the controller figure Corisca and, of course, onto the satyr as well, who lays the stone that entraps Mirtillo and Amarilli together in the cave. The tempering of different modal perspectives, represented by the tragic-heroic Silvio and the comic-pastoral Mirtillo, constitutes both the dramaturgy and the action of the play. Like the male and female forms in the hermaphrodite, the tragic and the comic modes temper one another and eventually dissolve into a greater synthesis, although not before a dialogic conflict between the two modes is staged.

MODAL CONTESTATION IN SHAKESPEARE'S LATE PLAYS

Like the contemporary *Mucedorus* exchange, Shakespeare's late plays take a contestatory approach to the Italian idea of modal contestation. Modal and generic interaction does not always issue in the final hermaphroditic blend theorized by Guarini. The private-theater audience inherited by the King's Men was used to modal "polyglossia," such as Marstonian parody, which mocks tragedic discourse, or Jacobean revenge tragedy, which counterpoints tragic registers with black humor and satire.

The ideal stasis expressed in the glowing characterizations of Posthumus and Imogen gives way, in *Cymbeline*, to interaction and contest between different kind-coded points of view. In addition to moving through different generic landscapes and their horizons of expectation, the play stages the *encounters* between different worlds. Posthumus is contaminated by Iachimo's cynical, materialistic world. Iachimo attempts to goad Imogen into tragedic action. With Caius Lucius, the world of Rome and the heroic mode tempers Cymbeline's tainted court and momentarily transforms the corrupt Queen and her son into voices of heroic defiance. The worlds of Cloten and Guiderius are not merely juxtaposed (thus providing different generic perspectives) but affect one another in various ways. Cloten tests Guiderius's world, and Guiderius rebukes Cloten's courtly corruption. A crude ritual combat would seem to declare Guiderius the absolute winner, but it becomes clear that Cloten's infiltration has contaminated, in a modal sense, Belarius's pastoral world. The worlds of Britain and Rome, of course, martially contest each other, only to mix together in a tragicomedic fusion something akin to Guarini's hermaphrodite: "the Roman eagle . . . Lessen'd herself and in the beams o' the sun / So vanish'd; which foreshadow'd our princely eagle, / Th'imperial Caesar, should again unite / His favour with the radiant Cymbeline" (5.5.471–76). Especially in this final mixture of Britain and Rome, the play dramatizes the process of something like the Italian fusion of kinds. At the same time, the encounter of different modes sometimes issues in grotesque conjunctions as unsettling as those found in modern tragicomedy. Cloten's entry into the pastoral world yields the grotesque display of his head and, even more disturbingly, Imogen's strange lament over the headless body of Cloten, whom she supposes to be Posthumus. These grotesque moments result from the encounter of incompatible worlds, and suggest the more contestatory relations between Shakespearean modes relative to Italian ones.

Critics have argued whether acts 1 to 3 of *The Winter's Tale* should be seen as tragedic, comprising a kind of compressed tragedy, or as tragicomic, suggesting to the audience early on that the play will have felicitous issue.[17] This debate turns on whether one emphasizes generic or modal features. Leontes attempts, fairly successfully, to construct the generic "world" of a pure tragedy, but is vigorously contested by satiric and comic modes. The first three acts of the play do present a schematic, telescoped tragedic genre-world, but also dramatize a conflict between different modal points of view. Leontes is obsessed with the purity of his wife, the absolute identity between him and Mamillius (1.2.119–22, 128–35, 153–60), and the certainty of his tragic interpretation of the events around him. His public denunciation of Hermione affirms the principles of purity and degree:

> O thou thing—
> Which I'll not call a creature of thy place,
> Lest barbarism, making me the precedent,
> Should a like language use to all degrees,
> And mannerly distinguishment leave out
> Betwixt the prince and beggar.
>
> (2.1.82–87)

Leontes here fears both stylistic breaches of decorum and the mingling of kings and clowns. Camillo's crime, according to Leontes, is that he violates the king's tragedic decorum, foolishly taking serious things for jest (1.2.246–49). His greatest fear is the prospect of being laughed at, as a comic gull, by Camillo and Polixenes (2.3.23–26). Leontes attempts to banish laughter from his public, court tragedy, but comedy still operates as subversive aside:

> LEON. Come follow us:
> We are to speak in public; for this business
> Will raise us all.
> ANT. [*Aside*] To laughter, as I take it,
> If the good truth were known.
>
> (2.2.196–99)

As if in response to Antigonus's aside, Paulina enters. Her opposition to Leontes' "tragedy" takes a primarily comic and satiric turn. She resembles Malevole in Marston's tragicomedy *The Malcontent* in that she punishes the tyrant not with the direct physical violence of the revenger but with language. Breaking past the sycophantic courtiers, she assumes the "office" of the sharp-tongued truth-teller, eschewing "honey-mouth'ed talk" for "red-look'd anger" (2.2.33–35). And she is also something of a comic shrew. As Joan Hartwig argues, Leontes' tragic project is opposed by comic typology: a shrew, a henpecked husband, and Paulina's casting of Leontes himself as a tyrant more comic than tragic.[18] So the characters' perceptions of one another become typological:

> LEON. A gross hag!
> And lozel, thou art worthy to be hang'd
> That wilt not stay her tongue.
> ANT. Hang all the husbands
> That cannot do that feat, you'll leave yourself
> Hardly one subject.
>
> (2.3.107–11)

Comic generalizations oppose tragic particularity.

The pastoral section of the play includes the famous debate between Polixenes and Perdita about art and nature, which turns on the social coding of kind and will be discussed in the following chapter. In the pastoral episode, rhetorically opposing modalities of kind may be seen in the bawdy, low-comic tonalities of Autolycus; the heroic rhetoric of Florizel as he first reacts to Polixenes' interdiction (4.4.477–82); and the providential, tragicomedic resolution suggested by Camillo to the desperate lover (4.4.542–55). The pastoral arenas of the late plays play with gender as well as genre, as we have already seen in our discussion of Guiderius and the "wench-like" Arviragus, both boys liminal in regard to vocal register. Florizel and Ferdinand oscillate between a pseudoheroic braggadocio inappropriate to the pastoral decorum and a feminized submission to their lovers. The most finely blended, hermaphroditic character of the late plays, as frequently exploited in late-twentieth-century productions, is Ariel: nominally male, but performing the female roles of sea nymph, harpy, and Ceres.[19]

Prospero, as we have seen, deploys generically coded spectacles in the manipulation of his audience. His overall project amounts to a grand, tragicomedic synthesis on the order of the wedding masque, which attempts the union of goddesses, minor deities, aristocrats, and rustics. Prospero is unable to control all of the genres of the play, however, opposed as he is by tragedic conspiracy, comic buffoonery parodying tragedic action, and the satiric dissent of the satyr and of Antonio and Sebastian.

The long scene among the shipwreck victims that begins act 2 stages a kind of debate in a pastoral arena. The strangeness of the place and the indeterminacy of the pastoral locus allow for a kind of play between different kind-coded perspectives. Gonzalo, as we have discussed, represents a utopian, pastoral point of view, with his optimistic vision of the golden age and his sense of the beauty and fertility of the land. Antonio and Sebastian's hard-nosed perspective functions as satirical "countermode" to Gonzalo's visionary pastoral. As a king who grieves for the apparent loss of his son, Alonso evokes, in small, the perspective of tragedy. The grim physicality of his language ("what strange fish / Hath made his meal on thee?" [2.1.108-9]) briefly suggests Hamlet's tortuous memento mori (*Hamlet* 4.3.19-31). The function of Francisco's speech ("I saw him beat the surges under him" [2.1.110–18]) cannot possibly be to inform us about a character in which Shakespeare clearly has no interest; it rather presents a heroic mode and attitude reminiscent of the Roman plays, a mode that sharply contrasts Alonso's melancholy and adds to the tonal multiplicity of the scene. For Sebastian and Alonso, Ariel establishes and, at the point of danger, interrupts an encapsulated tragedy during which they propose to reenact Antonio's tragedic act of usurpation performed in Milan twelve years before.

The analysis of modal dialogue in Shakespeare's late plays could, of course, be significantly expanded (and contested as well, for any modal analysis is interpretive) and my discussion makes no claim to be exhaustive. The point is that the networks of kind in Shakespeare's late plays are not static systems. To a greater degree than in Italian tragicomedy the dramatic kinds—tragedy, comedy, pastoral, and satire—are rhetorical performances transparently tied to speaking situations. Leontes' domestic tragedy and Iachimo's revenge tragedy are motivated, and they in turn provoke responses from other characters. In Shakespeare, especially in his most generically multiple plays, the kinds are not objective, determinative frames, but always interested points of view. The kinds come together on a more or less equal footing and infiltrate, contaminate, test, counter, and mix with one another in sharper and in more dialogic ways than in Italian tragicomedy.[20]

9

Social Negotiations

Because Renaissance kinds had recognizable, though flexible, social codings, a generically multiple form like tragicomedy could refer to social and political issues, either mediating or, in some cases, sharpening social difference. Here again, the pastoral mode is generically liminal and thus dramaturgically interesting because of the uncertain social and political status of its representative figures. Shakespeare dramatizes both the impulse towards social reconciliation implicit in pastoral's bridging of comedy and tragedy as theorized by the Italians, as well as the social energies that resist synthesis.

Aristotle's remark, in the *Poetics*, that "[comedy] sets out to represent men as worse than they are today, [tragedy] as better" actually refers to moral criteria and not necessarily to differences in social status.[1] But Renaissance commentators almost universally took Aristotle to be making social distinctions between tragedy and comedy. The Terentian commentaries attributed to Donatus, which distinguished tragedy and comedy according to ending, subject, and social station, played a major role in codifying this misreading of Aristotle.[2] As Madeleine Doran has shown, Donatus based generic social distinctions on his derivation of comedy from the Greek words κώμη (village) and ἀείδω (to sing).[3] In the Terentian-Donatan tradition, the domain of comedy was extended from the village to the city. Renaissance commentators, undemocratic in outlook, could further justify the distinction by arguing that common people were incapable of the noble and heroic actions of tragedy. Scaliger's elaborate system hierarchizes the genres according to the person represented by each kind of poem: the highest form is the hymn, followed by the ode, the epic, tragedy, comedy, and so on.[4] And the Serlian designation of the city as the scene of comedy and the court as the locus of tragedy certainly reinforced the social referentiality of genre. The Donatan social codification of genre pervaded Italian, English, Spanish, and French dramatic theory in the Renaissance.

It was largely due to the social codification of genres that the proposal of mixed forms could incite such vitriolic debate. Tragicomedy, for its opponents, constituted a "monster" in part because it implied a mixture of social classes. The hybrid form, theoretically, could challenge the social hierarchy implied by the hierarchy of kinds as codified by Denores and Scaliger. As Dominick LaCapra argues, "Genres generally come in hierarchies, and the objection to a mixture of genres often occults or conceals an attempt to retain or reinforce a dominant position or an authoritative perspective."[5] Guarini's very proposal to mix kinds violates Denores's hierarchical genre system. Guarini largely holds to the social coding of genres, claiming that "La differenza di questi duo poemi [tragedy and comedy] sta nelle persone imitate" [The difference between tragedy and comedy consists in the persons imitated] (Compendio 3:432). But in the wide-ranging critical discussion that begins the first Verato and the Compendio, he assents to social mixtures far more radical than anything actually deployed in Il pastor fido. For example, he approves of the mixtures of citizens, peasants, gods, and animals in the comedies of Aristophanes, appealing to them as a classical precedent for the social mixtures he would allow in tragicomedy (I Verato, 2:240). Oedipus the King becomes a precedent for the tragical-pastoral mixtures of courtiers and shepherds because of the crucial role Guarini attributes to the shepherd in resolving the plot. As in his discussion of the affective functions of tragedy, comedy, and tragicomedy, Guarini thinks of the social coding of genre not in the analytical, tripartite terms of Denores but according to a flexible continuum: the purest tragedies will not contain any persons of low status, nor will the purest comedies portray anyone of high standing, but an almost infinite number of intermediate registers may be created (Compendio, 3:432).

The mixing of pastoral with other kinds might also offend the conservatives' sense of social decorum and hierarchy. For Denores, it was primarily the social basis of pastoral that prevented it from representing the actions of tragedic or comedic drama. Concerning the lives of rustic villagers, pastoral had nothing to teach those of the court or the city: it was capable neither of tragedic grandeur nor of comedic deceit. As Jane Tylus has argued, when pastoral finally took the stage in the form of a full-length drama explanations were "demanded as to the possible links between the world of shepherds, now made glaringly visible on the Cinquecento stage, and that of its civic spectators."[6] How could rude shepherds possess the *civiltà* requisite for teaching citizens political and ethical lessons?

Whereas Denores considers the characters of pastoral to be of uniformly low status, Guarini argues for social lability and social difference in Arcadia, distinguishing between shepherds and the more humble farmers. Guarini locates social gradation in the microcosm of pastoral: "Gia tra Pastori furon quei medesimi gradi, e di costumi, e di condizione, che oggidi si vede ne' Cittadini" [Already among the shepherds there were the same degrees of custom and condition that one today sees among city dwellers] (*I Verato*, 2:282). Among shepherds, there are not only servants but also owners *(padroni)* whose responsibility over their flock and their inferiors could represent the duties of the Renaissance ruler. Shepherds, Guarini points out, have become political leaders (Romulus), tragedic heroes (Daphnis), and priests and prophets, as in the Bible and in the state of *Il pastor fido* itself, a theocracy led by the priest Montano (*I Verato*, 2:298–304).

For Guarini, shepherds' natural capacity for *meraviglia* renders them natural philosophers and thus capable of *civiltà*. And in the *Trattato della politica libertà*, he distinguishes between the first, uncivilized age, when men lived scattered throughout the countryside without government, and the more advanced period between Moses and Saul, when laws and government were instituted in pastoral societies.[7] The social negotiations of pastoral tragicomedy—a historically advanced genre as figured in the Jonson title page—refer not to the first but to the second stage of pastoral development. Orlando Pescetti, an early-Seicento defender of Guarini against partisans of Denores, discusses the mutual interaction of civic and pastoral worlds, by which civilization is introduced into the countryside.[8] As Tylus has shown, for Pescetti bucolic festivals such as the feast of Pales do not represent rustic spontaneity but the public *civiltà* requisite to the foundation of Rome.[9]

TRANSCENDING SOCIAL ESTRANGEMENT

Behind the dramaturgically innovative use of pastoral as a social bridge between comedy and tragedy, it is certainly possible to detect the unfortunate story of Italian neofeudalization in the late-sixteenth century. Some of *Il pastor fido* was indeed written in Guarini's family villa in northern Italy, where his retreat into "private life" and implicit critique of the court assumed the form of governing the local *contadini*.[10] Beginning in this period, the relative decline of agricultural productivity meant that many small landowners had to sell their property to aristocratic speculators.[11] Many feudal titles continued to be granted after 1500 in Lombardy and elsewhere, and feudal rights constituted a renewed source of income for noblemen in many parts of Italy. The same period saw a relative increase in the villa, an institution that proposes a myth of harmony between the court and the country not unlike that implicit in courtly pastoral. The great aristocratic villas were splendid but sterile islands in the country that actually "took away, in their magnificence, vital life-blood from the surrounding countryside."[12] The open opposition between *cittadino* and *contadino* dramatized in the early-Cinquecento drama of Ruzante, which was possible when small landowners were actually increasing their holdings, now had to give way to a myth of interclass harmony formulated by the aristocracy.[13] If, as Siro Ferrone has argued, the humanist, courtly theater was a utopian theater, projecting in its scenography images of the ideal city or court or in its dramaturgy the ideal Aristotelian tragedy, pastoral tragicomedy was the last great utopian project of sixteenth-century humanist theater.[14] Its dramaturgy and theory of generic reconciliation instantiated a "principle of courtship," described by Kenneth Burke as "the use of suasive devices for the transcending of social estrangement."[15] In *Il pastor fido* and many other late-sixteenth-century pastoral plays, the principle of courtship takes the form of an aristocratic sleight of hand; real *contadini*, who might critique the neofeudal structure, are eliminated, and courtiers are disguised as shepherds. This is a striking example of Empson's pastoral "trick," which puts the complex into the simple and stages the fiction of a "beautiful relationship between rich and poor."[16] Still, as Guarini hints in the *Compendio*, perhaps in a moment of frustration with his own servitude to the absolutist Este court and surely in a moment of utopian idealism, pastoral was at the same time theoretically capable of representing true social egalitarianism and mobility.[17]

The locus classicus of this social trick common to Renaissance pastoral drama may be found in Plautus's *Amphitryon*, an important classical precedent of tragicomedy for Guarini and others (*Compendio*, 3:398). In the prologue, Mercury conceives of genre and tragicomedy in social terms:

Now first as to the favour I have come to ask, and then you shall hear the argument of our tragedy. What? Frowning because I said this was to be a tragedy? I am a god: I'll transform it. I'll convert this same play from tragedy to comedy, if you like, and never change a line. Do you wish me to do it, or not? But there! how stupid of me! As if I didn't know that you do wish it, when I'm a deity. I understand your feelings in the matter perfectly. I shall mix things up: let it be tragi-comedy. Of course it would never do for me to make it comedy out and out, with kings and gods on the boards. How about it, then? Well, in view of the fact that there is a slave part in it, I shall do just as I said and make it tragi-comedy.[18]

As a god of change, a kind of omnipotent but eager-to-please playwright, Mercury boasts that he can easily manipulate the generic status of the play he is about to present, if the audience wishes. The easy commerce between a god and a human audience—accomplished by theatrical disguise—reflects Mercury's capacity to freely mix slaves, kings, and gods and thus create the new genre of tragicomedy for the pleasure of the audience. The social and generic codes of *Amphitryon* are highly paradoxical and labile, because the play is based on the disguises of Jupiter and Mercury as, respectively, king and servant.

In the prologue to Tasso's *Aminta*, Amore (Cupid) also functions as a quick-change artist of genre, one who demonstrates the close connection of genre and social rank in the Renaissance. The Empsonian trick of putting the complex into the simple assumes a mythological and genre-founding dimension, with a god assuming both human and pastoral disguise along the lines of *Amphitryon*: "Chi credería che sotto umane forme / e sotto queste pastorali spoglie / fosse nascosto un Dio?" [Who would believe that a god was hidden under human form and these pastoral clothes?] (prologo 1–3). Amore vows to subvert the hierarchy of the Olympian pantheon and prove himself more powerful than Jove, Mars, or Neptune. Amore has rejected Venus's command that he restrict his activity to the court and has decided to work on the "rozzi petti" [rough hearts] formally reserved for his minor assistants. This "Amor fuggito" myth (Cupid flees Venus and stirs up trouble in a new place) is called upon to explain the very founding of a new version of pastoral, one that mixes different kinds and the social stations upon which they are based. Amore claims love to be a force of social equalization, allowing humble pastoral dwellers to experience "noble" emotions:

>Spirerò nobil sensi a' rozzi petti,
>raddolcirò de le lor lingue il suono;

perché, ovunque i' mi sia, io sono Amore,
ne' pastori non men che ne gli eroi,
e la disagguaglianza de' soggetti
come a me piace agguaglio; e questa è pure
suprema gloria e gran miracol mio:
render simili a le più dotte cetre
le rustiche sampogne.

(Prologo 80–88)

[I will inspire noble sensibilities in rustic hearts, and I will sweeten their speech, because wherever I go, I am Cupid, as much among shepherds as heroes, and I will smooth out the differences among my subjects as I please. This is my supreme glory and miracle—to make rustic pipes sound like learned lyres.]

The new Ferraran pastoral employs the courtly fiction of pastoral egalitarianism based upon the common condition of being subject to eros. Amore is a kind of playwright, granting noble emotions to rustic figures and heightening the generic decorum of their style.

Festival

Just as early-Cinquecento theater appropriated civic and popular festivals for the court by performing comedies in the time of carnival, late-Cinquecento theater appropriated agrarian celebrations like May Day into pastoral drama, albeit in a highly purified form that neutralized the spring festivals of much of their egalitarian or sexually licentious possibilities. The ordered pastoral festival might demonstrate the *civiltà* of shepherds along the lines theorized by Pescetti. Certainly this reflects an idealized relationship between court and country (and neofeudal economic relationships between noblemen and *contadini* as well), and is comparable to the politics of pastoral in Stuart England, when James was attempting to appropriate the pastimes and traditions of merry, rustic England and striving to transcend social estrangement.

Sometimes Italian pastoral plays did clarify the courtly appropriation of festival. In pastoral exile, the usurped prince Edemondo of Leoni's *Roselmina* mounts an opulent joust and festival whose magnificence aims to demonstrate his political legitimacy—successfully, according to the duly impressed glutton Zizzalardone (4.4). As a grand, socially reconciling spectacle produced by an exiled pastoral figure, Edemondo's

festival compares with Prospero's wedding masque. But usually in
Cinquecento pastoral, universalizing mythology replaces the social and
political particularities of the pastoral *festa*. Set on May Day, Angelo
Ingegneri's *Danza di Venere* celebrates the feast of Venus, with the action
converging on the goddess's temple.[19] Two choruses of shepherds
and nymphs dominate the play's action, performing festival activities
such as singing competitions, athletic games, and, as the play's title
suggests, fertility dances around Venus's temple. The two festive games
of *Il pastor fido*—the kissing game and blindman's buff—are purely jocose and erotic, although interesting because of Mirtillo's transvestite
transgression into the female domain. Although the festive songs of
the Rozzi's 1546 *Il batecchio* preserve the aesthetic and social opposition
between real *contadini* and idealizing shepherds (*cittadini* in disguise),
often the communal *festa* that ends Italian pastoral plays appropriates
the peasant and neutralizes social difference.[20]

Intent to depict shepherds as owners and not hirelings and thus
capable of tragicomedic rather than low-comedic action, Fletcher in *The
Faithful Shepherdess* radically proscribes popular pastoral festival in his
"To the Reader." The chaste Clorin associates festive pastoral games
with lust:

> thus I free
> Myself from all ensuing heats and fires
> Of love; all sports, delights, and merry games,
> That shepherds hold full dear, thus put I off.
> Now no more shall these smooth brows be girt
> With youthful coronals, and lead the dance.
>
> (1.1.6–11)

Festivity is displaced offstage onto the divine realm of Pan, as reported
by the reverent and chaste satyr (3.1.167–79). Only the gods can engage
in "dancing, music, and a feast" (3.1.174). What is staged is a festival in
honor of Pan, a kind of temperance ritual on the lines of Prospero's
wedding masque, described by the Old Shepherd and administered by
the Priest: "Never more let lustful heat / Through your purged conduits beat" (1.2.23–24). Of course, the play must dramatize the chaos of
intemperance as well, and the Priest and Old Shepherd later wake to
find the shepherds out of their bed, drawn during the night to some
"lusty sport / Or spiced wassail bowl, to which resort / All the young
men and maids of many a cote, / Whilst the trim minstrel strikes his
merry note" (5.1.28–31). Respectful as Jonson was of Fletcher's "tragi-

comedy well done," he realized that the exclusion of "low" festivity was not a formula for theatrical success. As he did in the Comus antimasque to *Pleasure Reconciled to Virtue* and in *Bartholomew Fair*, Jonson incorporates rustic and plebeian festivity into the design of *The Sad Shepherd*. In *The Winter's Tale* Shakespeare appeals to his heterogeneous audience by including popular festivity, in which one can observe both the erotic element (Autolycus's bawdy songs, the frank sexual interplay between Perdita and Florizel) and a certain control of eros, suggested by Perdita's vain appeal that Autolycus "use no scurrilous words in's songs" (4.4.215), a control that looks forward both to Paulina's solemn, religious "festival" and to Prospero's austere festivity.

THE POLITICS OF TRAGICOMEDY: ITALIAN THEORY

Denores's notion of genre could not be more political, at least in theory.[21] Each of his three chief genres have been formulated, in ancient Greece, by philosophical and political principles and directly refer to specific forms of government. Epic presents images of virtue and teaches the nature of monarchy; tragedy warns against the dangers of tyranny and is governed by the principles of oligarchy; comedy is regulated by the principles of democracy and is designed to "disponergli alla vita politica" [prepare {man} for democratic life] (*Discorso*, 2:155–56). Denores's tripartite genre system fosters various political comparisons. For the Paduan professor, however, pastoral is an apolitical form, not worthy of the stage and not capable of presenting tragedic or comedic actions.

Even Cinquecento theorists like Castelvetro who championed the aesthetic over the political functions of poetry had difficulty remaining entirely consistent. Minturno and Scaliger, along with many other theorists, were eclectic and synthetic, claiming for poetry a complex mixture of utilitarian, rhetorical, and aesthetic functions. Guarini's opposition to Denores does not amount to a pure aestheticism, as has sometimes been claimed, but constitutes an indirect politics that synthetically responds to his opponent's political theory of genres.[22]

The most extended of several analogies used to illustrate tragicomedic dramaturgy is a political one. Tragicomedy may be *like* biological hybridization, music, painting, and metallurgical alloys, but it actually *constitutes* a kind of politics because it involves the governing of the different social classes represented by the different genres. Guarini argues that if governors can regulate social constituencies, poets ought to be able to do the same thing in the realm of the imagination (*I Verato*, 2:160). In particular, Guarini compares tragicomedy to the Venetian republic. For Guarini, the republic incorporates both democracy and oligarchy, not as two separate entities but as one integral form: "Tutti i cittadini unitamente si governino con forma contenente parte di Oligarchia, e parte di Dimocrazia" [All the citizens, in unison, govern themselves under a form containing parts of oligarchy, and parts of democracy] (*II Verato*, 3:163). The republic does not merely juxtapose the completely realized forms of oligarchy and democracy but carefully selects only the elements of each that can be plausibly combined. The point is not merely social mixture but the achievement of a form that regulates diverse social constituencies (163).

Not surprisingly, Guarini does not emphasize the social conflict implicit in such a system but rather the paradoxical quality of the hybrid political form. Both tragicomedy and the republic are rare forms achieved with difficulty (163), the result of a skillful, precarious, and paradoxical integration of the constituent forms of oligarchy and democracy: "Le persone atte in potenza a generare lo stato di pochi, in atto poi finiscano nel popolare, ed è converso" [The persons potentially ready to form the state of the few, in actuality generate the democratic state, and vice versa] (161). Neither the oligarchic nor the democratic forms are actualized to their fullest extent, just as neither the full form of comedy nor tragedy is realized in tragicomedy (163). Like tragicomedy, the republic negotiates and eventually synthesizes apparently contradictory tendencies. Following Aristotle, Guarini claims that "la mescolanza dello stato popolare, e de'pochi avrà conseguito bene il suo fine, quando la medesima repubblica potrà dirsi che sia, e stato popolare, e stato di pochi" [the mixing of the popular and the oligarchic state will have fully achieved its end when the same republic might be called both democratic and oligarchic] (161). Tragicomedic paradox is here theorized by Guarini, characterizing in particular the fragile political negotiations of the new form: it might seem at once oligarchic in its generic foregrounding of social difference and democratic in its social lability, its capacity to mix social kinds.

The pastoralism of tragicomedy might suggest egalitarianism, as it does for Gonzalo in his golden-age revelry. In ancient pastoral societies, argues Guarini, the shepherd-ruler was merely first among equals.[23] Montano, the priest of *Il pastor fido*, is also a shepherd and palpably subject to the same limitations as the other fallible humans in Guarini's fideistic world. But northern Italian court audiences saw far less political relevance in the lives of tragedic and tragicomedic princes than did English audiences a few years later at the Globe, and Italian tragicomedy does not pursue political issues very aggressively. Certainly the pastoral society of *Aminta* is a thinly disguised, *drame à clef* mirror of the Ferraran court, one that does not contest its aristocratic structure. It would be fair to say, with Marxist critics, that the political paradoxes of Italian tragicomedy actually mystify real social and political conflicts. In practice, pastoral egalitarianism in *Aminta* and *Il pastor fido* usually amounts to the *elision* of social difference, and the rustic element dominating earlier Cinquecento pastoral like that of Ruzante is relegated to the satyr.

But in Guarini's theory, tragicomedic dramaturgy certainly has political implications, and they are more liberal than one would expect for its courtly setting. It was left to English playwrights writing in a relatively less censored environment to dramatize social and political issues that are only implicit in Italian tragicomedy.

Social Negotiations in *The Winter's Tale*

The drama of Beaumont and Fletcher successfully appealed to the upwardly mobile audiences of the Blackfriars, many of whom had just achieved gentlemanly status. Richard Proudfoot identifies in their plays a newly "polite tone" spoken by ladies and gentleman, and cites Dryden's claim that they "understood and imitated the conversation of gentlemen much better than did Shakespeare."[24] Although this tendency might have influenced Shakespeare in his increased use of anonymous "gentlemen" in the late plays, Beaumont and Fletcher are less interested in social lability and interclass alliances than Shakespeare. If their version of pastoral, as we have seen, does not present an alternative mode, neither can it enable social lability (or its fiction) in the manner of Italian and Shakespearean tragicomedy. The citizens' revolt in *Philaster* and their near dismemberment of Pharamond crucially turn the plot but offer not even the illusion of interclass harmony. The captain enjoins his citizen charges to "forget your mother gibberish of what-do-you-lack" (5.4.2–3), so that they efface their low diction in the royal cry of "Philaster, brave Philaster." Pharamond's terrified designation of the citizens as "wild cannibals" is not refuted as he beseeches the noble and thus humane soul of Philaster for forgiveness (5.4.100–103). His revolt successful, the Captain calls his troupes back their taverns for "music and the red grape" but there is no attempt, on the play-wrights' part, to sublimate such festivity to the court.

The only late play of Shakespeare with real shepherds and all of the external trappings of pastoral, *The Winter's Tale* most clearly deploys the social lability theorized in Guarini and tentatively enacted in courtly, Ferraran tragicomedy. The pastoral section of the play is insistently concerned with social issues, which should be evaluated in the context of Italian tragicomedy. Whereas there is more interclass fluidity in Shakespeare than in the Italians, the possibility of social conflict is also given sharper dramatic form by the English playwright.

As the *Aminta* prologue suggests, the disguises implicit in the pastoral mode may negotiate different social levels, bridging the gap between rich and poor in the fiction of a "beautiful relationship" as the courtier impersonates a shepherd. There is a theatrical component to pastoral, then, that allows it to play out possibilities of social mixture. In the tragic section of *The Winter's Tale*, Leontes denies both theatrical and sexual "play" (1.1.187–89) and the possibility of social mixture (2.1.82–87). The pastoral section of the play provides a positive view of theatricality that is only broken with a diminished reprisal of Leontes' antitheatricality in the person of Polixenes, who suddenly causes the pastoral disguises to drop. Notwithstanding this tragic intrusion into the pastoral "stage," various pastoral disguises explore possibilities of social lability in the play's middle section.

Pastoral is staged as theatrical and social disguise in the form of the sheep-shearing festival. Adding to the metatheatrical complexity of a boy actor playing a shepherdess is the fact that, within the fiction of the play, a princess unknowingly disguised as a shepherdess impersonates a queen. What is merely assumed in Italian pastoral tragicomedy—the trick of courtiers disguising themselves as shepherds—is critically dramatized by Shakespeare in the person of Florizel, who plays at being a shepherd in his courtship of Perdita. Florizel's "play" is both theatrical and sexual, and should be seen as a salutary alternative to Leontes' rejection of both ludic forms. Naive and headstrong, he represents an absolute confidence in the social flexibility of pastoral disguise:

> These your unusual weeds, to each part of you
> Do give a life: no shepherdess, but Flora
> Peering in April's front. This your sheep-shearing
> Is as a meeting of the petty gods,
> And you the queen on't.
>
> (4.4.1–5)

And, in a later speech, he claims the prerogative of disguise for himself: "The gods themselves, / Humbling their deities to love, have taken / The shapes of beasts upon them" (4.4.25–27). For Florizel clothes magically confer a new identity for Perdita, now not only a queen but the very goddess Flora. If many Italian pastoral plays dramatize the supernatural metamorphoses derived from Ovid, Shakespeare offers a verisimilar version of this, the fictional evocation of supernatural transformation. The inclusion of the animal and divine realms extends the social reach of tragicomedy to a cosmic level, along the lines of the paradigmatic *Amphitryon*. As in *Aminta*, eros motivates such lability in the form of a pastoral disguise.

If the famous art and nature debate between Perdita and Polixenes falls along the lines of the Italian pastoral debates,[25] the earlier exchange between Florizel and Perdita turns on similar issues. Perdita's attitude toward the social transformations of pastoral disguise is more skeptical and realistic than that of Florizel. Pastoral costume, so she claims, cannot confer new identity but rather distorts one's "true" self. According to her, Florizel has "obscur'd" his "high self" in his pastoral habit and inappropriately "prank'd up" Perdita as a goddess (4.4.7–10). In opposition to Florizel's breezy confidence in the social flexibility of pastoral, Perdita seems to reaffirm social, and thus generic, boundaries:

> To me the difference forges dread (your greatness
> Hath not been us'd to fear): even now I tremble
> To think your father, by some accident
> Should pass this way, as you did: O the Fates!
> How would he look, to see his work, so noble
> Vilely bound up? What would he say? Or how
> Should I, in these my borrowed flaunts, behold
> The sternness of his presence?
>
> (4.4.17–24)

Perdita here affirms, as did Denores, the principle of theatrical, social, and generic difference, in language proper to tragedic discourse. If one thinks of her character and her ultimately felicitous destiny, she is anything but a tragedic figure, but her language expresses tragic modalities here in her debate with Florizel and in her more famous debate with Polixenes. Pastoral and festival license, for Perdita, cannot erase the social and generic difference between the "noble" and the "vile." The "stern" presence of Polixenes—a man greater than ourselves, in Aristotelian terms—would elicit the emotions of tragedy: "dread," "fear," and "trembling," at least to a social inferior such as Perdita. Fore-shadowing the incursion of Polixenes, Perdita suggests a horizon of tragedic rather than providentially tragicomedic expectations with her invocation of the "Fates." To Florizel's festive affirmation of the efficacy of disguise ("apprehend nothing but jollity"), Perdita continues in the language of difference and conflict:

> O, but sir,
> Your resolution cannot hold when 'tis
> Oppos'd, as it must be, by th' power of the king:
> One of these two must be necessities,
> Which then will speak, that you must change this purpose
> Or I my life.
>
> (4.4.35–40)

The either/or logic of Perdita's speech reflects an absolute, tragedic bifurcation, rather than the nuances, mediations, or transformations of tragicomedy. Royal power, in the person of the king, prevails over the limited power of the pastoral protagonist. The stakes, in Perdita's hypothesis, are those of tragedy: dynastic succession and Perdita's very life.

With often noted dramatic irony, Polixenes seems to assent to the principle of generic and social mixture in the famous debate with Perdita:

> You see, sweet maid, we marry
> A gentler scion to the wildest stock
> And make conceive a bark of baser kind
> By bud of nobler race. This is an art
> Which does mend nature—change it rather—but
> The art itself is nature
>
> (4.4.92–97)

Polixenes' famous metaphor, one that cunningly blends the artificial and the natural, is actually anticipated by Guarini, who describes generic production as a kind of grafting: tragedy was "grafted" *(innestato)* onto the trunk of the dithyramb (*I Verato*, 2:297), and tragicomedy itself is a kind of grafting (*Compendio*, 3:440). Ironically, Perdita assumes the Denorian position against Polixenes, reiterating the skepticism about social mixture expressed earlier to Florizel. Of course, the tragic horizon of expectations raised earlier by Perdita was only hypothetical, and in reality the sudden intrusion of Polixenes does not elicit real fear. Instead, it draws from Perdita a statement of pastoral egalitarianism, truer to the tone of the entire festival than her earlier avowed fears:

> I was not much afeard; for once or twice
> I was about to speak, and tell him plainly,
> The selfsame sun that shines upon his court
> Hides not his visage from our cottage, but
> Looks on all alike.

> (4.4.443–47)

And of course Perdita's own career as a royal foundling does not affirm Denores's position in the debate but rather the social fluidity of tragicomedy. Even before the recognition of the royal objects, Perdita is declared to be, paradoxically, both a shepherdess and a princess, as befits her role in the sheep-shearing festival. And she eventually does marry the "gentler scion," in a dynastic, political marriage typical of the late plays that aims to complete the reconciliation between the previously estranged families. Like Arviragus and Guiderius in *Cymbeline*, like her shepherd foster parents, she negotiates the transition from the pastoral to the courtly world.

At first, the shepherds are the victims of the social lability inherent in pastoral disguise, when Autolycus fobs himself off as a "great courtier" to the naive shepherds by presenting himself in Florizel's clothing. This scene dramatizes the opposition, especially important in early-Cinquecento pastoral, between the naive rustic and the sophisticated city or court dweller. Pastoral disguise here is not deliberate or structured around a festival occasion, as it is for Perdita and Florizel, but improvisatory. The shepherds, of course, have the last laugh in their next encounter with Autolycus. If *The Winter's Tale* is considered in the context of continental tragicomedy, the transportation of the shepherds to Sicilia (a mythic place of pastoral origins) and their translation into new gentlemen acquires increased significance. Because the shepherds clearly represent the pastoral mode, the raising of their social status elevates the generic prestige of pastoral—the very project of Tasso and Guarini. Whereas the disguises of the sheep-shearing festival (in particular, those of Perdita and Autolycus) are temporary, the shepherds actually rise in social status, with appropriate sartorial and emotional signifiers to prove it. The Clown marvels at the new kinship relations of the newly grafted pastoral-royal family:

> I was a gentleman born before my father; for the king's son took me by the hand, and called me brother; and then the two kings called my father brother; and then the prince, my brother, and the princess, my sister, called my father father; and so we wept; and there was the first gentleman-like tears that ever we shed. (5.2.139–45)

The new family constitutes a social and generic mixture. As in the grafting metaphor used by both Guarini and Polixenes, the mixture is paradoxically both natural ("gentleman *born*") and artificial, although it is the artificial, constructed quality of the new family resemblances that is most emphasized. Like tragicomedy, the new family constitutes a complex network of new social relationships. Their new clothes do not only signify but actually confer new identities for them; their four-hour-old "birth" is, one realizes, a beneficent (and well-deserved) social construction. Autolycus, earlier the genius of social transformation in the "low," farcical style of the cony-catcher or of the *commedia dell'arte zanni*, now is humbled before the new gentlemen. The emotional responses of low comedy—relaxation, dissolute laughter—now give way to the pathos-filled tonalities of Guarinian tragicomedy: "gentleman-like tears."

For the younger shepherd, gentlemanly status confers not only more refined emotional sensibilities but the prerogatives of fighting and swearing false oaths (5.2.129–35, 156–72). Shakespeare here satirizes the large numbers of newly created gentlemen in early-seventeenth-century London, many of whom formed an important component of the theater audience at the Globe and especially at the Blackfriars.[26] Many new London gentlemen were recent provincial transplants, and would have appreciated in *The Winter's Tale* a play that seems to accomplish an easy passage from country to courtly *civiltà*. Shakespeare himself, of course, traveled a not dissimilar social itinerary, from the son of a yeoman to a gentleman to a member of the King's Men, who wore the royal livery. For Shakespeare as for the shepherds, new clothing most conspicuously registers newly acquired status. But it may be autobiographical reticence that mitigates the satire, certainly in relation to Jonsonian standards, and allows the tragicomic, Guarinian pathos to stand, quite possibly move us, and anticipate the pathetic tonalities of both the narrated and enacted recognition scenes of act 5. The old shepherd corrects his impetuous son, reminding him of the decorous relationship between inner and outer "gentleness" ("we must be gentle, now we are gentlemen") (5.2.152–53). And by becoming permanently aligned to Leontes' royal family, the shepherds here enact a properly pastoral satire of the court: the rustics prove more "gentle" than gentlemen. If Marston transfers the emphasis from the shepherd to the bitter satyr/satirist, then Shakespeare returns to both the figure of the shepherd and the "gentler" tonalities of continental tragicomedy, in which satire is less sharp and more modally aligned with visionary pastoral.

10

Low Comedy

MOUNTEBANKS AND BUFFOONS

The *commedia dell'arte* exerts a greater presence in Guarinian tragicomedy than has been acknowledged.[1] Guarini felt himself in competition with the professional theater, which itself performed a species of pastoral tragicomedy, as we have seen. If Renaissance kinds were socially coded, "low" comedy carried a powerful social resonance and became an important dramaturgical term of tragicomedy. Just as tragic terror is, in tragicomedy, evoked in a partial way and then modulated into a different register, the kind of farce produced by "low," comic registers constitutes a dramaturgical material of tragicomedy, an element to be displaced or transformed into a different register. The function of low comedy as a dramaturgical element is demonstrated in Guarini's quotation of Donatus on Terence: "Illud quoque inter Terentianas virtutes mirabile, quod ejus fabulae eo sunt temperamento ut neque extumescant ad Tragicam celsitudinem, neque abjiciantur ad histrionicam" [And among Terence's virtues there is the admirable attribute that his plays are tempered and neither swell to the heights of tragedy nor are degraded to the depths of histrionic comedy] (*I Verato*, 2:273). Terence, for Donatus and Guarini (who saw in him a prototype of the "tempering," tragicomedic playwright), negotiates the extremes of tragic sublimity and histrionic farce. The featuring of "gentleman-like tears," such as we have seen in chapters 6, signals the diminution of low-comic registers, as Autolycus gives way to the shepherds. Low comedy is often associated with a degraded form of professionalism, clearly marked in Italy by the mountebank and the piazza versions of the *commedia dell'arte* and more subtly dramatized in Shakespearean theater by the brothel scene in *Pericles* and by figures like Autolycus. More socially heterogeneous than Italian tragicomedy and deriving from a theatrical milieu obviously more hospitable to the professional actor than the Italian courts, Shakespeare's late plays dramatize the opposition of low, professional comedy and the "higher" strains of pathos and tragedy, rather than stressing the sublimation of the first term.

This common dramaturgical practice derives from an important cultural homology in the two theaters: the uncertain and changing status of the professional player, and changing attitudes toward low-comedic forms of entertainment. The most striking similarity between English and Italian theater of the sixteenth century is the emergence of a theater even more fully professional than that of France or Spain of the same period, where public theater was usually sponsored by religious confraternities and other charitable organizations. In Italy as in England, it was the marked population growth of cities and the increased circulation of money that encouraged a market for the early-modern professional theater. Siro Ferrone argues that a fundamental shift occurred in European theater of the sixteenth century when performance was no longer tied to temporal cycles ("natural" calendrical festivals or political/religious authority naturalizing itself), and the sale of theater became its own sufficient authority, allowing performance all year long.[1] Professional actors in Italy, France, Spain, and England were no longer confined to the spatial and temporal matrix of the *festa* but became relatively autonomous in when and where they could play, although they still could exploit the crowds of fairs and festivals. Autolycus, the autonomous one, occupies exactly this liminal position between the festival and the professional theater; he is a free, itinerant agent, but exploits the sheep-shearing festival for profit.

For Ferrone, who follows Roberto Tessari, the mountebank is a crucial figure in the transition from *festa* to marketplace.[3] Especially during fairs and festivals like carnival, mountebanks exploited huge crowds, improvising a stage with platforms and banners. The mountebanks constitute a plausible early-modern "source" for the *commedia dell'arte* because they would often warm up the audience to their harangues by performing *arte*-like dialogues and routines with buffoons, establishing the basis, some say, of the Magnifico-Zanni opposition so central to the mature *commedia dell'arte*.[4] Like Autolycus, the charlatans sang ballads and sold printed songs, luxury items, and various kinds of healing elixirs. What counts for both the mountebank and Autolycus is the profit motive. As Tessari says of the early modern mountebank: "The relationship of occult persuasion, of fascination between the new vagabond and his public, then, would not be founded on faith, charity, or on the hope of traditional religion, but on a confidence based on a buy-sell relationship, on an illusion of happiness . . . promised by a belief in the power of acquisition."⁵ This illusion of happiness is precisely what Autolycus offers the shepherds at the festival. It is pointedly contrasted to the form of theater staged by Paulina at the play's end: a theater not dependent on a "buy-sell relationship" but on something like religious faith ("It is requir'd / you do awake your faith, " says Paulina to Leontes at 5.3.94–95).

The mountebank, the low buffoon, and the itinerant actor were all stigmatized by the new dramaturgy; they became a term in need of tempering or sublimating into a higher register. Antitheatricalists in England and Italy could easily associate itinerant professional actors with other disreputable entertainers: rope dancers, jugglers, ballad singers, magicians, bear wards, ape-keepers, and puppet masters (many of which professions Autolycus is said to practice). All of these popular entertainers, lacking the proper license, could be considered vagabonds and subject to new laws passed against vagrancy. For civic and ecclesiastical authorities, the popular player was threatening because of the transportability of his theater. In a carnival song written by Antonio Grazzini in 1559, a group of "buffoni e parasiti" [buffoons and parasites] announce that they will "gir dov' abbiam spacio l'arte nostra" [wander wherever our art can find the space], but this virtuosic boast was the authorities' fear.⁶

GUARINI AND THE *COMMEDIA DELL'ARTE*

The *commedia dell'arte*, although ultimately gaining the favor of European courts, could never quite free itself of associations with mountebanks and buffoons in the eyes of clerical, post-Tridentine antitheatricalists and of neoclassicists even within the theatrical arena. Certainly Guarini usually does not distinguish between *arte* actors and low popular entertainment. At the time of *Il pastor fido* and the Guarini-Denores quarrel, the increasingly successful *commedia dell'arte* was under attack by municipal and ecclesiastical authorities, as well as literary arbiters such as Guarini himself, who averred the superiority of their learned dramaturgy to the popular fare of the professional players. At the heart of Guarini's animosity toward the *arte* was its professionalism—the fact that the actors received money for their services and that they made a business out of theater by roaming like vagabonds. The high art of comedy has declined, according to Guarini, "per cagione di gente sordida, e mercenaria, che l'ha contaminata, e ridotta a vilissimo stato, portando quà e là per infamissimo prezzo quell' eccellente poema, che soleva già coronar di gloria e suoi facitori" [because of that sordid and mercenary people, who have contaminated {the ancient art of comedy} and reduced it to a vile state, carrying here and there for a disgraceful price that excellent poem, that used to crown its makers with glory] (*I Verato* 2:261–62).

Declaring that the common players had debased the ancient art of Terentian comedy, Guarini and many other amateur playwrights aimed to elevate the generic status of comedy and make it a worthy partner of tragedy. If, like Guarini, the *commedia dell'arte* theater mixes kinds, creating composite generic titles "longer than the work itself," it does it without attention to dramaturgical art (*II Verato*, 3:115). Countering Denores's charge that his hybrid is nothing but "laughing tragedy," Guarini conjures the spectacle of an *arte* troupe playing Greek tragedy:

> Sapete quali sarebbono le Tragedie beffarde? se nell'Edipo, o nelle Fenisse, o in alcun'altra tale s'introducesse un Zanni, un Graziano, un Magnifico, nella guisa, che fanno que' vostri sozzi dalla gazzetta ... questi sono essi i facitori delle Tragedie vituperate, nelle quali si truova in atto la persona, e l'azione tragica contenente il terribile, e il miserabile, contaminata dallo scherzo, dal riso de'buffoni, e de'giocolari. (164)

> [Do you know what mocking tragedy would be like? If in *Oedipus the King*, or the *Phoenicians*, or in any other similar tragedy one introduced a *zanni*, a Gratiano, a Magnifico, in the way that your filthy mercenary comedians do. ... These are indeed the makers of reviled tragedies in which one finds fully realized the tragedic person and action containing the terrible and the miserable, but contaminated by the jokes and laughter of the buffoons and jugglers.]

As Guarini sees the *commedia dell'arte*, no coherent dramaturgical principles inform the combination of tragedic and comedic elements. The extreme generic mixtures of the *arte* constitute a "contamination" of high-tragic emotions with low-comic registers, as well as a social contamination of the high persons of tragedy with the inferior personages of comedy.

As we have seen, however, *contaminatio* referred first to Terence's mixture of Greek New Comedy plots and then to the mixtures of theater-grams and kinds. Whereas Denores attacks Terentian *contaminatio*, Guarini defends it, locating Terence's source and plot mixtures as a classical prototype for his own hybrid. But from Denores's perspective, the generic *contaminatio* practiced by Guarini is not very different from that of the *commedia dell'arte*.

Denores persistently associates Guarini's hybrid with the *commedia dell'arte*, in ways that are sometimes palpably reactionary and sometimes rather convincing. Denores is right to see that both Guarini and the *commedia dell'arte* consider kind, not as a determinative frame, but as material to be recombined and transformed in various ways. In mixing the "magnificent" style of tragedy and the *tenuis* (low) style of comedy, Guarinian tragicomedy appears to Denores every bit as monstrous as the polydialectal *commedia dell'arte* (*Apologia*, 2:349). If, like Guarini, one rejects the premise that poetry is founded on philosophical and political principles, the way is not far to the slippery slope of *arte*-style *buffoneria* (341). For Denores, both Guarini and the professional troupes pander to their audiences with generic novelties. If, following his Ferraran predecessor Giraldi, Guarini calibrates generic changes to the "gusti diversi degli ascoltanti" [the different tastes of the audience] (*I Verato* 2:260), the *commedia dell'arte* similarly played to the "what you will" of the audience. And, for Denores, both Guarini and the mercenary actors entice the crowds with novel, Polonius-like hybrids like "tragicommedia, comicotragedia, tragicosatira, ed altre simili" [tragicomedy, comitragedy, tragisatire, and other of the like] (*Apologia*, 2:349). For a conservative like Denores, the similarities between high and low generic innovation are more important than the differences:

> Con questi nomi nuovi si procurano qualche guadagno, il quale perciocchè non veggono di poter conseguire con nomi semplici delle poesie, ricorrono alla moltiplicità de'nomi composti, per mostrarsi inventori di cose nuove, e per ingannar la moltitudine. (351)

> [With these new-fangled names they make a profit, because seeing that they can't succeed with the simple names of poetry, they have recourse to composite names, to show that they are inventors of new things, and to cheat the crowds.]

Denores specifically associates Guarini with *arte* troupes recently active in the Veneto, which he claims have performed "tragicommedie pastorali." In particular, he mentions the actor Battista Veronese, who in Ferrara and throughout the continent had performed a pastoral tragi-comedy based on the madness of Ariosto's Orlando (325–26). Denores, then, clearly saw the practical implications of Guarini's theory of combinatory dramaturgy.

HIGH AND LOW CULTURE

Denores's argument is often convincing because the sharp boundaries that Guarini wishes to maintain between high and low theater, between the *commedia erudita* and the *commedia mercenaria*, simply do not hold up for the period. Even Guarini's own *Il pastor fido* includes a scene of *arte*-like physical farce between the evil, city-bred Corisca and her frustrated lover the satyr. And *arte* troupes actually performed the plays of Tasso and Guarini. Tasso's *Aminta* was an important part of the Gelosi's repertoire, as well as that of other *commedia* troupes. Guarini's comedy *La idropica* was twice performed by professional troupes—by the Fedeli in 1608 and by the Accesi in 1618—and *Il pastor fido* itself was played by the Accesi, also in 1618. For their part, *arte* pastorals such as *L'albore Incantata* freely borrowed from the learned pastoral plays of Tasso and Guarini.[7]

Perhaps due to the power of its rich pictorial tradition, the *commedia dell'arte* has often been associated merely with farce and buffoonery, but its golden age (roughly corresponding to Shakespeare's lifetime) was characterized by an extremely rich dialogue between what might loosely be called "learned" and "popular" strains. There was a great deal of contact between the amateur and the professional theaters, as evidenced by the *commedia* productions of *Aminta* and *Il pastor fido*. The plot scenarios used by the professional troupes, as well as the roles themselves, were largely drawn from the *commedia erudita*.[8] The *comici* were aware of neoclassical precepts, subtle points of dramatic theory, and, as Denores indicates, avant-garde experiments in mixed kinds. Individual actors prepared for their improvisatory monologues and dialogues with speeches extracted and adapted from high literature.[9] If *comici* referred to books for performance, they also wrote full-length, scripted plays, as well as collections of conceits and dialogues, such as Francesco Andreini's *Le bravure del Capitano Spavento*.[10] On the other side, amateur actors, playwrights, and entrepreneurs such as Leone De'Sommi (1527–92) were intrigued and influenced by the professional theater.

Just as the English professional theater was attacked by Puritan pamphleteers and civic authorities, the emerging *commedia dell'arte* was besieged by a vigorous antitheatrical movement represented by post-Tridentine ecclesiastics such as Carlo Borromeo, archbishop of Milan from 1565 to 1584.[11] In response to attacks that the professional theater was escapist, trivial, and immoral, many professional actors answered their attackers in treatises, poems, prefaces, and reminiscences. Such apologists for the *arte* as Pier Maria Cecchini, Nicolò Barbieri, and Giovanni Battista Andreini carefully distinguished the trained actor from the mountebanks, jugglers, and urban buffoons entertaining in the streets and piazzas of Italian cities.[12] At the heart of the literate *comici*'s defense was the notion of dramaturgy—the idea that their art was founded upon the same neoclassical principles invoked by *erudita* playwrights such as Guarini and Tasso: temperance, generic decorum, concatenation of action, verisimilitude, mimesis, and moral utility. And in order to distance themselves further from the low farce, the *arte* apologists claimed another prerogative of *erudita* playwrights like Guarini: generic versatility. Just like Polonius extolling the generic virtuosity of the traveling company at Elsinore, Francesco Andreini boasted that his prestigious Gelosi company could "recitar Comedie, Tragicomedie, Tragedie, Pastorali, intermedii apparenti, e altre inventioni rappresentative" [perform comedies, tragicomedies, tragedies, pastorals, *intermezzi*, and other dramatic inventions].[13] The boast was realized in such plays as the forty-second day of Scala's collection, entitled *Comical, Pastoral, and Tragical Events, a Mixed Opera*.[14] The point is that for Polonius, Guarini, Andreini, and *commedia* apologists, generic versatility itself was seen to confer value and elevate the professional theater above the street performer, who could presumably play only one note. Not merely a legitimizing tag, generic virtuosity was also a drawing card, in particular for the new divas said to be great because they could play so many different generic registers, including the newly codified one of tragicomic or pastoral pathos. The actor and writer Adriano Valerini praises the actress Vincenza Armani for her protean skill in mastering three different modal styles (comedy, tragedy, and pastoral).[15] Indeed, Ferdinando Taviani has argued that the *commedia dell'arte*, which before 1560 was male, farcical, and artisanal, only became capable of generic diversity after its assimilation of the actress, who like the courtesan was skilled in courtly registers of poetry and music.

Improvisation itself may be seen as inherently tragicomic. High diction, concatenated plot, and sustained seriousness of tragedy are difficult to maintain in improvisational theater. The report of an actress who in 1576 played in the tragedy of *Dido* "mutata in tragi-commedia" [changed into a tragicomedy] suggests the general truth that tragedy tended to modulate into tragicomedy when handled by the players.[16] Like Guarini, the *comici* tempered the extremities of tragedy when they took on the mode. Certainly their rhetorical project resembled Guarini's in that they were modulating the affective extremes of tragedy. As with the *erudita* theater, *arte* pastoral plays, with amatory themes treated less cynically than in comedy, tended to generate sentimental, pathetic registers. Like Shakespeare, especially in his recapitulatory late plays, the *commedia dell'arte* played with genre, appropriating and modulating high modes like the tragic.

GL'INTRICATI

The marginalization of buffoonery is aptly demonstrated by Pasqualigo's 1581 *Gl'intricati*, a play that precariously balances the *commedia dell'arte* and the new tonalities of courtly pastoral. The buffoonish, *arte*-like clowns—the Bolognese Graciano, the Spanish Calabaza, and the Maremma *villano*—are not native to Arcadia. The mere fact that they are allowed to enter the charmed space, seek love after their own fashion, and attend a supper with the refined nymphs and shepherds does bespeak an extended social spectrum along the lines of *A Midsummer Night's Dream*, although their fantasy of interclass alliances is doomed to frustration. Although their perceptions of love are limited by typically plebeian parameters—it is a matter not of spirit but appetite—they conceive love to confer an elevated social status. Thinking he is about to possess the *maga's* magic stones that guarantee success in love, the *villano* fantasizes that he will be raised to gentlemanly rank:

> Diventarò pu'hora un gentilhuomo,
> Sarò pur ricco, e fortunato à pieno.
> Voglio che quante donne sono al mondo
> Habbian di gratia d'esser mie massare,
> E di servirmi anchor per concubine.
>
> (3.7)

[I will become a gentleman, and I will be very prosperous and rich. I want all the women of the world to consent to be my farmhands and also to serve me as concubines.]

This carnivalesque fantasy of social elevation seems to be confirmed by the presumed convivial equality of the supper to which the buffoons are invited to join and contribute some entertainment. Like Graciano, Calabaza attempts sublime Petrarchan registers in his song, but the *villano* confirms the mercenary, buffoonish nature of his entertainment:

> Così cantan gli Mori di Granata,
> E gli buffoni del paese nostro,
> Di modo che in un loco, over ne l'altro
> Sei sicuro d'haver cantando il vitto.

(4.4)

[That's the way the Moors of Granada and the buffoons of our country sing, so that in one place or another you can be sure of singing for your supper.]

It is the mercenary and the ambulatory stigmas—he sings for money, wherever he can—that identify the Spaniard as a low buffoon and distance him from the refined lovers, reconfirming the clowns as itinerant strangers in Arcadia.

The final rebuke and expulsion of the buffoons from Arcadia is delivered by the *maga* at the end of the play, who declares, "Non si convien l'Amor con gente vile / Come voi sete" [Love is not for lower class people like you] (5.5). The sorcerer orders the *villano* to work the plow, Graciano to feed farm animals, and Calabaza to pursue another socially low occupation:

> E tu spagnuol, và vendi balle in banco,
> Per far rider le genti per le piazze,
> E amor lasciate tra gli spirti eletti,
> Tra gli animi gentili, e tra Signori,
> Ove sempre regna, e siate certi, ch'egli
> Non può alberger con cui bisogno tiene
> Di procacciarsi, mendicando, il pane.

(5.5)

[And you, Spaniard, go sell pills on the bench to make the people in the piazza laugh, and leave love to the elect spirits of gentle souls and lords where it reigns forever, and be assured that love cannot dwell with those who need to earn a living, begging for their bread.]

Mercenary buffoonery is an important dramaturgical element in
Gl'intricati, but one to be "tempered" by the *maga,* who functions somewhat like a playwright. Tempering takes the radical form of marginalization and reconfiguration outside the Arcadian space. The clowns are
then given the heads of a ram, a bull, and an ass so that they may see
their true images *sub specie amoris,* and are allowed to regain their former
shapes only on condition that they forego their aspirations to eros. They
are outside the tragicomedic syntheses of the play's end: the therapeutic dreams that realign erotic vectors and grant to each lover his or her
true desire. More clearly than most late-Cinquecento pastoral playwrights, Pasqualigo dramatizes the grotesque impossibility of a grand
social synthesis.

SHAKESPEARE

That Shakespeare understood, if not advocated, a polarization between dramaturgy and buffoonery is demonstrated by Hamlet's famous
speech to the players (*Hamlet* 3.2.1–45). Very like the literate *comici,*
Hamlet opposes both technique (proper diction, gesture, movement)
and dramaturgy (verisimilitude, imitation, decorum, temperance) to
the undisciplined practice of the town crier and the improvisatory clown.
Hamlet's sophisticated neoclassicism, belied of course by his own rough
theatrics, bespeaks a sophisticated awareness of the pan-European
theories of acting and dramaturgy being disseminated at the end of the
sixteenth century. Dramatizing the tension rather than taking sides,
Shakespeare maintains both the neoclassicist and the buffoon in the
very figure of Hamlet. In the late plays, especially in *The Winter's Tale*
and *The Tempest,* he has it both ways as well. Most obviously, the unities enacted in *The Tempest* and alluded to in the Time speech of *The
Winter's Tale* oppose the improvisatory plots of Autolycus and the *Tempest* buffoons.

The brothel scenes in *Pericles* provide a kind of sublimation of low
comedy in the manner of Italian tragicomedy. As Steven Mullaney has
shown, the first part of Pericles occludes the mercantile traces of a probable source, Lawrence Twine's *Patterne of Painefull Adventures.*[17] Whereas
Twine's Apollonius first expects payment for his gift of grain to the city
of Tharsus, only then to reject it in favor of a symbolic reward, a statue
erected in the marketplace, this transformation of a material form of

exchange into a symbolic one is effaced in Shakespeare's version of the story. Only the brothel scene, says Mullaney, stages mercantilism and at the same time connects it with another type of economic exchange that generates social mobility: the theater. Staged in front of, rather than inside, a brothel in the manner of New Comedy decor, the scene features the typical denizens of urban comedy: a bawd, a pander, his servant, and a nobleman whose disguise facilitates his downward social passage. The brothel has become a place of easy social lability, where "lord and lown" (4.6.17) and "gentlemen of all fashions" (4.2.74–75) are accommodated. There is a keen sense here of the marketplace—continual circulation of money and of women as commodities. As for Italian and English antitheatricalists, Boult aligns prostitution and acting: Marina is enjoined to "seem to do that forcefully which you commit willingly" and "weep that you live as you do" (4.2.116–18).

Mullaney is wrong, however, to say that theatricality is only assigned to the role that Marina would have acted, and thus altogether displaced from her.[18] In fact, Boult's initial observation that Marina "speaks well" is borne out by her persuasiveness in preventing Lysimachus and others from enjoying her. For her speech, Lysimachus gives Marina gold, which she accepts and then gives later to Boult: a circulation that she hopes will enable honest economy. Marina's circulation of gold (curiously not mentioned by Mullaney) not only recalls that of Apollonius in *The Paineful Adventures* but also represents the ambivalent but real relationship with financial exchange characteristic of Isabella Andreini and other *commedia* divas, who straddled the economies of professional exchange and courtly patronage. Like the *arte* actresses, Marina does not efface but rather sublimates the market to another theatrical and moral level. The licentious suburbs of *Measure for Measure* are no more transformed by the end of the play than is Angelo by the speech of Isabella—noted, like Marina, for her eloquence. But in *Pericles*, two anonymous gentlemen depart from the brothel transformed, one supposes, back into real "gentlemen" by what Marina has turned into a kind of virginal temple. As in *The Winter's Tale*, we are prepared, not for a world denuded of theatricality, but for the solemn theatricality of the final scene in front of the temple of Diana. Shakespeare has dramatized a kind of "tempering" of low comedy.

As a singer and seller of ballads, ape-bearer, puppet master, frequenter of wakes, fairs, and bear baitings, Autolycus evokes not just the underworld of the London cony-catcher but the world of popular entertainment, continually under siege by ecclesiastical and civic authorities in England as in Italy. Autolycus is a liminal figure between the court and the country, once wearing courtly attire in Prince Florizel's service but now living by his wits. His hoodwinking of the young shepherd is a sparkling theatrical gag, a virtuosic physical feat along the lines of *commedia dell'arte lazzi*. As someone who boasts "We may do anything extempore" (4.4.677), especially anything of a profit-making nature, Autolycus bears comparison with the mercenary actor and in particular with mountebank entertainment.

During the sheep-shearing festival, the prince and future queen oppose "high" theatrical registers to Autolycus's mercenary theater. Perdita only allows Autolycus into her feast on condition that he "use no scurrilous words in's tunes" (4.4.215–16). Associating the itinerant performer with obscenity and immorality, Perdita attempts to sublimate low comedy, much like the many *arte* actresses who in the 1560s and afterwards were seen to rescue comedy from its perceived decadence and raise it to a higher moral and generic register. The princely Florizel explicitly raises himself above the economy of desire circulating between Mopsa, Dorcas, and the Clown—an economy fully exploited by Autolycus. His love for Perdita is of a higher order, he claims, because she "prizes not such trifles as these are: / The gifts she looks from me are pack'd and lock'd / Up in my heart" (4.4.358–60). As we have seen, the social transformations of Guarinian tragicomedy, performed both by the royal marriage and by the socially sublimated shepherds, displace Autolycus from the center of the play, a position he comes close to achieving in the pastoral section. In the last act of the play, theater belongs not to Autolycus but to Paulina; it occurs neither on the piazza or the road but in the fixed, indoor, and reverent space of Paulina's chapel. Her wondrous spectacle is reminiscent of both the masque and the serious endings of the Italian *commedia grave*.

The theatrical pleasure produced by Autolycus, of course, contradicts any moralistic reading of the play along social lines. Unlike Fletcher in the prefatory note to the publication of *The Faithful Shepherdess*, unlike the more severe Italian playwrights, Shakespeare does not suppress the popular energies represented by Autolycus and the sheep-shearing festival but allows them to stand alongside "higher" versions of theater. *The Winter's Tale* dramatizes different theaters: (1) the disreputable theatrics of the popular entertainer; (2) the popular-festive theatricality of the pastoral festival; (3) Guarinian, pastoral drama of complex social negotiations; (4) the solemn theater of Paulina's chapel. Indeed, in his protean capacity to appropriate theaters of varying cultural range, Shakespeare is rather like Autolycus and the *comici*.

Comparisons of the *commedia dell'arte* scenarios discussed earlier and *The Tempest* have focused on the Stephano-Trinculo-Caliban subplot, for which there are the most distinct resemblances. But the striking resemblances between the Italian and Shakespearean pastorals, even if not due to direct influence, interpretively bear upon the entire play. In general, *The Tempest* continually counterposes deliberation and improvisation in ways that reflect the dual traditions of *erudita* and *improvvisa* pastoral tragicomedy. The conspiracy of the Stephano group is a tragicomic version of tragedic conspiracies both in Shakespeare's previous works and in *The Tempest*. (Like *Hamlet*'s Claudius, Caliban knows that his intended victim's custom of sleeping in the afternoon will provide a good occasion for murder.) What Prospero has deliberately and painstakingly planned against Antonio—revenge for usurpation—Caliban improvises with the buffoons: "I say, by sorcery he got this isle; / From me he got it. If thy greatness will / Revenge it on him . . . Thou shalt be lord of it, and I'll serve thee" (3.2.51–53, 56). The buffoons' plot to steal Prospero's learned book—a central element of the *commedia* scenarios, where it is actually carried through—may stand for the way in which the *commedia dell'arte* appropriated the learned scripts of the *commedia erudita*.

If the improvisational conspiracy of the buffoons actually seems to pose no real threat to Prospero, who is more powerful than the *mago* of the *arte*, it does recall more threatening conspiracies in the play. Antonio seizes power, as Prospero puts it to Miranda, "to have no screen between the part he played and him he played it for" (1.2.107–8). Deliberately, Prospero had created Antonio's role as a theatrical cover behind which he could become rapt in secret studies; improvisationally, Antonio appropriates the theatrical role for himself. The conspiracy of Sebastian and Antonio to kill the sleeping Alonso, improvisatory and self-consciously theatrical ("What's past is prologue, what to come / In yours and my discharge") (2.1.248–49) recalls and attempts to replay the Milan tragedy. After the dilatory exchange between the members of the court party, the tragic moment comes suddenly, as Antonio plays upon Sebastian's imagination.

At moments the usually deliberate Prospero himself becomes an improviser. At first, Prospero's approach to the initial encounter between Ferdinand and Miranda is premeditated, as befits his plans for a dynastic marriage. Prospero's invitation to Miranda to lift the "fringèd curtains" of her eyes evokes a discovery scene and lends the moment a self-consciously theatrical quality.[19] When, observing the quick success of his matchmaking project, Prospero decides to defer the comedic denouement "lest too light winning / Make the prize light" (1.2.454–55), he assumes the guise of a New Comedy or *arte* blocking father in relation to Ferdinand. (In the scenario *Pantaloncino*, in fact, we find a *mago* who is instinctively hostile to love and jealously guards his daughter.) Comically, Prospero projects onto the innocent Ferdinand Antonio's prior crime of usurpation:

> Thou dost here usurp
> The name thou ow'st not, and hast put thyself
> Upon this island as a spy, to win it
> From me, the lord on't
>
> (1.2.456–59)

Here is an improvisation of a tragedic topos, in the manner of the *commedia dell'arte*.

Prospero, in fact, is as much *arte mago* as deliberate and learned playwright/magician. His petulance and capriciousness, the perverse pleasure he takes in tormenting his enemies with mischievous pranks and physical pain, smack much more of the *mago* than of the protocolonialist. To consider Prospero as anticipating the European colonialist certainly addresses many serious issues of the play. But politically earnest readings of the play risk moralizing Prospero's very unserene deficiencies, which probably gave contemporary audiences great theatrical pleasure, for better or for worse. Like Prospero, the *mago* both plays pranks and utters grand declarations of power, thus strangely alternating between low-comic and quasi-tragic registers. In short, the scenarios provide a relevant international context for the comedic business of the play.

CONCLUSION

The low-comic registers of *The Tempest* are marginalized but not "tempered" to the degree that they are in Italian tragicomedy. This is not only due to Shakespeare's extraordinary imaginative generosity but to the presence of the actor on the English Renaissance stage, and in particular the presence of Robert Armin, who played Cloten, Autolycus, and Caliban. The Italian erudite theater, written for courtly and academic theaters, does not dramatize the presence of the actor, and in the *commedia dell'arte* we must look beyond the scenarios to discover his or her presence. It was easier for the Italians than for the English to think of a grand tragicomedic synthesis reconciling the genres, which in Italy were less animated by the bodies of individual actors. In Shakespeare's late plays, genres are more palpably tied to actors and speaking situations.

For Guarini, the genres of tragedy and comedy may be combined because of an inherent *amicizia*, or friendship, between them based on the common elements attributed to them in Cinquecento theory such as verisimilitude, reversal, and recognition (*I Verato*, 2:239). If, according to Alastair Fowler following Wittgenstein, genres are less like classes than families, whose members share certain family resemblances,[20] the mixed kind of tragicomedy is formed by establishing family resemblances between tragedy and comedy. As the Jonson title page suggests, tragicomedy is the offspring of tragedy and comedy, in which the likenesses of the parents might be detected. Indeed, Guarini speaks of tragicomedy as the "child" of tragedy and comedy, a genuinely new creation formed by the seeds of its parents (*II Verato*, 3:167).

Shakespeare's late plays implicitly enliven this analogy because the fate of genres, or kinds, is intimately connected with that of families. "Kindness," in the dual sense of "kinship" and "the quality of being humane," eventually unites families and political kingdoms earlier severed by "unkindness." If, according to the opening scene of *The Winter's Tale*, "Bohemia" and "Sicilia" have been "over-kind" (1.1.21) to one another, the generically analytic play splits the two king-places (person standing for place, as we have seen in chapter 7) into two separate kinds: Sicilian tragedy and Bohemian pastoral. This is not only a dramaturgical or technical operation (as it usually is in Italian theater) but an animated, personal action: the generic split issues from Leontes' "unkindness." Paulina knows that the only way to prevent the tragic rift between the families is for Leontes to be "kindly" and to recognize family resemblances between himself and his infant daughter (2.3.95–107), as he obsessively had done with Mamillius (1.2.128–35). The reconciliation of literary kinds, families, and political kingdoms begins with Leontes' recognition of family resemblances between Florizel and Polixenes (5.1.123–27). Then the young couple remind the old king of the son he has lost and the daughter that he believes to be gone (5.1.130–33). Here— and this is a key difference between Shakespeare and the Italians—the reestablishment of family resemblances both bespeaks tragicomedic reconciliation, in the father recognizing the daughter, and irrevocable tragic loss, in the father recognizing the dead son. Leontes' "unkind-ness" has issued in a tragedy whose personal and political weight (Leontes has lost his male heir) can never be tempered, diminished, reconciled, or synthesized. And the same can be said for the years lost with Hermione. Tragicomedic redemption does not efface tragic memory, as one moves beyond tragedy without denying it.

The marriage of the gentler scion Florizel and the only apparently wild Perdita rejoins the two family-kingdoms and promises future off-spring that will solidify the generic, familial, and political union. The prospectively fertile marriage achieves a structural function in tragi-comedy that it does not have in comedy: the union of Florizel and Perdita heal a tragic rift and sustain a political dynasty; the marriage of Benedict and Beatrice does neither. If Perdita's royal nature really belies the arti-ficiality implicit in the "gillyvors" analogy (reminiscent of Guarini's "grafting" metaphor), the gentling of the shepherd foster-parents—now endowed with "kindly" pathos—does reflect the tragicomedic art of generic and social blending. Our laughter, however, at the shepherd's claim to have shed "gentleman-like tears" registers the incongruity between the claim and the reality, an admission that "kindness" is not absolute and totalizing. A more ethically earnest—and valid—response to this moment might register the incongruity of the courtly appropria-tion of pastoral: James's attempt to incorporate into the royal body politic old country holidays and pastimes. And the other recalcitrantly pasto-ral figure, the comical-satirical Autolycus, still is at large despite his translation to Sicily. He still represents the itinerant mercenary actor whom civic, courtly, and ecclesiastical authorities could never com-pletely contain. Most immediately for London audiences, he is Robert Armin, whose short and grotesque body also enlivened Cloten and, most powerfully, Caliban.

In the quarrel, Denores frequently likens tragicomedy to the "mostro" [monster] described by Horace as a negative example of po-etic composition, a human head joined to the neck of a horse, and a woman ending in a "turpiter atrum . . . piscem" [black and ugly fish].[21] If, for Denores, tragicomedy was a monstrous form of species corrup-tion,[22] it resembles the goat-man satyr, who becomes for Guarini an allowably monstrous mixture, but one effaced by the end of the play. As we have seen, the mythological hybrid ideally representative of Guarinian tragicomedy is not the satyr but the hermaphrodite, who perfectly blends male and female forms and sensibilities. Even to the end of *The Tempest*, Shakespeare enlivens both the monstrous hybrid in the satyrlike Caliban and the harmonious mixture in the hermaphroditic Ariel (a fine blend of the four elements).[23] The well-tempered Ariel, whom the "gentle" Gonzalo describes as among those supernatural beings whose "manners are more gentle, kind, than of / Our human generation you shall find" (3.3.32–33), enables Prospero to be "kindlier moved" to those of his kind. In his pathos-filled account of the penitent court party, Ariel functions as a tragicomedic agent who reconciles kinds, families, and political kingdoms. Prospero's grudging acknowledgment of "this thing of darkness" as his own is less convincing as a tragicomedic synthesis and demonstrates the exclusion of the grotesque Caliban (to whom we might add the unrepentant Antonio and Sebastian) from the play-ending reconciliation. Shakespeare's consummate greatness consists of his ability to stage both Ariel and Caliban. In Ariel, we can see the well-blended, pathos-filled, hermaphroditic ideal of Italian tragicomedy. In Caliban, Shakespeare takes the ambivalent, monstrous mixture and gives it a grotesquely tragicomic power anticipatory of modern tragicomedy, a power all the more enlivened on the London stage by the body of the actor-clown.

Notes

CHAPTER 1. INTRODUCTION

1. See Eugene M. Waith, *The Pattern of Tragicomedy in Beaumont and Fletcher* (New Haven: Yale University Press, 1952), 45–46; W.H. Herendeen, "A New Way to Pay Old Debts: Pretexts to the 1616 Folio," in *Ben Jonson's 1616 Folio*, ed. Jennifer Brady and W. H. Herendeen (Newark: University of Delaware Press, 1991); and Lawrence Danson, "Jonsonian Comedy and the Discovery of the Social Self," *PMLA* 99 (1984): 179–80, 184. Not printed until 1641, *The Sad Shepherd* was probably written in 1636–37, just before Jonson's death.

2. For a detailed description of the illustration, see Margery Corbett and Ronald Lightbown, *The Comely Frontispiece: The Emblematic Title-Page in England, 1550–1660* (London: Routledge and Kegan Paul, 1979), 145–50.

3. Horace, "The Art of Poetry," in *Horace: Satires, Epistles, and Ars Poetica*, trans. H. R. Fairclough, Loeb Classical Library (1929; reprint, Cambridge: Harvard University Press, 1978), 458–59. Unless otherwise indicated, translations from Latin and Greek Loeb Classical Library texts are those of the translator.

4. Ibid., 472–73. In Fairclough's translation of Horace, I have changed "tragic" to "tragedic," for reasons that will be explained below.

5. For the connection between the satyr and satire in the Renaissance, see my discussion in chapter 4, as well as Waith, *Pattern of Tragicomedy*, 43–85; and Alfred Kernan, *The Cankered Muse: Satire of the English Renaissance* (New Haven: Yale University Press, 1959), 90–140.

6. My discussion of the Jonson title page is especially indebted to Joseph Loewenstein's superb "Guarini and the Presence of Genre," in *Renaissance Tragicomedy: Explorations in Genre and Politics*, ed. Nancy Klein Maguire (New York: AMS Press, 1987), 33–55.

7. This point has been argued by Barbara Kiefer Lewalski, *Paradise Lost and the Rhetoric of Literary Forms* (Princeton: Princeton University Press, 1985), 11.

8. Alastair Fowler, *Kinds of Literature: An Introduction to the Theory of Genres and Modes* (Cambridge: Harvard University Press, 1982), 58ff. I base my distinction between genre and mode, and my use of the category of subgenre, on Fowler. Austin Warren and René Wellek use the terms "outer form" and "inner form." See their *Theory of Literature*, 3d ed. (New York: Harcourt Brace Jovanovich, 1956), 241.

9. Empson, for example, locates the pastoral mode in unexpected places like Carroll's *Alice in Wonderland*. See his *Some Versions of Pastoral* (1935; reprint, New York: New Directions, 1974).

10. Group terms like "genre" and "mode" are not categories with absolute boundaries and so my choice of, say, "comic" or "comedic" for a given phenomenon may be challenged by alternative definitions or usages of "genre" and "mode."

11. Hayden White demonstrates the spatial liminality of the satyr and the wild man in "The Forms of Wildness: Archaeology of an Idea," in *The Wild Man Within: An Image in Western Thought from the Renaissance to Romanticism*, ed. Edward Dudley and Maximillian E. Novak (Pittsburgh: University of Pittsburgh Press, 1972), 3–38.

12. John Marston, *The Malcontent*, ed. G. K. Hunter (London: Methuen, 1975), xli–xlvi.

13. Much Renaissance tragicomedy, of course, has neither pastoral or satire, and the illustration cannot be taken as an exhaustive iconography of the Renaissance genre.

14. Leo Salingar discusses homological developments in Italian and English Renaissance theaters in "Elizabethan Dramatists and Italy: A Postscript," in *Theatre of the English and Italian Renaissance*, ed. J. R. Mulryne and Margeret Shewring (New York: St. Martin's Press, 1991), 221–37.

15. For the presence of satiric elements in Siennese theater, see Nino Borsellino, *Rozzi e Intronati: Esperienze e forme di teatro dal "Decameron" al "Candelaio,"* 2d ed. (Rome: Bulzoni, 1976), 99.

16. In the facsimile editions of the Poetiken Cinquecento series, see Francesco Robortello, *In librum Aristotelis de arte poetica explicationes paraphrasis in librum Horatii, qui vulgo de arte poetica ad Pisones inscribitur* (1548; reprint, Munich: Wilhelm Fink Verlag, 1971); and Antonio Sebastiano Minturno, *L'arte poetica* (1564; reprint, Munich: Wilhelm Fink Verlag, 1971). A useful modern abridged edition of Castelvetro is *Castelvetro on the Art of Poetry: An Abridged Translation of Lodovico Castelvetro's "Poetica d'Aristotele Vulgarizzata et Sposta,"* ed. Andrew Bongiorno (Binghamton, N.Y.: Medieval and Renaissance Texts and Studies, 1984). Giraldi's treatise, entitled "Discorso intorno al comporre delle commedie e delle tragedie," may be found in G. B. Giraldi Cinzio, *Scritti critici*, ed. Camillo Guerrieri Crocetti (Milan: Marzorati, 1973), 169–224.

17. A good, concise account of Italian Renaissance tragedy is that of Marzia Pieri in *La nascita del teatro moderno in Italian tra XV e XVI secolo* (Turin: Bollati Boringhieri, 1989), 135–55.

18. The evolution of late-Cinquecento comedy into *commedia grave* is magisterially discussed by Louise George Clubb in *Italian Drama in Shakespeare's Time* (New Haven: Yale University Press, 1989), 29–89.

19. See Marvin T. Herrick, *Comic Theory in the Sixteenth Century* (Urbana: University of Illinois Press, 1964).

20. Ferdinando Taviani has copiously documented the attacks on the *commedia* in *La Commedia dell'Arte e la società barocca: La fascinazione del teatro* (Rome: Bulzoni, 1969).

21. See Ingegneri's "Della Poesia Rappresentativa," which is conveniently collected with all of the major documents of the quarrel between Battista Guarini and Giason Denores (described below), in *Delle opere del cavalier Battista Guarini* (Verona, 1738), 3:483–85. I will refer to this edition as *Opere*.

22. Ingegneri, "Della Poesia Rappresentativa" (*Opere*, 3:483). Tasso's play was written in 1572, probably first performed in 1573, and published in an illustrated edition in Venice in 1583. Guarini wrote *Il pastor fido* between 1580 and 1585 and published it in 1590 and then, in a definitive edition, in 1602. Both *Il pastor fido* editions were published in Venice.

23. Il Fumoso, *Il batecchio, commedia di maggio composta per il pellegrino ingegno del Fumoso* (Siena, 1546). For a brilliant discussion of this play and the role of class and gender in Italian pastoral drama, see Jane Tylus, "Colonizing Peasants: The Rape of the Sabines and Renaissance Pastoral," *Renaissance Drama*, n.s., 23 (1992): 113–38.

24. Vittorio Rossi details the tortuous production history of *Il pastor fido* in *Battista Guarini ed Il pastor fido: Studio biografico-critico* (Turin: Ermanno Loescher, 1886), 179–89, 223–38.

25. This treatise was published in Padua and is found in the second volume of the *Opere*.

26. *Il Verato ovvero difesa di quanto ha scritto M. Giason Denores contra le tragicomedie, et le pastorali, in un suo discorso di poesia* (Ferrara, 1588). Found in the second volume of the *Opere*, this treatise will be referred to as *I Verato*.

27. The *Apologia contra l'auttor del Verato di Iason De Nores di quanto ha egli detto in un suo discorso delle tragicomedie, e delle pastorali* was published in 1590 and is located in the second volume of the *Opere*.

28. The full title of this treatise is *Il Verato secondo ovvero replica dell'attizzato accademico ferrarese in difesa del pastorfido*, completed by 1591 but not published until 1593 in Florence, and collected in the third volume of the *Opere*. I will refer to it as *II Verato*. Finally, in 1601 Guarini published a work incorporating the major points of his two earlier treatises, the *Compendio della poesia tragicomica, tratto dai duo Verati, per opera dell'autore del pastor fido, colla giunta di molte cose spettanti all'arte* (Venice, 1601), which is located in the third volume of the *Opere*. A good account of the quarrel has been given by Bernard Weinberg, *A History of Literary Criticism in the Italian Renaissance* (Chicago: University of Chicago Press, 1961), 2:1074–1105.

29. Arthur Kirsch compares Jonson and Guarini in *Jacobean Dramatic Perspectives* (Charlottesville: University Press of Virginia, 1972), 7–15

30. Loewenstein, "Guarini," 37.

31. All citations from the quarrel documents refer to the *Opere*. I indicate whether the citation is from the first or second *Verato* and then specify the volume from the eighteenth-century *Opere* in which the treatise is included. *II Verato*, 3:163, then, would refer to page 163 of the second *Verato*, located in the third volume of the eighteenth-century edition. Unless otherwise noted, translations of Italian theoretical and dramatic materials are my own.

32. This argument has persuasively been made by James J. Yoch, "A Greater Power Than We Can Contradict: The Voice of Authority in the Staging of Italian Pastorals," in *The Elizabethan Theatre, VIII*, ed. George R. Hibbard (Port Credit, Ont.: P. D. Meany Co., 1982), 164–87.

33. For a study of the roles played by Robert Armin for the King's Men, see David Wiles, *Shakespeare's Clown: Actor and Text in the Elizabethan Playhouse* (Cambridge: Cambridge University Press, 1987), 136–63. Armin's parts in *Cymbeline, The Winter's Tale*, and *The Tempest* are discussed at 153–77. As Chambers has shown, he appears in the actor list of Jonson's *Alchemist* (performed by the King's Men in 1610), but in none after that. E. K. Chambers, *The Elizabethan Stage* (Oxford:

Clarendon Press, 1923), 2:299–300. There is no evidence, however, that Armin dropped out of Shakespeare's company immediately after 1610.

34. See Glynne Wickham, "From Tragedy to Tragicomedy: *King Lear* as Prologue," *Shakespeare Survey* 26 (1973): 33–48 and Robert W. Uphaus, *Beyond Tragedy: Structure and Experience in Shakespeare's Romances* (Lexington: University Press of Kentucky, 1981), 12–33.

35. Citations refer to *The Tempest*, ed. Frank Kermode (London and New York: Methuen, 1954).

36. Jonathan Dollimore, *Radical Tragedy: Religion, Ideology, and Power in the Drama of Shakespeare and his Contemporaries* (Brighton, U.K.: Harvester, 1984).

37. Concurrent with Sidney's great pastoral romance *The Arcadia*, the 1570s and 1580s had seen the appearance of pastoral drama on the English stage, in Sidney's 1579[?] masque *The Lady of May*, George Peele's 1584 *The Arraignment of Paris*, and Lyly's *Gallathea* (probably written between 1584 and 1588, and printed in 1592).

38. For print and performance dating of *Mucedorus*, see Arvin H. Jupin, ed., *A Contexual Study and Modern-Spelling Edition of "Mucedorus"* (New York and London: Garland Publishing, 1987), 1–12.

39. In an analysis of *As You Like It*, *King Lear*, *The Winter's Tale*, and *The Tempest*, (which includes a discussion of *Cymbeline*), David Young astutely argues that Shakespeare was interested in the subject and emotional focus of pastoral rather than in its external characteristics. See *The Heart's Forest: A Study of Shakespeare's Pastoral Plays* (New Haven and London: Yale University Press, 1972).

40. For the Wales scenes as hard pastoral, see Michael Taylor, "The Pastoral Reckoning in *Cymbeline*," *Shakespeare Survey* 36 (1983): 97–106.

41. For the introductory note, see *The Dramatic Works in the Beaumont and Fletcher Canon*, ed. Fredson Bowers (Cambridge: Cambridge University Press, 1976), 3:497.

42. See the introduction to *The Politics of Tragicomedy: Shakespeare and After*, ed. Gordon McMullan and Jonathan Hope (London and New York: Routledge, 1992), 1–7.

43. For Moretti's account of Tudor/Stuart tragedy, see "The Great Eclipse: Tragic Form as the Deconsecration of Sovereignty," in *Signs Taken for Wonders: Essays in the Sociology of Literary Forms*, trans. Susan Fischer, David Forgacs, and David Miller (London and New York: Verso, 1988), 42–82.

44. I take the term "courtly aesthetic" from Gary Schmidgall, *Shakespeare and the Courtly Aesthetic* (Berkeley: University of California Press, 1981). Schmidgall discusses these and other Italian influences on the early-Stuart court, which he sees as crucial. See 140–42.

45. For Italian influence on the English masque, see Enid Welsford, "Italian Influence on the English Court Masque," *MLR* 28 (1923): 394–409; A. M. Nagler, *Theatre Festivals of the Medici* (New Haven and London: Yale University Press, 1964), 119–25; and John Peacock, "Inigo Jones and the Florentine Court Theatre," *John Donne Journal* 5 (1986): 200–234.

46. Leah Marcus, *The Politics of Mirth: Jonson, Herrick, Milton, Marvell, and the Defense of Old Holiday Pastimes* (Chicago and London: University of Chicago Press, 1986), 1–23.

47. Ibid., 11.

48. *The Workes of the Most High and Mightie Prince James* (London, 1616), sig. X3, p. 245.

49. Peter Force, ed., *Tracts and Other Papers Relating Principally to the Origin, Settlement, and Progress of the Colonies in North America* (Washington, D.C., 1836), 3:11.

50. "In generic resemblance," argues Alastair Fowler, "the direct line of descent is not so dominant that genre theory can be identified with source criticism. See Fowler, *Kinds of Literature*, 43.

51. David Orr, *Italian Renaissance Drama in England Before 1625: The Influence of Erudite Tragedy, Comedy, and Pastoral on Elizabethan and Jacobean Drama* (Chapel Hill: University of North Carolina Press, 1970), vii.

52. Ibid., viii.

53. These have been collected by Kathleen Lea in *Italian Popular Comedy: A Study in the Commedia dell'Arte, 1560–1620, with Special Reference to the English Stage* (Oxford: Clarendon Press, 1934), 2:374–81.

54. Contact between Italian and English actors is also documented in ibid., 2:350–52.

55. For character studies of Italian and English drama, see O. J. Campbell, "*Love's Labor's Lost* Revisited" and "*The Two Gentlemen of Verona* and Italian Comedy," in *Studies in Shakespeare, Milton, and Donne* (New York: Macmillan, 1925), 1–64; Daniel C. Boughner, *The Braggart in Renaissance Comedy: A Study in Comparative Drama from Aristophanes to Shakespeare* (Minneapolis: University of Minnesota Press, 1954); Allardyce Nicoll, *The World of Harlequin: A Critical Study of the Commedia dell'Arte* (Cambridge: Cambridge University Press, 1963); Robert C. Melzi, "From Lelia to Viola," *Renaissance Drama* 9 (1966): 67–81. Robert S. Miola, in two fine articles, has examined both comedic characters and dramatic traditions in "*The Merry Wives of Windsor*: Classical and Italian Intertexts," *Comparative Drama* 27 (1993): 364–76 and "New Comedy in *All's Well That Ends Well*," *Renaissance Quarterly* 46 (1993): 23–43.

56. Clubb, *Italian Drama*, 6.

57. See Polonius's famous litany of Renaissance *genera mista*, in *Hamlet* 2.2.392–98, which serves as the epigraph to Clubb's book. The citation refers to William Shakespeare, *Hamlet*, ed. Harold Jenkins (London and New York: Methuen, 1982).

58. Leo Salingar, *Shakespeare and the Traditions of Comedy* (Cambridge: Cambridge University Press, 1972). For Salingar's discussion of Shakespeare and Italian comedy, see *Shakespeare and the Traditions of Comedy*, 175–242.

59. Most prominent among such studies is Marvin T. Herrick's encyclopedic *Tragicomedy: Its Origins and Development in Italy, France, and England* (Urbana: University of Illinois Press, 1955).

60. Alastair Fowler and others have applied Ludwig Wittgenstein's notion of "family resemblance" (used by Wittgenstein to discuss common elements in language games and games in general) to genre theory. See Ludwig Wittgenstein, *Philosophical Investigations*, trans. G. E. M. Anscombe (New York: Macmillan, 1953), secs. 65, 66, 67; and Fowler, *Kinds of Literature*, 41.

61. Clubb explores the tonal and generic resonance of animals in *The Winter's Tale* and Italian pastoral drama in her *Italian Drama*, 140–52.

62. Guidubaldo Bonarelli, *Filli di Sciro, favola pastorale* (Ferrara, 1607). There is a modern edition of the play: *Filli di Sciro, discorsi, e appendice*, ed. Giovanni Gambarin (Bari: Laterza, 1941).

63. Most Anglo-American critics use the abridged translation of Allan H. Gilbert, found in his *Literary Criticism: Plato to Dryden* (1940; reprint, Detroit, Mich.:

Wayne State University Press, 1962), 504–33. Some useful studies of Guarini's theory and Renaissance English drama, in addition to those already cited, are Madeleine Doran, *Endeavors of Art : A Study of Form in Elizabethan Drama* (Madison: University of Wisconsin Press, 1963), 186–215; G. K. Hunter, "Italian Tragicomedy on the English Stage," *Renaissance Drama*, n.s., 6 (1973): 123–48; and David L. Hirst, *Tragicomedy* (London and New York: Methuen, 1984), 3–8, 18–21. Herrick does use the eighteenth-century *Opere* edition, although he concentrates on the *Compendio* and on passages found in Gilbert's abridged translation. Yoch has read Guarini quite carefully, including citations from the latter's annotations to *Il pastor fido*. Some critics, like Kirsch, refer also to Weinberg's many quotations from Guarini, some indeed taken from the *Verati*. (Weinberg himself has read all of the quarrel documents.) Hirst and Doran do refer to the complete *Compendio*, which they have consulted in Italian. The excellent essays by John T. Shawcross, Barbara A. Mowat, Verna Foster, James J. Yoch, and especially Joseph Loewenstein, edited by Nancy Klein Maguire in *Renaissance Tragicomedy*, probably constitute the best recent work on Guarini and tragicomedy, but do not refer to the *Verati*. Two doctoral dissertations relate Shakespeare's late plays to Guarini's theory of tragicomedy: May E. Cambell, *"The Winter's Tale: A Study in Shakespeare's Late Plays with Special Reference to Guarini's Theory of Tragicomedy"* (diss., University of North Carolina at Chapel Hill, 1970); and Jane Haney Collura, "Guarini's Theory of Tragicomedy and Shakespeare's Last Three Plays" (diss., The Catholic University of America, 1979).

64. The useful term "unwritten poetics" is taken from Claudio Guillén, *Literature as System: Essays Toward the Theory of Literary History* (Princeton: Princeton University Press, 1971).

65. In his discussion of Guarini's legacy to the early-Stuart "courtly aesthetic," Gary Schmidgall concentrates mainly on style. See Schmidgall, *Shakespeare and the Courtly Aesthetic*, 59. In "A Greater Power Than We Can Contradict," James J. Yoch admirably analyzes the effect of the *intermezzi* on Italian courtly audiences, but I think underestimates the importance of the plays themselves.

66. The argument that Fletcher was concerned about the dramaturgical integrity of his pastoral tragicomedy is made by William Proctor Williams in "Not Hornpipes and Funerals: Fletcherian Tragicomedy," in Maguire, *Renaissance Tragicomedy*, 139–54. I quote from Beaumont and Fletcher, *Dramatic Works*, ed. Bowers, 3:497.

67. Richard Proudfoot, "Shakespeare and the New Dramatists of the King's Men, 1606–1613," in *Later Shakespeare*, ed. John Russell Brown and Bernard Harris (New York: St. Martin's Press, 1967), 240.

68. Stanley Wells reviews these attacks on romance in "Shakespeare and Romance," in Brown and Harris, *Later Shakespeare*, 52–53. See also Salingar, *Shakespeare and the Traditions of Comedy*, 71–75.

69. See Kirsch, *Jacobean Dramatic Perspectives*; R. A. Foakes, "Tragicomedy and Comic Form," in *Comedy from Shakespeare to Sheridan: Change and Continuity in the English and European Dramatic Tradition: Essays in Honor of Eugene Waith*, ed. A. R. Braunmuller, and J. C. Bulman (Newark: University of Delaware Press, 1986), 74–88; and Barbara Mowat, *The Dramaturgy of Shakespeare's Romances* (Athens: University of Georgia Press, 1976).

70. See Walter Cohen, "The Politics of Golden Age Tragicomedy" in Maguire, *Renaissance Tragicomedy*, 154–75; and "Prerevolutionary Drama," in McMullan and Hope, *Politics of Tragicomedy*, 122–50.

71. See, for example, Cohen's reference to "tearful aristocratic reconciliation" in "Prerevolutionary Drama," 136.

72. Verna Foster, for example, sees wonder as the central tragicomedic response in *The Winter's Tale* in her illuminating "The 'Death' of Hermione: Tragicomic Dramaturgy in *The Winter's Tale*," *Cahiers Elizabethains* 43 (1993): 43–56.

73. See Northrop Frye, *A Natural Perspective: The Development of Shakespearean Comedy and Romance* (New York: Columbia University Press, 1965); Salingar, *Shakespeare and the Traditions of Comedy*, 28–75; Howard Felperin, "Romance and Romanticism: Some Reflections on *The Tempest* and *The Heart of Darkness*, or When is Romance no longer Romance?" in *Shakespeare's Romances Reconsidered*, ed. Carol McGinnis Kay and Henry E. Jacobs (Lincoln: University of Nebraska Press, 1978), 60–76; Howard Felperin, *Shakespearean Romance* (Princeton: Princeton University Press, 1972); Stanley Wells, "Shakespeare and Romance," in Brown and Harris, *Later Shakespeare*, 49–80.

74. In the late-nineteenth century, Dowden initiated the interpretive use of "romance" for the late plays. See his *Shakespeare* (New York, 1877), 55–56. For Jameson on romance, see *The Political Unconscious: Narrative as a Socially Symbolic Act* (Ithaca: Cornell University Press, 1981), 103–50, esp. 148.

75. Mowat, *Dramaturgy*, 69–94.

76. Salingar, *Shakespeare and the Traditions of Comedy*, 30–33.

77. Ibid., 28–75.

78. See "Towards a 'Philosophy' of Renaissance Theatre," in *Comparative Critical Approaches to Renaissance Comedy*, ed. Donald Beecher and Massimo Ciavolella (Ottawa: Dovehouse Editions, 1986), 10.

79. Jameson, *Political Unconscious*, 110.

80. Felperin, *Shakespearean Romance*, 52. It is very seldom, in Robert W. Uphaus's *Beyond Tragedy*, that we get actual romance: romance is skeletal and conventional in *Pericles*, parodic in *Cymbeline*, and not fully presented until the fifth act of *The Winter's Tale*.

81. Harry Berger, "Miraculous Harp: A Reading of Shakespeare's *Tempest*," *Shakespeare Studies* 5 (1969): 253–83.

82. *The Place of the Stage: License, Play, and Power in Renaissance England* (Chicago and London: University of Chicago Press, 1988), 135.

83. Wells, "Shakespeare and Romance," 66.

84. *Pericles* citations refer to *Pericles*, ed. F. D. Hoeniger (London and New York, Methuen, 1963).

85. The term, very useful in thinking about the mediation of genre concepts between the work and the reader/audience, is from Hans Robert Jauss, "Literary History as a Challenge to Literary Theory," *New Literary History* 2 (1970): 14–15.

CHAPTER 2. ITALIAN-ENGLISH TRANSMISSIONS AND ENGLISH CONTEXTS

1. Samuel Schoenbaum, *William Shakespeare: A Compact Documentary Life* (Oxford: Oxford University Press, 1977), 169.

2. Roger Ascham, *The Schoolmaster* (1570), ed. Lawrence V. Ryun (Charlottesville: University Press of Virginia, 1967), 71.

3. Frances A. Yates, *John Florio: The Life of an Italian in Shakespeare's England* (Cambridge: Cambridge University Press, 1934), 267.

4. R. C. Simonini, *Italian Scholarship in Renaissance England* (Chapel Hill: University of North Carolina Press, 1952), 102.

5. For Florio's furnishing Jonson with information about Italian culture of special importance in *Volpone*, see Brian Parker, "Jonson's Venice," in Mulryne and Shewing, *Theatre*, 95–112.

6. For information on John Wolfe, see Harry R. Hoppe, "John Wolfe, Printer and Publisher, 1579–1601," *Library*, 4th ser., 14 (1933–34): 241–48; Harry Sellers, "Italian Books Printed Before 1640," *Library*, 4th ser., 5 (1924–25): 105–25; Clifford Chalmers Huffman, *Elizabethan Impressions: John Wolfe and His Press* (New York: AMS Press, 1988); Joseph Loewenstein, "For a History of Literary Property: John Wolfe's Reformation," *English Literary Renaissance* 18 (1988): 389–412.

7. For the interesting life and literary career of Castelvetro, see Sheila A. Dimsey, "Giacopo Castelvetro," *MLR* 23 (1928): 424–31; Eleanor Rosenberg, "Giacomo Castelvetro, Italian Publisher in Elizabethan London and His Patrons," *HLQ* 6 (1943): 119–48; and K. T. Butler, "Giacomo Castelvetro," *Italian Studies* 5 (1950): 1–42.

8. Judith Kennedy, "Il pastor cortese: Tasso, Guarini, and Shakespeare's 'Courtly' Comedies," paper presented at the annual meeting of the Shakespeare Association of America, Philadelphia, April 1990. I am grateful to Louise George Clubb for sharing this paper with me.

9. See William Shakespeare, *King Richard II*, ed. Peter Ure (London and New York: Methuen, 1956), xlii–iv; and William Shakespeare, *Antony and Cleopatra*, ed. M. R. Ridlely (London and New York: Methuen, 1954), xxiv–vi.

10. Mark Eccles, "Samuel Daniel in France and Italy," *Studies in Philology* 44 (1937), 148–67.

11. Elizabeth Story Donno, ed., *Three Renaissance Pastorals: Tasso, Guarini, Daniel* (Binghamton, N.Y.: Medieval and Renaissance Texts and Studies, 1993), xxviii.

12. See John Peacock, "Ben Jonson's Masques and Italian Culture," in Mulryne and Shewring, *Theatre*, 73–94.

13. Donno has argued that the probable translator was Tailboys Dymoke, the brother of Edward. A member of Lincoln's Inn in the 1580s, Tailboys was accused by his uncle, the earl of Lincoln, as being a "common contriver and publisher of infamous pamphlets and libells" (Donno, *Three Renaissance Pastorals*, xxi–xxiv). One of these libels must have been a May Day play produced by Tailboys in which he impersonated the earl in front of an audience of several hundred.

14. Johanna Procter, "The *Queenes Arcadia* (1606) and *Hymen's Triumph* (1615): Samuel Daniel's Court Pastoral Plays," in *The Renaissance in Ferrara and Its European Horizons*, ed. J. Salmons (Cardiff: University of Wales Press, 1984), 107 n. 18.

15. I quote from *The Complete Works in Verse and Prose of Samuel Daniel*, ed. Alexander Grosart (New York: Russell and Russell, 1963), 3:26.

16. See, for example, Roberto Tessari, *Commedia dell'Arte: la maschera e l'ombra* (Milan: Mursia, 1981), 31–47.

17. Ben Jonson, *Volpone*, ed. Philip Brockbank (New York: W. W. Norton, 1968). For the performance dates of *Volpone*, see Jonson, *Volpone*, ed. Brockbank, xxvii.

18. Quoted by Peacock, "Ben Jonson's Masques," 74.

19. For Jonson's poem, see Beaumont and Fletcher, *Dramatic Works*, ed. Bowers, 3:492.

20. The notion of a generic idea as an "invitation to form," or an incitement to the writer to refashion the genre with each individual response, is that of Guillén, *Literature as System*, 129.

21. G. K. Hunter, "English Folly and Italian Vice," in *Jacobean Theatre* (New York: St. Martin's Press, 1960), 85–111.

22. For the dates of *The Malcontent*'s early performances, see Marston, *The Malcontent*, ed. Hunter, xli–xlvi.

23. "Italian Tragicomedy on the English Stage," 123–48.

24. For an illuminating account of these two plays and their relationship to tragedy, see Moretti, *Signs Taken for Wonders*, 57–61.

25. In her "Shakespearean Tragicomedy," Barbara A. Mowat argues that Shakespeare's "problem plays" lay at least as much claim to follow Guarini's precepts as do the late plays. She sees in the "problem plays" careful, Guarinian blends of the "conventionally comic and the conventionally tragic" (88), while acknowledging certain departures from Guarinian dramaturgy as well. I would depart from Mowat in stressing what recent productions of these plays have been staging: their sharp and ironic contrasts of tragic and comic modalities. And I would argue that it is not only the problem plays' omission of pastoral but the lack of several other generic (rather than modal) features of tragicomedic dramaturgy that makes the Italian precedent less important for the *Measure For Measure* group than for the late plays. Mowat's article is found in Maguire, *Renaissance Tragicomedy*, 80–96.

26. Philip J. Finkelpearl, *Court and Country Politics in the Plays of Beaumont and Fletcher* (Princeton: Princeton University Press, 1990), 102.

27. I quote from Beaumont and Fletcher, *Dramatic Works*, ed. Bowers, 3:497.

28. "La maggior parte amica / fu de le sacre Muse, amore e studio" [Most {of the ancient shepherds} were friends of the sacred muses, love, and study.] All *Il pastor fido* citations are from *Opere di Battista Guarini*, ed. Marziano Guglielminetti (Turin: UTET, 1971).

29. The approximate dates of Beaumont and Fletcher's two greatest tragicomedies and Shakespeare's late plays are the following: *Cymbeline* and *Philaster*, 1609; *The Winter's Tale*, 1610; *The Tempest* and *A King and No King*, 1611.

30. For a good comparative study of Shakespeare with Beaumont and Fletcher, see Lee Bliss, "Tragicomic Romance for the King's Men, 1609–1611: Shakespeare, Beaumont, and Fletcher," in Braunmuller and Bulman, *Comedy from Shakespeare to Sheridan*, 148–64. Bliss argues that Beaumont and Fletcher's plays signficantly reduce the functional importance of pastoral, "not offering pastoral interludes rich in alternative possibilities" as do Shakespeare's late plays (151).

31. *A King and No King* citations refer to Russell A. Fraser and Norman Rabkin, eds., *Drama of the Renaissance*, vol. 2 (New York: Macmillan, 1976). The Shakespeare citation refers to *The Winter's Tale*, ed. J. H. P. Pafford (London and New York: Methuen, 1963).

32. Waith, *Pattern of Tragicomedy*, 53.

33. Citation refers to *Philaster*, ed. Dora Jean Ashe (Lincoln: University of Nebraska Press, 1974).

34. Citation refers to *Ben Jonson's Plays and Masques*, ed. Robert M. Adams (New York: Norton, 1979).

35. Marcus, *Politics of Mirth*, 1–139.

36. For example, Amarillis refers to Perigot's pursuit of country sports (1.2.148).

37. See Winifred Smith, *The Commedia dell'Arte: A Study in Italian Popular Comedy* (New York: Columbia University Press, 1912), 170–99; Lea, *Italian Popular Comedy*,

2:339–455; Ninian Mellamphy, "Pantaloons and Zanies: Shakespeare's 'Apprenticeship' to Italian Professional Comedy Troupes," in *Shakespearean Comedy*, ed. Maurice Charney (New York: New York Literary Forum, 1980), 141–51; Andrew Grewar, "Shakespeare and the Actors of the *Commedia dell'Arte*," in *Studies of the Commedia dell'Arte*, ed. David J. George and Christopher J. Gossip (Cardiff: University of Wales Press, 1993), 13–48.

38. For a study of Shakespeare's use of *arte* character types in his early comedies, see Campbell, *Studies*, 1–64.

39. See Grewar, "Shakespeare and the Actors."

40. Lea lists English references to the *commedia* in her *Italian Popular Comedy*, 2:374–90.

41. *Documents Relating to the Office of Revels in the Time of Queen Elizabeth*, ed. A. Feuillerat (Louvain: A. Uystpruyst, 1908), 225–28. Quoted by Lea, *Italian Popular Comedy*, 2:353.

42. E. K. Chambers, "The Integrity of *The Tempest*," *Review of English Studies* 1 (1925): 129–50.

43. The report is quoted by Lea, *Italian Popular Comedy*, 2:357.

44. For a study of Kemp's relationship to the *commedia dell'arte*, see Louis B. Wright, "Will Kemp and the *Commedia dell'Arte*," *MLN* 41 (1926): 516–20. For the exchange between Kemp and the Arlecchino, see *The Works of John Day*, ed. A. H. Bullen (1881; reprint, London: Holland Press, 1963), 369–73.

45. Lea, *Italian Popular Comedy*, 2:350–52.

46. The *commedia dell'arte* scenarios collected by Scala can be found in Flaminio Scala, *Il teatro delle favole rappresentative*, ed. Ferruccio Marotti, 2 vols. (1611; Milan: Il Polifilo, 1976).

47. For the Locatelli manuscript in the Casanatense, see MS. F. IV 12–13. The Corsini collection is now located in the Biblioteca of the Accademia dei Lincei, Rome.

48. In *Scenari delle maschere in Arcadia* (Castello: S. Lapi, 1913), Ferdinando Neri includes the texts of five of these Arcadian scenarios. Lea includes nine scenarios in the second volume of her study. All of the scenarios that I cite may be found in Lea, *Italian Popular Comedy*, 2:610–74. There is one other pastoral scenario, *L'Arcadia Incantata*, which is located in the Passanti collection of scenarios in the Biblioteca Nazionale of Naples. *L'Arcadia Incantata* is also included in Lea's appendix. There is a variant of this *scenario* in the eighteenth-century collection of *arte* materials made by Placido Adriani, located in the Biblioteca Comunale in Perugia.

49. E. K. Chambers, *William Shakespeare: A Study of Facts and Problems* (Oxford: Clarendon Press, 1930), 1:493–94. Shakespeare, *The Tempest*, ed. Kermode, lxvi–lxix.

50. *Gl'intricati, pastorale* (Venice, 1581); *La fiammella, pastorale* (Paris, 1584).

51. Clubb discusses the play in *Italian Drama*, 93–95.

52. *The Tempest*, ed. Kermode, lxvii.

53. In *Pantaloncino*, the magician has a daughter whom he jealously guards. See Lea, *Italian Popular Comedy*, 2:636–42.

54. In *Arcadia incantata*, there are explicit stage directions for a tempest, a "stormy sea with a sinking ship."

55. In *Arcadia incantata* (Lea, *Italian Popular Comedy*, 672), flames issue from a fruit tree when the travelers start to pick it. In this scenario, the Italians are the victims of exhaustion and fear, becoming terrified in the labyrinthine woods.

56. The concept of "dramatic competence" is discussed in Keir Elam, *The Semiotics of Theatre and Drama* (London: Methuen, 1989), 98–99.

57. Andrew Gurr, *The Shakespearean Stage, 1574–1642,* 2d ed. (Cambridge: Cambridge University Press, 1980), 17–18.

58. Alfred Harbage, *Shakespeare and the Rival Traditions* (New York: Macmillan, 1952); Ann Jennalie Cook, *The Privileged Playgoers of Shakespeare's London, 1576–1642* (Princeton: Princeton University Press, 1981).

59. Gerald Eades Bentley, "Shakespeare and the Blackfriars Theatre," *Shakespeare Survey* 1 (1948): 38–50.

60. Schoenbaum, *William Shakespeare,* 266.

61. Keith Sturgess, *Jacobean Private Theatre* (London and New York: Routledge and Kegan Paul, 1987), 12.

62. Ibid., 17.

63. Ibid., 12.

64. Ibid., 24.

65. Gurr, *Shakespearean Stage,* 199.

66. Quoted by ibid., 199.

67. Ibid., 53.

68. Ibid., 160.

69. *The Malcontent,* induction, 84.

70. From Marston's *Antonio's Revenge,* quoted by Gurr, *Shakespearean Stage,* 95.

71. Harley Granville-Barker, *Prefaces to Shakespeare,* 2d ser. (London: Sidgwick and Jackson, 1930), 249–50.

CHAPTER 3. THEORY AND PRACTICE IN THE CINQUECENTO

1. A few did, such as Leone De'Sommi, who claimed that those performing scripted plays can learn from the improvisatory players. See Leone De'Sommi, *Quattro dialoghi in materia di rappresentazioni sceniche,* ed. Ferruccio Marotti (Milan: Il Polifilo, 1968).

2. See Ferdinand Braudel, "L'Italian fuori d'Italia," in *Storia d'Italia,* vol. 2, *Dalla caduta dell'Impero romano al secolo XVIII* (Turin: Einaudi, 1974), 2092–248; Eric Cochrane, "Counter-Reformation or Tridentine Reformation?: Italy in the Age of Carlo Borromeo," in *San Carlo Borromeo: Catholic Reform and Ecclesiastical Politics in the Second Half of the Sixteenth Century,* ed. John M Headley and John B. Tomaro (Washington, D.C.: Folger Shakespeare Library, 1988), 31–46; and Paul F. Grendler, *The Roman Inquisition and the Venetian Press, 1540–1605* (Princeton: Princeton University Press, 1977).

3. Braudel, "L'Italian fuori d'Italia," 2161–71.

4. See F. C. Lane, "The Mediterranean Spice Trade: Further Evidence of its Revival in the Sixteenth Century," *American Historical Review* 45 (1940): 581–90.

5. Grendler, *Roman Inquisition,* 201–52.

6. The term "distinterment" is that of Thomas Greene, *The Light in Troy: Imitation and Discovery in Renaissance Poetry* (New Haven: Yale University Press, 1982), 92.

7. Grendler, *Roman Inquisition,* 291.

8. The works published in Venice were the *Lettere* (1593), *Il Segretario* (1594), the *Rime* (1598), the *Compendio* (1601), and the definitive edition of *Il pastor fido* (1602). For a complete list of Guarini's works, see *Opere di Battista Guarini,* ed. Guglielminetti, 71–73.

9. "Self-Justifying Norms in the Genre Theories of Italian Renaissance Poets," *Philological Quarterly* 67 (1988): 195–218.

10. For an account of these quarrels, see Weinberg, *History of Literary Criticism*, 2:819–1112.

11. Guillén, *Literature as System*, 109.

12. Ibid., 107.

13. This point has been made most forceably by Weinberg, *History of Literary Criticism*, 1:502–11, although Andrew Bongiorno takes issue with Weinberg's argument that Castelvetro bases the unities on the psychological needs of the audience (*Castelvetro on the Art of Poetry*, ed. Bongiorno, xlii).

14. Marco De Marinis, "Dramaturgy of the Spectator," *Drama Review* 31 (1987): 101.

15. Barbara Kiefer Lewalski sees Sidney here anticipating the modern concept of mode. See *Paradise Lost and the Rhetoric of Literary Forms*, 10. I cite Sidney from *An Apology for Poetry*, ed. Geoffrey Shepherd (London: Thomas Nelson and Sons, 1965), 116–17.

16. The phrase is from Rosalie Colie's *Resources of Kind: Genre-Theory in the Renaissance*, ed. Barbara Kiefer Lewalski (Berkeley: University of California Press, 1973).

17. Citation refers to *King Lear*, ed. Kenneth Muir (London and New York: Methuen, 1972).

18. For a study of the practical, interventionary function of rhetoric in the Renaissance, see Nancy S. Struever, *Theory as Practice: Ethical Inquiry in the Renaissance* (Chicago: University of Chicago Press, 1992).

19. Javitch, "Self-Justifying Norms," 195–218.

20. Daniel Javitch, "Pioneer Genre Theory and the Opening of the Humanist Canon," *Common Knowledge* 3 (1994): 54–66.

21. Clubb, *Italian Drama*, 153–90.

22. See Giacopo Mazzoni, *On the Defense of the Comedy of Dante. Introduction and Summary*, trans. Robert L. Montgomery (Tallahassee: University Presses of Florida, 1983), 24, 46. John Peacock, in "Ben Jonson's Masques and Italian Culture," provides a good account of Mazzoni's views on imitation as they relate to English theories about the court masque.

23. Greene, *Light in Troy*, 92.

24. See Tzvetan Todorov, "The Origin of Genres," *New Literary History* 8 (1976): 159–70, for the argument that new genres are produced from old.

25. The translation is that of Gilbert at 511.

26. The argument of Clubb.

27. Colie, *Resources of Kind*, 1–31.

CHAPTER 4. PASTORAL AS TRAGICOMEDIC

1. M. Chialbò and F. Doglio, eds., *Origini del dramma pastorale in Europa* (Viterbo: Centro studi sul teatro medioevale e rinascimentale, 1985). The collection includes a copious and well-annotated bibliography on Renaissance pastoral drama, particularly as regards Italy.

2. Enrico Carrara, *La poesia pastorale* (Milan: Vallardi, 1909); Marzia Pieri, *La scena boschereccia nel rinascimento italiano* (Padua: Liviana Editrice, 1983).

3. For a text of *Cefalo*, see Niccolò da Correggio, *Opere*, ed. Antonia Tissoni Benvenuti (Bari: Laterza, 1969), 7–45.

4. Pieri, *La scena boschereccia*, 44.

5. Ibid., 65–83.

6. The definitive edition of Ruzante is *Teatro*, ed. Ludovico Zorzi (Turin: Einaudi, 1967). For a survey, in English, of the life and theatrical production of Ruzante, see Linda L. Carroll, *Angelo Beolco (Il Ruzante)* (Boston: Twayne Publishers, 1990).

7. For Diomedes' account of *satira*, see Henricus Keil, *Grammatici Latini* (Hildesheim and New York: Georg Olms Verlag, 1981), 1:485–86.

8. Dana F. Sutton lists marvelous and magical elements that appear in satyr plays, including a magical flute and headgear that bestows invisibility in Sophocles' *Inachus*. See his "The Satyr Play," in *The Cambridge History of Classical Drama*, ed. P. E. Easterling and B. M. W. Knox (Cambridge: Cambridge University Press, 1989), 1:99.

9. Horace, "The Art of Poetry," 468–71.

10. The medieval references to Vitruvius are collected by Ferruccio Marotti, ed., *Lo spettacolo dall'umanesimo al Manierismo* (Milan: Feltrinelli, 1974), 25 n. 1. A good discussion of Quattrocento notions of the *satira* may be found in Antonia Benvenuti Tissoni and Maria Pia Missini Sacchi, eds., *Teatro del Quattrocento: Le corte padane* (Turin: UTET, 1983), 9–26.

11. Vitruvius, *The Ten Books on Architecture*, trans. Morris Hicky Morgan (Cambridge: Harvard University Press, 1916).

12. Marotti, *Lo spettacolo*, 63. On 28 n. 8, Marotti addresses the dating of this treatise, located in an undated manuscript, codex Lat. 466, V, 1, 6 in the Biblioteca Estense of Modena. See 28 n. 8.

13. Lyon, 1510, fol. vi. v.

14. This is from Poliziano's commentary on Statius. See the edition of Lucia Cesarini Martinelli, *Commento inedito alle Selve di Poliziano* (Florence: Sansoni, 1978), 55.

15. Marotti, *Lo spettacolo*, 127. See *Di Lucio Vitruvio Pollione, De architectura libri decem tradducti de Latino in vulgare affigurati: commentati . . .* (Como, 1521).

16. Quoted by Marotti, *Lo spettacolo*, 201–3.

17. It is possible to see in Giraldi's choice of the satyr over the shepherd a rejection of pastoral, although I believe that this view attaches too many generic constraints to the pastoral mode. See the excellent discussions of Riccardo Bruscagli, "G.B. Giraldi: comico, satirico, tragico," in *Il teatro italiano del rinascimento*, ed. Maristella De Panizza Lorch (Milan: Edizioni di comunità, 1980), 261–83; and Jane Tylus, "Purloined Passages: Giraldi, Tasso, and the Pastoral Debates," *Modern Language Notes* 99, no. 1 (1984): 101–24.

18. The play and the treatise are collected by Carla Molinari, ed., *Egle, Lettera sovra il comporre le satire atte alla scena, favola pastorale* (Bologna: Commissione per i testi di lingua, 1985).

19. Molinari, *Egle*, 153.

20. Ibid., 158.

21. *Castelvetro*, ed. Bongiorno, 254.

22. Molinari, *Egle*, 157. According to Adriano Cavicchi, "Ferraran theatrical machinery from the mid-sixteenth to the mid-seventeenth century distinguished itself as one of the most fantastic and spectacular of European theater." See Cavicchi's "La scenografia dell' *Aminta* nella tradizione scenografica pastorale ferrarese del sec. XVI," in *Studi su teatro veneto fra Rinascimento ed età barocca*, ed. Maria Teresa Muraro (Firenze: Olschki, 1971), 56.

23. See the discussion of Pasqualigo's play by Clubb, *Italian Drama*, 93–96. The play was printed in Venice.

24. These plays are discussed by ibid., 93–123, 153–87; Pietro Cresci, *Tirena, favola pastorale* (Venice, 1584); Gieronimo Vida, *Filliria, favola boscareccia* (Venice, 1587); Camillo Della Valle, *Gelosi amanti, favola pastorale* (Ferrara, 1585).

25. Leoni's play was printed in Venice.

26. See the scenario *Pantaloncino*, collected in Lea, *Italian Popular Comedy*, 2:636–42.

27. *Aminta* literary criticism has marginalized this and the other three *intermezzi* often performed with the play. Bàrberi Squarotti follows Bartolo Tommaso Sozzi in not including the *intermezzi* in his critical edition. Evidence suggests, however, that beginning with a 1579 performance of the play, the *intermezzi* came to be considered an important part of the performance event. See the entry of Elena Povoledo dedicated to Ferrara in the *Enciclopedia dello spettacolo* (Rome: Le Maschere, 1954–58), 5:173–86. For the *intermezzi* texts, see Torquato Tasso, *Opere*, ed. Bruno Marer (Milan: Rizzoli, 1963), lines 205–8.

28. See *Il pastor fido* (Venice, 1602), 255.

29. Citation refers to the first volume of the *Opere*.

30. For a discussion of comedic structures in Italian pastoral plays excepting *Aminta* and *Il pastor fido* and written between 1573–90, see Clubb, *Italian Drama*, 93–123.

31. Weinberg, *History of Literary Criticism*, 2:1077.

32. Tasso had begun working on *Gerusalemme Liberata* in the 1560s. *Aminta* was first performed in 1573.

33. All *Aminta* citations are from Torquato Tasso, *Aminta*, ed. Giorgio Bàrberi Squarotti (Padova: R.A.D.A.R., 1968). Line numbers are cumulative.

34. Of *Aminta*, Marziano Guglielminetti observes that "although the play alternates, like all of the productions of dramatic pastoral, between comedy and tragedy, it leans rather to the latter and only treats a few comedic situations." See Torquato Tasso, *Teatro*, ed. Marziano Guglielminetti (Milan: Garzanti, 1983), xx. For the tragicity of *Aminta*, see also Giorgio Bàrberi Squarotti, "La tragicità dell' *Aminta*," in *Fine dell'idyllio. Da Dante al Marino* (Genova: Il Melangolo, 1978), 139–73.

35. Sophocles, *Antigone*, trans. F. Storr, in *Sophocles*, Loeb Classical Library (1912; reprint, London: William Heinemann, 1968), 390–93.

36. See Sebastiano Serlio, *Tutte l'opere d'architettura et prospettiva* (1619; reprint, Ridgewood, N.J.: Gregg Press, 1964), 45–47. Serlio's remarks on theatrical scenes are also collected in E. K. Chambers, *The Elizabethan Stage* (Oxford: Clarendon Press, 1923), 4:353–65.

37. Joseph Loewenstein has commented on the insistent nature of the demonstratives in the prologue. "Guarini and the Presence of Genre," 45.

38. In Sassuolo in 1587, Beccari's *Il Sacrificio* was performed on the occasion of the wedding between Marco Pio Savoia and Clelia Farnese. (For the performance, Guarini wrote the prologue and the *intermezzi*.) An anonymous observer of the production noted the capaciousness of the pastoral set, in ways that echo Serlio's description of the *scena satyrica*: "The art of perspective, with which [the set] was done, did not represent a theatrical scene, but a large country full of woods, of fertile mountains, of well-cultivated fields, of great distances, of huts, of cottages. . . ." He goes on to describe a city depicted at the fork of the river, mountainous terrain, and a temple dedicated to the god Pan. See Armando Favio Ivaldi, *Le nozze Pio-Farnese e gli apparati teatrali di Sassuolo del 1587. Studio su una rappresentazione del primo dramma pastorale italiano, con intermezzi di G.B Guarini* (Genova: E.R.G.A., 1974), 9.

39. Antonio Ongaro, *Alceo, favola pescatoria* (Venice, 1582).

40. Whether actually painted on panels fronting the *skene,* or merely verbally invoked, temples and statues did figure prominently in Greek tragedy.

41. Daniel citations refer to vol. 3 of *The Complete Works in Verse and Prose of Samuel Daniel,* ed. Alexander B. Grosart (1885; reprint, New York: Russell and Russell, 1963). Line numbers are cumulative.

42. Citation refers to William Shakespeare, *King Henry VI, Part 3,* ed. Andrew S. Cairncross (London and New York: Methuen, 1964).

43. Citation refers to *A Midsummer Night's Dream,* ed. Harold F. Brooks (London and New York: Methuen, 1979).

44. Mellamphy, "Pantaloons and Zanies," 141–42.

45. Citation refers to William Shakespeare, *Cymbeline,* ed. J. M. Nosworthy (London and New York: Methuen, 1955).

46. Jameson, *Political Unconscious,* 110.

47. Citation refers to William Shakespeare, *All's Well That Ends Well* (London and New York: Methuen, 1959).

48. Rosalie L. Colie, *Shakespeare's Living Art* (Princeton: Princeton University Press, 1974), 243–83; Taylor, "The Pastoral Reckoning."

49. James Edward Siemon, "'But it Appears She Lives'; Iteration in *The Winter's Tale,*" *PMLA* 74 (1974): 13.

50. For the marginalization of the London theater, see Mullaney, *Place of the Stage.*

51. For colonialist readings, see Stephen Greenblatt, "Learning to Curse: Aspects of Linguistic Colonialism in the Sixteenth Century," in *Learning to Curse: Essays in Early Modern Culture* (London: Routledge, 1992), 16–39; and Francis Barker and Peter Hulme, "Nymphs and Reapers Heavily Vanish: The Discursive Con-texts of *The Tempest,*" in *Alternative Shakespeares,* ed. John Drakakis (London: Methuen, 1985), 191–205. Kermode rightly considers the play as a pastoral drama because of its broad thematic interest in problems typically addressed in Renaissance pastoral—art versus nature, nurture and civilization versus nature, the corrupting influence of the court, etc. William Shakespeare, *The Tempest,* ed. Frank Kermode (1954; reprint, London and New York: Methuen, 1958), xxiv. *Tempest* citations refer to this edition.

52. Clubb, *Italian Drama,* 112–13.

53. Yoch, "A Greater Power," 166.

54. *The Tempest,* ed. Orgel, 49.

55. G. K. Hunter contrasts the political turn taken by English tragicomedy with the merely theocratic apparatus of Italian tragicomedy. In the main, Hunter's argument is persuasive, although there are certainly political implications in Guarini's theory. See Hunter's "Italian Tragicomedy on the English Stage."

CHAPTER 5. THE TRAGICOMEDIC SATYR

1. See the essay of Greenblatt, and that of Barker and Hulme.

2. Montaigne's famous essay, "Des Cannibales," which Shakespeare read in John Florio's translation, is a well-known subtext for Shakespeare's play. In particular, Gonzalo's "golden age" speech (2.1.143–52, 155–60) is partly lifted from a passage in Florio's translation.

3. The term "species corruption" is that of Hayden White, "The Forms of

Wildness." White argues that unlike the Hellenic monsters generated from the union of humans and animals (e.g., the Minotaur), which are spatialized in altogether nonhuman places, satyrs inhabit the friendlier confines of meadows and pools just across the boundaries of civilization, representing both the pleasures afforded by the release of civilized repressions and the punishments that might ensue from such a liberation.

4. The most thorough investigation of both historical and literary backgrounds relevant to Caliban has been done by Alden T. Vaughan and Virginia Mason Vaughan, *Shakespeare's Caliban: A Cultural History* (Cambridge: Cambridge University Press, 1991). They only briefly mention the satyr. See 62, 78–79.

5. *Oberon* was performed on 1 January 1611. *The Winter's Tale* must have been written before 15 May 1611, when Simon Foreman saw the play at the Globe, and was probably composed earlier in the same year. *The Tempest* was first performed at Whitehall in October 1611.

6. My account of the Greek satyr play is indebted to Richard Seaborg's excellent introduction to the *Cyclops*.

7. For a good reproduction of the Pronomos vase, see *The Cambridge History of Classical Drama*, ed. Easterling and Knox (Cambridge: Cambridge University Press, 1989), 21.

8. The passage is from *Oeneus* or possibly *Schoeneus*, and is quoted by Sutton, "The Satyr Play," 95.

9. Seaborg, *Cyclops*, 30.

10. David Konstan, "An Anthropology of Euripides' *Kyklops*," in *Nothing To Do With Dionysos?*, ed. John J. Winkler and Froma I. Zeitlin (Princeton: Princeton University Press, 1990), 208.

11. Richard Bernheimer, *Wild Men in the Middle Ages* (Cambridge: Harvard University Press, 1952).

12. Molinari, *Egle*, 155.

13. *The Landscape of the Mind: Pastoralism and Platonic Theory in Tasso's "Aminta" and Shakespeare's Early Comedies* (Oxford: Clarendon Press, 1969), 52.

14. Molinari, *Egle*, 156.

15. Ibid., 161.

16. Citation refers to *Vergil. Eclogues, Georgics, Aeneid 1–6*, trans. H. R. Fairclough, Loeb Classical Library (Cambridge: Harvard University Press, 1916), 42–45.

17. Molinari, *Egle*, 160

18. The phrase is that of Hayden White, "The Forms of Wildness," 24.

19. For a discussion of rape in the pastoral space, see Tylus, "Colonizing Peasants," 120.

20. Ornella Garaffo provides a good survey of the satyr in Ferraran pastoral in "Il satiro nella pastorale ferrarese del Cinquecento," *Italianistica* 14 (1985): 185–201.

21. Agostino Beccari, *Il sacrificio, favola pastorale* (Ferrara, 1555).

22. Leone De'Sommi, *Hirfile, pastorale*. Extracts of this play (probably written in 1555–56) may be found in Abd-El-Kader Salza, "Un dramma pastorale inedito del Cinquecento (*L'Irfile* di Leone De'Sommi)," *Giornale storico della letteratura italiana* 27 (1909): 103–20. The play may be found in the Biblioteca Nazionale of Turin, in a miscellaneous manuscript collection of De'Sommi (Segnatura N IV 18). I quote from Garrafo, "Il Satiro," 194.

23. I use the translation of Lea, *Italian Popular Comedy*, 2:644.

24. Vaughan and Vaughan, *Shakespeare's Caliban*, 65–71.

25. Citations refer to *Hamlet*, ed. Harold Jenkins (London and New York: Methuen, 1982).

26. W. J. Lawrence, "Notes on a Collection of Masque Music," *Music and Letters* (1922): 49–58.

CHAPTER 6. "GENTLEMAN-LIKE TEARS": TRAGICOMEDY AND AFFECTIVE RESPONSE

1. Jan Mukarovsky discusses the notion of "internal audience": "After all, the roles of the actor and the spectator are much less distinguished than it might seem at first glance. Even the actor to a certain extent is a spectator for his partner at the moment when the partner is playing. . . ." See his *Structure, Sign, and Function*, trans. John Burbank and Peter Steiner (New Haven and London: Yale University Press, 1978), 218–19.

2. Susan Bennett, *Theatre Audiences: A Theory of Production and Reception* (London and New York: Methuen, 1990), 4.

3. For an interpretation of Aristotelian catharsis that does not refer to the audience, see Gerald F. Else, *Aristotle's Poetics: The Argument* (Cambridge: Harvard University Press, 1957), 224–32.

4. See, for example, section 14 of the *Poetics*: "Fear and pity sometimes result from what is seen on the stage and are sometimes aroused by the actual arrangement of the incidents, which is preferable and the mark of the better poet." I quote from Aristotle, *The Poetics*, trans. W. Hamilton Fyfe, in *Aristotle: The Poetics, "Longinus": On the Sublime, Demetrius: On Style*, Loeb Classical Library (London: William Heinemann, 1927), 48–49.

5. Stephen Orgel argues, "The notion of tragedy as a genre defined by its therapeutic effect on the audience is a Renaissance one: Aristotle may have conceived of the form in that way, but he did not say so." See his "Shakespeare and the Kinds of Drama," *Critical Inquiry* 6 (1979): 117.

6. For the theory, see *I Verato*, 2:247–52.

7. A selection of Scaliger's *Poetics* may be found in *Select Translations from Scaliger's Poetics*, ed. Frederick Morgan Padelford, Yale Studies in English 26 (New York: Henry Holt and Co., 1905).

8. Several Italian scholars have commented on the musicality of *Il pastor fido* and Guarini's theory of tragicomedic style. Gianfranco Folena argues that Guarinian tragicomedy exploits a "multiplicity of tones, approaching a mediating harmony, of a musical and pathetic nature." See his "La mistione tragicomica e la metamorfosi dello stile nella poetica del Guarini," in *La critica stilistica e il Barocco letterario*, Atti del secondo Congresso Internazionale di studi italiani a cura della Associazione Internazionale per gli studi di lingua e letteratura italiana (Florence: Le Monnier, 1957), 344–49. See also Mario Fubini, "L'*Aminta* intermezzo alla tragedia della 'Liberata'," *Giornale storico della letteratura italiana* 145 (1968), 45; and Deanna Battaglin, "Il linguaggio tragicomico del Guarini e l'elaborazione del *Pastor fido*," in *Lingua e strutture del teatro italiano del Rinascimento*, Quaderni del circolo filologico linguistico padovano (Padova: Liviana, 1970), 2:293–94.

9. *Structure, Sign, and Function*, 206–7.

10. Clubb, *Italian Drama*, 153–90.

11. Isabella Andreini, *Mirtilla, pastorale* (Venice, 1598).

12. *Violence and the Sacred*, trans. Patrick Gregory (1972; reprint, Baltimore and London: Johns Hopkins University Press, 1977).

13. Says Gloucester, "As flies to wanton boys, are we to th'Gods; / They kill us for their sport" (*King Lear* 4.1.36–37).

14. See, for example, 1.2.338–341.

15. The argument of Waith, *Pattern of Tragicomedy*, 86–98.

16. Quoted by ibid., 39.

17. The argument was first made by A. H. Thorndike in *The Influence of Beaumont and Fletcher on Shakespeare* (Worcester, Mass: Oliver B. Wood, 1901). Harold Wilson, among others, contests Thorndike's thesis in *"Philaster* and *Cymbeline,"* in *Shakespeare's Contemporaries*, ed. Max Bluestone and Norman Rabkin (Englewood Cliffs, N.J.: Prentice-Hall, 1961), 250–62.

18. The concern with decorum that pervades the scene might explain Belarius's odd care, after Fidele's dirge, to grant Cloten a funeral decorously appropriate to his high station (4.2.243–51).

19. The theatergram is common in Italian pastoral drama. See, for example, *Danza di Venere* 1.5. Hamlet, of course, addresses Ophelia as a "Nymph" just before the "get thee to a nunnery" tirade (3.1.89).

20. *Hamlet* 4.3.19–31.

21. As Clubb has shown, the many animals populating the world of Italian pastoral drama conveyed various and nuanced tonal and generic codes, the bear providing a distinctively tragicomedic theatergram. See Clubb, *Italian Drama*, 140–52.

22. Kenneth Burke, *A Rhetoric of Motives* (1950; reprint, Berkeley and Los Angeles: University of California Press, 1969), 50–51.

23. *The Tempest*, ed. Orgel, 102.

24. Margreta de Grazia discusses the peculiarly internal nature of this reversal scene in *"The Tempest*: Gratuitous Movement or Action Without Kibes and Pinches," *Shakespeare Studies* 14 (1981): 249–65.

CHAPTER 7. PLACE, GENRE, AND "HORIZONS OF EXPECTATION"

1. Thomas Middleton, *The Works*, ed. A. H. Bullen (Boston, 1884), 7:145.

2. In Clubb's view, Polonius's speech indicates Shakespeare's Italianate awareness of the resources of genre.

3. For a study of various analogies used in genre theory, see David Fishelov, *The Role of Analogy in Genre Theory* (University Park: Pennsylvania State University Press, 1994).

4. Rosalie Colie considers Renaissance genres as "habitats" (*Resources of Kind*, 115–16). For the spatial metaphor in genre theory, see also John R. Shawcross, "Literary Revisionism and a Case for Genre," *Genre* 18 (1985): 413–34.

5. Weinberg discusses this theory of Scaliger in *History of Literary Criticism*, 2:745–48.

6. Kenneth Burke, *A Grammar of Motives* (1945; reprint, Berkeley and Los Angeles: University of California Press, 1969).

7. Jameson, *Political Unconscious*, 112.

8. Ibid., 111.

9. Ibid., 112.

10. The translation is that of Morris Hicky Morgan. Morgan's translation of

Vitruvius uses "tragic" and "comic," which I have altered in conformity to my genre/mode distinction.

11. These comic moments are multiplied in Ongaro's *Alceo*, a post-Tassan play in which the pastoral mode is translated to a piscatory venue.

12. Yoch, "A Greater Power," 168.

13. See Bernard Knox, "*The Tempest* and the Ancient Comic Tradition," in *English Stage Comedy*, ed. W. K. Wimsatt Jr. (New York: Columbia University Press, 1955), 52–73.

14. This point has been made by a critic who also sees *Cymbeline* staging different genre-coded outlooks: Joan C. Marx, "The Encounter of Genres: *Cymbeline's* Structure of Juxtaposition," in *The Analysis of Literary Texts: Current Trends in Methodology*, ed. Randolph D. Pope (Ypsilanti, Mich.: Bilingual Press, 1980), 138–44. I differ from Marx in comparing the genre networks of *Cymbeline* to those of Italian pastoral tragicomedy and in seeing substantial dialogic interplay between genres, in addition to the multigeneric perspectivism that Marx emphasizes.

15. *In Shakespeare's Tragicomic Vision* (Baton Rouge: Louisiana State University Press, 1972), Joan Hartwig discusses the contrast between tragic particularity and comic generalization.

16. Stephen Orgel makes this point in his introduction to *The Tempest*, 5.

17. Daniel C. Boughner, "Jonsonian Structure in *The Tempest*," *Shakespeare Quarterly* 21 (1970): 3–10.

18. See James Black, "Shakespeare and the Comedy of Revenge," in *Comparative Critical Approaches to Renaissance Comedy*, ed. Donald Beecher and Massimo Ciavolella (Ottawa: Dovehouse Editions, 1986), 137–52.

19. Clubb discusses the transformation of pagan fate into Christian providence in Italian comedies and tragicomedies written during the Counter-Reformation period. See *Italian Drama in Shakespeare's Time*, 41.

Chapter 8. Modal Dialogues

1. Gérard Genette, "Genres, 'types', modes," *Poetique* 32 (1977): 389–421.

2. Javitch, "Self-Justifying Norms," 213–14.

3. Baxter Hathaway, *The Age of Criticism: The Late Renaissance in Italy* (Ithaca: Cornell University Press, 1962). Hathaway provides a good account of Cinquecento debates about imitation at 3–125. See also Genette on imitation and classical genres.

4. Denores, of course, could not but acknowledge ancient genres such as pastoral and lyric. Believing, however, that they were not governed by the principles of "grammar," and not by political and philosophical principles, he considered them much less important than the three major genres.

5. Ralph Cohen, "History and Genre," *New Literary History* 17 (1986): 207.

6. Francis Cairns, *Generic Composition in Greek and Roman Poetry* (Edinburgh: Edinburgh University Press, 1972), 34.

7. Guillén, *Literature as System*, 71–106.

8. Colie, *Resources of Kind*, 103.

9. Theoretically implicit in Guarini's genre system is the kind of dialogic interplay between kinds that Bakhtin considered a distinguishing characteristic of the late-sixteenth century. Bakhtin opposed the preferred Saussurean unit of study, the *langue*-based sentence, to the "utterance," which is marked by a change of

speakers (the "dixi," in Bakhtin's words). What characterizes the utterance is that it invites and awaits a response. The utterance, a link in a continuous chain of speech performances, is itself formed in response to previous utterances and anticipates subsequent responses—objection, agreement, modification—in its very formation. Utterances are socially inflected, organized according to categories of "speech genres." For Bakhtin, literary, or "secondary," genres incorporate speech genres and often derive from them, and so can be seen to observe the same dialogic behavior as the "primary" speech genres. See M. M. Bakhtin, "The Problem of Speech Genres," in *Speech Genres and other Essays,* ed. Caryl Emerson and Michael Holquist, trans. Vern W. McGee (Austin: University of Texas Press, 1986), 60–102; and V. N. Voloshinov, *Marxism and the Philosophy of Language,* trans. Ladislav Matejka and R. Titunik (Cambridge: Harvard University Press, 1986).

    10.   Printed in 1571 in Siena as *L'Hortensio, Comedia de gl'Academici Intronati.*

    11.   Oddi's play was written ca. 1570 and printed in Florence in 1590.

    12.   See Jupin, *Mucedorus,* 1–12. Parts of the prologue and epilogue excluding the address to James have been taken to refer to the so-called Wars of the Theaters of 1601–2 and could have thus been made before the 1606 edition, in which they do not appear.

    13.   Joseph Loewenstein argues that the figure of Echo in Guarini's *Pastor fido* converts the solipsistic Silvio from monody to dialogue. "Guarini and the Presence of Genre," 43.

    14.   Guarini uses the verb *temperare* at least as much as the participle *temperato.* For example, "il dolce . . . tempera quella grandezza, e sublimità, che è propria del puro Tragico" [the sweet style {of pastoral} tempers that greatness and sublimity that is proper to the tragedic style] (*I Verato,* 2:274).

    15.   "E come il rozzo e intrattabil ferro, / temprato con più tenero metallo, / effina sì, che sempre e più resiste, / e per uso più nobile s'adopra; / così vigor indomito e feroce, / e con le sue dolcezze Amor i tempra, / diviene a l'opra generoso e forte" [Just as the rough and intractable iron, tempered with a pliant metal, is refined to a greater strength, and adapts itself to worthier tasks, so wild and fierce vigor, if tempered by the sweetness of love, becomes generous and strong] (*Il pastor fido* 1.1).

    16.   Giovanni Battista Della Porta, *Gli duoi fratelli rivali, comedia nuovamente data in luce, dal Signor Gio. Bat. Della Porta Gentilhuomo Napolitano* (Venice, 1601). For the Ginevra story in *Orlando Furioso,* see Lodovico Ariosto, *Orlando Furioso,* ed. Marcello Turchi and Edoardo Sanguineti (Milan: Garzanti, 1984), vol. 1, canto 5: 5–74.

    17.   Foster, Mowat.

    18.   Hartwig, *Shakespeare's Tragicomic Vision,* 104–17.

    19.   *The Tempest,* ed. Orgel, 27. For example, the Berkeley Shakespeare Festival production of *The Tempest* in 1989 divided the role of Ariel into male and female parts.

    20.   In an article entitled "Neck Riddle as a Dialogue of Genres: Applying Bakhtin's Genre Theory," John Dorst considers the dialogic relationship between folk genres that come together on equal and contestory terms. See *Journal of American Folklore* 96 (1983): 413–33.

Chapter 9. Social Negotiations

    1.   *Poetics,* Loeb Classical Library, 10–11.

    2.   In Donatus's commentary on Terence there are two essays, one titled "De

Fabula" and now attributed to Evantius, and another titled "De Comoedia" and credited to Donatus himself. The two essays fundamentally shaped Renaissance ideas about classical tragedy and comedy. By convenience and by established convention, I refer to the authors of these commentaries as "Donatus." See Marvin Herrick, *Comic Theory in the Sixteenth Century* (Urbana: University of Illinois Press, 1964), 57–60 for a discussion of these essays and for relevant bibliographical information.

3. Madeleine Doran, *Endeavors of Art: A Study of Form in Elizabethan Drama* (Madison: University of Wisconsin Press, 1964), 166–67. Most modern scholars, however, derive "comedy" from κωμάζειν, to revel.

4. See Weinberg, *History of Literary Criticism*, 2:745.

5. LaCapra, "Comment," *New Literary History* 17 (1986): 221.

6. Tylus, "Purloined Passages," 113.

7. See G. A. Ruggieri's edition (Venice, 1818), 70–71.

8. Pescetti published three treatises defending Guarini, all published in Verona in 1601. He discusses the capacity of shepherds for *meraviglia* and the pastoral festival in *Difesa del Pastor fido*, pp. 57, 59.

9. Tylus, "Purloined Passages," 116–17.

10. Tylus, "Colonizing Peasants," 113–14, 131–32.

11. See Aldo De Maddalena, "Il mondo rurale italiano nel Cinque e nel Seicento," *Rivista storia italiana* 76 (1964): 362.

12. Ibid.

13. For the changing fortunes of small landowners, see B. Caizzi, "Le classi sociali nella vita milanese," in *Storia di Milano*, vol. 2, *Il declino spagnolo* (Milan: Foundazione Treccani degli Alfieri per la Storia di Milano, 1953–62), 334–73.

14. See *Attori Mercanti Corsari: La Commedia dell'Arte in Europa tra Cinque e Seicento* (Turin: Einaudi, 1993), xv–xvii.

15. Burke, *A Rhetoric of Motives*, 208.

16. Empson, *Some Versions of Pastoral* (1935; reprint, New York: New Directions, 1974), 11.

17. *Compendio*, in Gilbert, *Literary Criticism*, 530. For Guarini's frustrations, see Guglielminetti's introduction to his edition of Guarini's works.

18. Plautus, *Amphitryon*, in *Plautus in Five Volumes*, trans. Paul Nixon, Loeb Classical Library (Cambridge: Harvard University Press, 1979), 1:8–12.

19. *Danza di Venere*, pastorale (Vicenza, 1584).

20. Tylus, "Colonizing Peasants."

21. Because politics is not my chief focus in this study, I refer the reader to the anthologies of Nancy McGuire and McMullan/Hope, which emphasize the politics of tragicomedy. See especially the excellent essays, in both anthologies, of Walter Cohen. The essays of James J. Yoch, already cited, discuss political aspects of Italian pastoral drama.

22. Guiseppe Toffanin has argued that despite Guarini's opposition to Denores's didactic and political approach, he too "recognized the dependence of poetry on politics as much as Denores." See his *La fine dell'umanesimo* (Milan: Fratelli Bocca, 1920), 154ff.

23. See the *Compendio*, in Gilbert, *Literary Criticism*, 530.

24. Quoted by Proudfoot, "Shakespeare and the New Dramatists," 247.

25. Colie makes this argument in *Shakespeare's Living Art*, 266.

26. The larger object of satire is the increasingly suspect social mobility of the

period, most scandalously represented by James's liberal granting of new peerages.

CHAPTER 10. LOW COMEDY

1. See, however, Marzia Pieri, "*Il pastor fido* e i comici dell'Arte," *Biblioteca teatrale* 17 (1991): 1–15.

2. Siro Ferrone, "La vendita del teatro: Tipologie Europee tra Cinque e Seicento," in *The Commedia dell'Arte from the Renaissance to Dario Fo: The Italian Origins of European Theatre*, ed. Christopher Cairns (Lewiston, N.Y.: Edwin Mellen Press, 1988), 37.

3. See Tessari, *Commedia dell'Arte,* 31–47.

4. Mario Apollonio, *Storia della Commedia dell'Arte* (1930; reprint, Florence: Sansoni, 1982), 71–84.

5. Ibid., 40.

6. Antonio Grazzini, "Canto di Buffoni e Parasiti," collected in *Tutti i trionfi, carri, mascherate, o canti carnascialeschi andati per Firenze dal tempo del Magnifico Lorenzo De'Medici fino all'anno 1559* (Florence, 1750), 450.

7. From Scala, *Il teatro delle favole rappresentative..*

8. See Douglas Radcliff-Umstead, "The Erudite Comic Tradition of the *Commedia dell'Arte*," in *The Science of Buffoonery: Theory and History of the Commedia dell'Arte*, ed. Domenico Pietropaolo (Toronto: Dovehouse Editions, 1989), 33–58.

9. See, for example, one of Domenico Bruni's prologues, in which a character who is the servant of her fellow actors complains of being an overworked librarian: Domenico Bruni, *Prologhi* (Turin, 1621), cited in *La Commedia dell'Arte e la società barocca. La professione del teatro*, ed. Ferrucio Marotti and Giovanna Romei (Rome: Bulzoni, 1991), 388–89; and quoted by Allardyce Nicoll, *The World of Harlequin* (Cambridge: Cambridge University Press, 1963), 32.

10. Francesco Andreini, *Le bravure del Capitano Spavento divise in molti ragionamenti in forma di dialogo* (Venice, 1607). Many of these dialogues are included in Marotti and Romei, *La Commedia dell'Arte,* 213–302.

11. For a concise account of attacks and defenses of the *commedia dell'arte*, including relevant primary documents, see Richards and Richards, *Commedia dell'Arte,* 235–55.

12. Pier Maria Cecchini, *Discorso sopra l'arte comico,* circa 1612; Pier Maria Cecchini, *Frutti delle moderne comedie et avvisi a chi le recita* (Padua, 1628); Nicolò Barbieri, *La Supplica, discorso famigliare di Niccolo Barbieri detto Beltrame diretto a coloro che scrivendo o parlando trattano de' comici trascurando i meriti delle azzioni virtuose* (Venice, 1634). Both Cecchini treatises are in Marotti and Romei, *La Commedia dell'Arte,* 67–92. A modern edition of Barbieri has been done by Ferdinando Taviani, ed. *La supplica discorso familiare a quelli che trattano de' comici* (Milan: Il Polifilo, 1971).

13. Andreini, *Le bravure,* in Moretti and Romei, *La Commedia dell'Arte,* 218.

14. See Scala, *Il teatro delle favole rappresentative,* ed. Marotti, 433–46.

15. Adriano Valerini, *Oratione D'Adriano Valerini Veronese, In morte della divina Signora Vincenza Armani, comica eccellentissima et alcune rime dell'istesso, e d'altri auttori, in lode della medesima con alquante leggiadre e belle compositioni di detta Signora Vincenza* (Verona, n.d.). Valerini's oration can be found in Marotti and Romei, *La Commedia dell'Arte,* 31–41.

16. For the reference to *Dido*, see A. D'Ancona, *Origini del teatro italiano* (Turin: E. Loescher, 1891), 2:449. For the connection between improvisation and tragicomedy, see Lea, *Italian Popular Comedy*, 1:196–97.

17. Mullaney, *Place of the Stage*, 135–51.

18. Ibid., 145.

19. Although, as Stephen Orgel says, stage curtains were not raised until the 1630s, "fringéd curtains" do "suggest the theatrical metaphor of a discovery scene" (*The Tempest*, ed. Orgel, 123).

20. Fowler, *Kinds of Literature*, 40–42.

21. Horace, "The Art of Poetry," lines 1–5.

22. As Dominick LaCapra says, "Texts that combine or mix genres may appear to be a cultural monstrosity: such a text may be attacked or made a scapegoat." See "Comment," 220.

23. This has been noticed by G. Wilson Knight, who describes Ariel as a "delicate mixture of earth, air, fire, and lightly apprehended sea." See *The Crown of Life: Essays in Interpretation of Shakespeare's Final Plays* (London: Methuen, 1947), 208.

Bibliography

PRIMARY WORKS

Andreini, Francesco. *Le bravure del Capitano Spavento divise in molti ragionamenti in forma di dialogo.* Venice, 1607.

Andreini, Isabella. *Mirtilla, pastorale.* Venice, 1598.

Ariosto, Lodovico. *Orlando Furioso.* Edited by Marcello Turchi and Edoardo Sanguineti. Milan: Garzanti, 1984.

Aristotle: The Poetics, "Longinus": On the Sublime, Demetrius: On Style. Loeb Classical Library. London: William Heinemann, 1927.

Ascham, Roger. *The Schoolmaster* (1570). Edited by V. Ryan. Charlottesville: University Press of Virginia, 1967.

Barbieri, Nicolò. *La supplica discorso famigliare a quelli che trattano de'comici.* Edited by Ferdinando Taviani. Milan: Il Polifilo, 1971.

Beaumont and Fletcher. *The Dramatic Works in the Beaumont and Fletcher Canon.* Edited by Fredson Bowers. 5 vols. Cambridge: Cambridge University Press, 1976.

———. *Philaster.* Edited by Dora Jean Ashe. Lincoln: University of Nebraska Press, 1974.

Beccari, Agostino. *Il sacrificio, favola pastorale.* Ferrara, 1555.

Bonarelli, Guidubaldo. *Filli di Sciro, favola pastorale.* Ferrara, 1607.

Bruni, Domenico. *Prologhi.* Turin, 1621.

Castelvetro, Lodovico. *Castelvetro on the Art of Poetry: An Abridged Translation of Lodovico Castelvetro's "Poetica d'Aristotele Vulgarizzata et Sposta."* Edited by Andrew Bongiorno. Binghamton, N.Y.: Medieval and Renaissance Texts and Studies, 1984.

Cecchini, Pier Maria. *Frutti delle moderne comedie et avvisi a chi le recita.* Padua, 1628.

Cesariano, Cesare. *Di Lucio Vitruvio Pollione, de architectura libri decem tradducti de Latino in vulgare affigurati: commentati . . .* Como, 1521.

Correggio, Niccolò da. *Opere.* Edited by Antonia Tissoni Benvenuti. Bari: Laterza, 1969.

Cresci, Pietro. *Tirena, favola pastorale.* Venice, 1584.

Daniel, Samuel. *The Complete Works in Verse and Prose of Samuel Daniel.* Edited by Alexander Grosart. 5 vols. 1885. Reprint, New York: Russell and Russell, 1963.

Day, John. *The Works of John Day.* Edited by A. H. Bullen. 1881. Reprint, London: Holland Press, 1963.

Della Porta, Giovanni Battista. *Gli duoi fratelli rivali, comedia nuovamente data in luce, dal Signor Gio. Bat. Della Porta Gentilhuomo Napolitano.* Venice, 1601.

Della Valle, Camillo. *Gelosi amanti, favola pastorale.* Ferrara, 1585.

De'Sommi, Leone. *Quattro dialoghi in materia di rappresentazioni sceniche.* Edited by Ferruccio Marotti. Milan: Il Polifilo, 1968.

Feuillerat, A., ed. *Documents Relating to the Office of Revels in the Time of Queen Elizabeth.* Louvain: A. Uystpruyst, 1908.

Fraser, Russell A., and Norman Rabkin, eds. *Drama of the Renaissance.* 2 vols. New York: Macmillan, 1976.

Force, Peter, ed. *Tracts and Other Papers Relating Principally to the Origin, Settlement, and Progress of the Colonies in North America.* Washington, D.C., 1836.

Il Fumoso. *Il Batecchio, commedia di maggio composta per il pellegrino ingegno del Fumoso.* Siena, 1546.

Giraldi Cinzio, Giambattista. *Egle, Lettera sovra il comporre le satire atte alla scena, Favola pastorale.* Edited by Carla Molinari. Bologna: Commissione per i testi di lingua, 1985.

———. *Scritti critici.* Edited by Camillo Guerrieri Crocetti. Milan: Marzorati, 1973.

Gilbert, Allan H, ed. *Literary Criticism: Plato to Dryden.* 1940. Reprint, Detroit, Mich.: Wayne State University Press, 1962.

Grazzini, Anton Francesco "Canto di Buffoni, e Parasiti." In *Tutti i trionfi, carri, mascherate, o canti carnascialeschi andati per Firenze dal tempo del Magnifico Lorenzo De'Medici fino all'anno 1559.* Florence, 1750.

Guarini, Battista. *Delle opere del cavalier Battista Guarini.* 4 vols. Verona, 1738.

———. *Opere di Battista Guarini.* Edited by Marziano Guglielminetti. Turin: UTET, 1971.

———. *Il pastor fido.* Venice, 1602.

———. *Trattato della politica libertà.* Edited by G. A. Ruggieri. Venice, 1818.

Horace. *Satires, Epistles, and Ars Poetica.* Translated by H. R. Fairclough. 1929. Loeb Classical Library. Reprint, Cambridge: Harvard University Press, 1978.

Intronati, Accademica degli. *L'Hortensio, Comedia de gl'Academici Intronati.* Siena, 1571.

James I. *The Workes of the Most High and Mightie Prince James.* London, 1616.

Jonson, Ben. *Ben Jonson's Plays and Masques.* Edited by Robert M. Adams. New York: Norton, 1979.

———. *Volpone.* Edited by Philip Brockbank. New York: W. W. Norton, 1968.

Keil, Henricus. *Grammatici Latini.* 8 vols. Hildesheim and New York: Georg Olms Verlag, 1981.

Marotti, Ferruccio, ed. *Lo spettacolo dall'umanesimo al Manierismo*. Milan: Feltrinelli, 1974.

Marotti, Ferruccio, and Giovanna Romei, eds. *La Commedia dell'Arte e la società barocca. La professione del teatro*. Rome: Bulzoni, 1991.

Marston, John. *The Malcontent*. Edited by G. K. Hunter. London: Methuen, 1975.

Mazzoni, Giacopo. *On the Defense of the Comedy of Dante. Introduction and Summary*. Translated by Robert L. Montgomery. Tallahassee: University Presses of Florida, 1983.

Middleton, Thomas. *The Works*. Edited by A. H. Bullen. Boston, 1884.

Minturno, Antonio Sebastiano. *L'arte poetica*. 1564. Poetiken Cinquecento. Reprint, Munich: Wilhelm Fink Verlag, 1971.

Oddi, Sforza. *I morti vivi*. Perugia, 1576.

———. *Prigione d'amore*. Florence, 1590.

Ongaro, Antonio. *Alceo, favola pescatoria*. Venice, 1582.

Pasqualigo, Luigi. *Gl'intricati, pastorale*. Venice, 1581.

Plautus. *Amphitryon*. In *Plautus in Five Volumes*. Translated by Paul Nixon. Loeb Classical Library. Cambridge: Harvard University Press, 1979.

Poliziano. *Commento inedito alle Selve di Poliziano*. Edited by Lucia Cesarini Martinelli Florence: Sansoni, 1978.

Puttenham, George. *The Arte of English Poesie*. Edited by Edward Arber. 1589. Westminister, U.K.: A. Constable, 1895.

Robortello, Francesco. *In librum Aristotelis de arte poetica explicationes paraphrasis in librum Horatii, qui vulgo de arte poetica ad Pisones inscribitur*. Poetiken Cinquecento. 1548. Reprint, Munich: Wilhelm Fink Verlag, 1971.

Rossi, Bartolomeo. *La fiammella, pastorale*. Paris, 1584.

Scala, Flaminio. *Il teatro delle favole rappresentative*. Edited by Ferruccio Marotti. 2 vols. 1611. Reprint, Milan: Il polifilo, 1976.

Scaliger, Julius Caesar. *Select Translations from Scaliger's Poetics*. Edited by Frederick Morgan Padelford. Yale Studies in English 26. New York: Henry Holt and Co., 1905.

Serlio, Sebastiano. *Tutte l'opere d'architettura et prospettiva*. 1619. Reprint, Ridgewood, N.J.: The Gregg Press, 1964.

Shakespeare, William. *All's Well That Ends Well*. London and New York: Methuen, 1959.

———. *Anthony and Cleopatra*. Edited by M. R. Ridlely. London and New York: Methuen, 1954.

———. *Cymbeline*. Edited by J. M. Nosworthy. London and New York: Methuen, 1955.

———. *Hamlet*. Edited by Harold Jenkins. London and New York: Methuen, 1982.

———. *King Henry VI, Part 3*. Edited by Andrew S. Cairncross. London and New York: Methuen, 1964.

———. *King Lear*. Edited by Kenneth Muir. London and New York: Methuen, 1972.

———. *King Richard II*. Edited by Peter Ure. London and New York: Methuen, 1956.

———. *A Midsummer Night's Dream*. Edited by Harold F. Brooks. London and New York: Methuen, 1979.

———. *Pericles*. Edited by F. D. Hoeniger. London and New York: Methuen, 1963.

———. *The Tempest*. Edited by Frank Kermode. London and New York: Methuen, 1954.

———. *The Winter's Tale*. Edited by J. H. P. Pafford. London and New York: Methuen, 1963.

Sidney, Philip. *An Apology for Poetry*. Edited by Geoffrey Shepherd. London: Thomas Nelson and Sons, 1965.

Sophocles. *Antigone*. Translated by F. Storr. Loeb Classical Library. 1912. Reprint, London: William Heinemann, 1968.

Tasso, Torquato. *Aminta*. Edited by Giorgio Bàrberi Squarotti. Padova: R.A.D.A.R.,1968.

———. *Opere*. Edited by Bruno Maier. 5 vols. Milan: Rizzoli, 1963–65.

Vergil. *Eclogues, Georgics, Aeneid 1–6*. Loeb Classical Library. Translated by H. R. Fairclough. Cambridge: Harvard University Press, 1916.

Vida, Gieronimo. *Filliria, favola boscareccia*. Venice, 1587.

Vitruvius. *The Ten Books on Architecture*. Translated by Morris Hicky Morgan. Cambridge: Harvard University Press, 1916.

SECONDARY WORKS

Apollonio, Mario. *Storia della Commedia dell'Arte*. 1930. Reprint, Florence: Sansoni, 1982.

Bakhtin, M. M. "The Problem of Speech Genres." In *Speech Genres and other Essays*, edited by Caryl Emerson and Michael Holquist, translated by Vern W. McGee, 60–102. Austin: University of Texas Press, 1986.

Bàrberi, Giorgio Squarotti. *Fine dell'idyllio. Da Dante al Marino*. Genova: Il Melangolo, 1978.

Barker, Francis, and Peter Hulme. "Nymphs and Reapers Heavily Vanish: the Discursive Con-texts of *The Tempest*." In *Alternative Shakespeares*, edited by John Drakakis, 191–205. London: Methuen, 1985.

Battaglin, Deanna. "Il linguaggio tragicomico del Guarini e l'elaborazione del 'Pastor fido'." In *Lingua e strutture del teatro italiano del Rinascimento*, 2:291–353. Quaderni del circolo filologico linguistico padovano. Padova: Liviana, 1970.

Bennett, Susan. *Theatre Audiences: A Theory of Production and Reception*. London and New York: Methuen, 1990.

Bentley, Gerald Eades. "Shakespeare and the Blackfriars Theatre." *Shakespeare Survey* 1 (1948): 38–50.

Berger, Harry. "Miraculous Harp: A Reading of Shakespeare's *Tempest*." *Shakespeare Studies* 5 (1969): 253–83.

Bernheimer, Richard. *Wild Men in the Middle Ages*. Cambridge: Harvard University Press, 1952.

Black, James. "Shakespeare and the Comedy of Revenge." In *Comparative Critical Approaches to Renaissance Comedy*, edited by Donald Beecher and Massimo Ciavolella, 137–52. Ottawa: Dovehouse Editions, 1986.

Borsellino, Nino. *Rozzi e Intronati: Esperienze e forme di teatro dal "Decameron" al "Candelaio."* 2d ed. Rome: Bulzoni, 1976.

Boughner, Daniel C. *The Braggart in Renaissance Comedy: A Study in Comparative Drama from Aristophanes to Shakespeare*. Minneapolis: The University of Minnesota Press, 1954.

———. "Jonsonian Structure in *The Tempest.*" *Shakespeare Quarterly* 21 (1970): 3–10.

Braudel, Ferdinand. "L'Italian fuori d'Italia." In *Dalla caduta dell'Impero romano al secolo XVIII*, 2092–2248. Vol. 2 of *Storia d'Italia*. Turin: Einaudi, 1974.

Braunmuller, A. R., and J. C. Bulman, eds. *Comedy from Shakespeare to Sheridan: Change and Continuity in the English and European Dramatic Tradition: Essays in Honor of Eugene Waith*. Newark: University of Delaware Press, 1986.

Brown, John Russell, and Bernard Harris, eds. *Later Shakespeare*. New York: St. Martin's Press, 1967.

Bruscagli, Riccardo. "G. B. Giraldi: comico, satirico, tragico." In *Il teatro italiano del rinascimento*, edited by Maristella De Panizza Lorch, 261–83. Milan: Edizioni di comunità, 1980.

Burke, Kenneth. *A Grammar of Motives*. 1945. Reprint, Berkeley and Los Angeles: University of California Press, 1969.

———. *A Rhetoric of Motives*. 1950. Reprint, Berkeley and Los Angeles: University of California Press, 1969

Butler, K. T. "Giacomo Castelvetro." *Italian Studies* 5 (1950): 1–42.

Cairns, Francis. *Generic Composition in Greek and Roman Poetry*. Edinburgh: Edinburgh University Press, 1972.

Caizzi, B. "Le classi sociali nella vita milanese." In *Il declino spagnolo*, 334–73. Vol. 11 of *Storia di Milano*. Milan: Foundazione Treccani degli Alfieri per la Storia di Milano, 1953–62.

Campbell, May E. "*The Winter's Tale*: A Study in Shakespeare's Late Plays with Special Reference to Guarini's Theory of Tragicomedy." Diss., University of North Carolina at Chapel Hill, 1970.

Campbell, O. J. "Love's Labor's Lost Revisited" and "The Two Gentlemen of Verona and Italian Comedy." In *Studies in Shakespeare, Milton, and Donne*. University of Michigan Publications in Language and Literature. New York: Macmillan, 1925.

Carrara, Enrico. *La poesia pastorale*. Milan: Vallardi, 1909.

Cavicchi, Adriano. "La scenografia dell' "Aminta" nella tradizione scenografica pastorale ferrarese del sec. XVI." In *Studi su teatro veneto fra Rinascimento ed età barocca*, edited by Maria Teresa Muraro, 53–72. Firenze: Olschki, 1971.

Chambers, E. K. *The Elizabethan Stage*. 4 vols. Oxford: Clarendon Press, 1923.

———. "The Integrity of *The Tempest.*" *The Review of English Studies* 1 (1925): 129–50.

———. *William Shakespeare: A Study of Facts and Problems*. 2 vols. Oxford: Clarendon Press, 1930.

Chialbò, M., and F. Doglio, ed. *Origini del dramma pastorale in Europa*. Viterbo: Centro studi sul teatro medioevale e rinascimentale, 1985.

Clubb, Louise George. *Italian Drama in Shakespeare's Time*. New Haven: Yale University Press, 1989.

Cochrane, Eric. "Counter-Reformation or Tridentine Reformation? Italy in the Age of Carlo Borromeo." In *San Carlo Borromeo: Catholic Reform and Ecclesiastical Politics in the Second Half of the Sixteenth Century*, edited by John M Headley and John B Tomaro, 31–46. Washington, D.C.: Folger Shakespeare Library, 1988.

Cody, Richard. *The Landscape of the Mind: Pastoralism and Platonic Theory in Tasso's "Aminta" and Shakespeare's Early Comedies*. Oxford: Clarendon Press, 1969.

Cohen, Ralph. "History and Genre." *New Literary History* 17 (1986): 203–18.

Colie, Rosalie L. *The Resources of Kind: Genre-Theory in the Renaissance*. Edited by Barbara Kiefer Lewalski. Berkeley: University of California Press, 1973.

———. *Shakespeare's Living Art*. Princeton: Princeton University Press, 1974.

Cook, Ann Jennalie. *The Privileged Playgoers of Shakespeare's London, 1576–1642*. Princeton: Princeton University Press, 1981.

Collura, Jane Haney. "Guarini's Theory of Tragicomedy and Shakespeare's Last Three Plays." Diss., The Catholic University of America, 1979.

Corbett Margery, and Ronald Lightbown. *The Comely Frontispiece: The Emblematic Title-Page in England, 1550–1660*. London: Routledge and Kegan Paul, 1979.

D'Ancona, Alessandro. *Origini del teatro italiano*. Turin: Ermanno Loescher, 1891.

Danson, Lawence. "Jonsonian Comedy and the Discovery of the Social Self." *PMLA* 99 (1984): 179–93.

De Maddalena, Aldo. "Il mondo rurale italiano nel Cinque e nel Seicento." *Rivista storia italiana* 76 (1964): 349–426.

De Marinis, Marco. "Dramaturgy of the Spectator." *Drama Review* 31 (1987): 100–114.

Dimsey, Sheila A. "Giacopo Castelvetro." *MLR* 23 (1928): 424–31.

Dollimore, Jonathan. *Radical Tragedy: Religion, Ideology, and Power in the Drama of Shakespeare and his Contemporaries*. Brighton, U.K.: Harvester, 1984.

Donno, Elizabeth Story, ed., *Three Renaissance Pastorals: Tasso, Guarini, Daniel*. Binghamton, N.Y.: Medieval and Renaissance Texts and Studies, 1993.

Doran, Madeleine. *Endeavors of Art : A Study of Form in Elizabethan Drama*. Madison: University of Wisconsin Press, 1963.

Dowden, Edward. *Shakespeare*. New York, 1877.

Elam, Keir. *The Semiotics of Theatre and Drama*. London and New York: Methuen, 1989.

Else, Gerald F. *Aristotle's Poetics: The Argument*. Cambridge: Harvard University Press, 1957.

Empson, William. *Some Versions of Pastoral*. 1935. Reprint, New York: New Directions, 1974.

Eccles, Mark. "Samuel Daniel in France and Italy." *Studies in Philology* 34 (1937): 148–67.

Felperin, Howard. "Romance and Romanticism: Some Reflections on *The Tempest* and *The Heart of Darkness*, or When is Romance no longer Romance?" In *Shakespeare's Romances Reconsidered*, edited by Carol McGinnis Kay and Henry E. Jacobs, 60–76. Lincoln: University of Nebraska Press, 1978.

———. *Shakespearean Romance*. Princeton: Princeton University Press, 1972.

Ferrone, Siro. *Attori Mercanti Corsari: La Commedia dell'Arte in Europa tra Cinque e Seicento*. Turin: Einaudi, 1993.

———. "Dalle parti 'scannate' al testo scritto. La *commedia dell'arte* all'inizio del secolo xvii." *Paragone* 34 (1983): 38–68

———."La vendita del teatro: Tipologie Europee tra cinque e seicento." In *The Commedia dell'Arte from the Renaissance to Dario Fo: The Italian Origins of European Theatre*, edited by Christopher Cairns, 35–73. Lewiston, N.Y.: Edwin Mellen Press, 1988.

Finkelpearl, Philip J. *Court and Country Politics in the Plays of Beaumont and Fletcher*. Princeton: Princeton University Press, 1990.

Fishelov, David. *The Role of Analogy in Genre Theory*. University Park: Pennsylvania State University Press, 1994.

Folena, Gianfranco. "La mistione tragicomica e la metamorfosi dello stile nella poetica del Guarini." In *La critica stilistica e il Barocco letterario*, 344–49. Atti del secondo Congresso Internazionale di studi italiani a cura della Associazione Internazionale per gli studi di lingua e letteratura italiana. Florence: Le Monnier, 1957.

Foster, Verna. "The 'Death' of Hermione: Tragicomic Dramaturgy in *The Winter's Tale*." *Cahiers Elizabethains* 43 (1993): 43–56.

Fowler, Alastair. *Kinds of Literature: An Introduction to the Theory of Genres and Modes*. Cambridge: Harvard University Press, 1982.

Frye, Northrop. *A Natural Perspective: The Development of Shakespearean Comedy and Romance*. New York: Columbia University Press, 1965.

Fubini, Mario. "L'*Aminta* intermezzo alla tragedia della *Liberata*." *Giornale storico della letteratura italiana* 145 (1968): 38–52.

Garaffo, Ornella. "Il satiro nella pastorale ferrarese del Cinquecento." *Italianistica* 14 (1985): 185–201.

Genette, Gérard. "Genres, 'types', modes." *Poetique* 32 (1977): 389–421.

Girard, René. *Violence and the Sacred*. Translated by Patrick Gregory. 1972. Reprint, Baltimore and London: The Johns Hopkins University Press, 1977.

Granville-Barker, Harley. *Prefaces to Shakespeare*. 2d ser. London: Sidgwick and Jackson, 1930.

Grazia, Margreta de. "*The Tempest*: Gratuitous Movement or Action Without Kibes and Pinches." *Shakespeare Studies* 14 (1981): 249–65.

Greenblatt, Stephen. *Learning to Curse: Essays in Early Modern Culture*. London: Routledge, 1992.

Greene, Thomas. *The Light in Troy: Imitation and Discovery in Renaissance Poetry*. New Haven: Yale University Press, 1982.

Grendler, Paul F. *The Roman Inquisition and the Venetian Press, 1540–1605*. Princeton: Princeton University Press, 1977.

Grewar, Andrew. "Shakespeare and the Actors of the *Commedia dell'Arte*." In *Studies of the Commedia dell'Arte*, edited by David J. George and Christopher J. Gossip. Cardiff: University of Wales Press, 1993.

Guglielminetti, Marziano, ed. *Teatro*, by Torquato Tasso. Milan: Garzanti, 1983.

Guillén, Claudio. *Literature as System: Essays Toward the Theory of Literary History*. Princeton: Princeton University Press, 1971.

Gurr, Andrew. *The Shakespearean Stage, 1574–1642*. 2d ed. Cambridge: Cambridge University Press, 1980.

Harbage, Alfred. *Shakespeare and the Rival Traditions*. New York: Macmillan, 1952.

Hartwig, Joan. *Shakespeare's Tragicomic Vision*. Baton Rouge: Louisiana State University Press, 1972.

Hathaway, Baxter. *The Age of Criticism: The Late Renaissance in Italy*. Ithaca: Cornell University Press, 1962.

Herendeen, W. H. "A New Way to Pay Old Debts: Pretexts to the 1616 Folio." In *Ben Jonson's 1616 Folio*, edited by Jennifer Brady and W. H. Herendeen, 38–63. Newark: University of Delaware Press, 1991.

Herrick, Marvin T. *Comic Theory in the Sixteenth Century*. Urbana: University of Illinois Press, 1964.

———. *Tragicomedy: Its Origins and Development in Italy, France, and England*. Urbana: University of Illinois Press, 1955.

Hirst, David. *Tragicomedy*. London and New York: Methuen, 1984.

Hoppe, Harry R. "John Wolfe, Printer and Publisher, 1579–1601." *The Library*, 4th ser., 14 (1933–34): 241–48.

Huffman, Clifford Chalmers. *Elizabethan Impressions: John Wolfe and His Press*. New York: AMS Press, 1988.

Hunter, G. K. "English Folly and Italian Vice." In *Jacobean Theatre*, 85–111. New York: St. Martin's Press, 1960.

———. "Italian Tragicomedy on the English Stage." *Renaissance Drama*, n.s., 6 (1973): 123–48.

Ivaldi, Armando Favio. *Le nozze Pio-Farnese e gli apparati teatrali di Sassuolo del 1587. Studio su una rappresentazione del primo dramma pastorale italiano, con intermezzi di G.B Guarini*. Genova: E.R.G.A., 1974.

Jameson, Fredric. *The Political Unconscious: Narrative as a Socially Symbolic Act*. Ithaca: Cornell University Press, 1981.

Jauss, Hans Robert. "Literary History as a Challenge to Literary Theory." *New Literary History* 2 (1970): 7–37.

Javitch, Daniel. "Pioneer Genre Theory and the Opening of the Humanist Canon." *Common Knowledge* 3 (1994): 54–66.

———. "Self-Justifying Norms in the Genre Theories of Italian Renaissance Poets." *Philological Quarterly* 67 (1988): 195–218.

Jupin, Arvin H., ed. *A Contexual Study and Modern-Spelling Edition of "Mucedorus."* New York and London: Garland Publishing, 1987.

Kay, Carol McGinnis, and Henry E. Jacobs, eds. *Shakespeare's Romances Reconsidered*. Lincoln and London: University of Nebraska Press, 1978.

Kennedy, Judith. "Il pastor cortese: Tasso, Guarini, and Shakespeare's 'Courtly' Comedies." Paper presented at the annual meeting of the Shakespeare Association of America, Philadelphia, April 1990.

Kernan, Alfred. *The Cankered Muse: Satire of the English Renaissance*. New Haven: Yale University Press, 1959.

Kirsch, Arthur. *Jacobean Dramatic Perspectives*. Charlottesville: University Press of Virginia, 1972.

Knight, G. Wilson. *The Crown of Life: Essays in Interpretation of Shakespeare's Final Plays*. London: Methuen, 1947.

Knox, Bernard. "*The Tempest* and the Ancient Comic Tradition." In *English Stage Comedy*, edited by W. K. Wimsatt Jr., 52–73. New York: Columbia University Press, 1955.

Konstan, David. "An Anthropology of Euripides' *Kyklops*." In *Nothing To Do With Dionysos?*, edited by John J. Winkler and Froma I. Zeitlin, 207–27. Princeton: Princeton University Press, 1990.

LaCapra, Dominick. "Comment." *New Literary History* 17 (1986): 219–21.

Lane, F. C. "The Mediterranean Spice Trade: Further Evidence of its Revival in the Sixteenth Century." *The American Historical Review* 45 (1940): 581–90.

Lawrence, W. J. "Notes on a Collection of Masque Music." *Music and Letters* 3 (1922): 49–58.

Lea, Kathleen. *Italian Popular Comedy: A Study in the Commedia dell'Arte, 1560–1620, with Special Reference to the English Stage*. 2 vols. Oxford: Clarendon Press, 1934.

Lewalski, Barbara Kiefer. *Paradise Lost and the Rhetoric of Literary Forms*. Princeton: Princeton University Press, 1985.

Loewenstein, Joseph. "For a History of Literary Property: John Wolfe's Reformation." *English Literary Renaissance* 18 (1988): 389–412.

———. "Guarini and the Presence of Genre." In *Renaissance Tragicomedy: Explorations in Genre and Politics*, edited by Nancy Klein Maguire, 33–55. New York: AMS Press, 1987.

Maguire, Nancy Klein, ed. *Renaissance Tragicomedy: Explorations in Genre and Politics*. New York: AMS Press, 1987.

Marcus, Leah. *The Politics of Mirth: Jonson, Herrick, Milton, Marvell, and the Defense of Old Holiday Pastimes*. Chicago and London: The University of Chicago Press, 1986.

Marx, Joan C. "The Encounter of Genres: *Cymbeline*'s Structure of Juxtaposition." In *The Analysis of Literary Texts: Current Trends in Methodology*, edited by Randolph D. Pope, 138–44. Ypsilanti, Mich.: Bilingual Press, 1980.

McMullan, Gordon, and Jonathan Hope, eds. *The Politics of Tragicomedy: Shakespeare and After*. London and New York: Routledge, 1992.

Mellamphy, Ninian. "Pantaloons and Zanies: Shakespeare's 'Apprenticeship' to Italian Professional Comedy Troupes." In *Shakespearean Comedy*, edited by Maurice Charney. New York: New York Literary Forum, 1980.

Melzi, Robert C. "From Lelia to Viola." *Renaissance Drama* 9 (1966): 67–81.

Miola, Robert S. "*The Merry Wives of Windsor*: Classical and Italian Intertexts." *Comparative Drama* 27 (1993): 364–76.

———. "New Comedy in *All's Well That Ends Well*." *Renaissance Quarterly* 46 (1993): 23–43.

Moretti, Franco. *Signs Taken for Wonders: Essays in the Sociology of Literary Forms.* Translated by Susan Fischer, David Forgacs, and David Miller. London and New York: Verso, 1988.

Mowat, Barbara. *The Dramaturgy of Shakespeare's Romances.* Athens: University of Georgia Press, 1976.

———. "Shakespearean Tragicomedy." In *Renaissance Tragicomedy: Explorations in Genre and Politics*, edited by Nancy Klein Maguire, 80–96. New York: AMS Press, 1987.

Mukarovsky, Jan. *Structure, Sign, and Function.* Translated by John Burbank and Peter Steiner. New Haven and London: Yale University Press, 1978.

Mullaney, Steven. *The Place of the Stage: License, Play, and Power in Renaissance England.* Chicago and London: The University of Chicago Press, 1988.

Nagler, A. M. *Theatre Festivals of the Medici.* New Haven and London: Yale University Press, 1964.

Neri, Ferdinando. *Scenari delle maschere in Arcadia.* Castello: S. Lapi, 1913.

Nicoll, Allardyce. *The World of Harlequin: A Critical Study of the Commedia dell'Arte.* Cambridge: Cambridge University Press, 1963.

Orgel, Stephen. "Shakespeare and the Kinds of Drama." *Critical Inquiry* 6 (1979): 107–23.

———, ed. *The Tempest*, by William Shakespeare. Oxford: Oxford University Press, 1987.

Orr, David. *Italian Renaissance Drama in England Before 1625: The Influence of Erudite Tragedy, Comedy, and Pastoral on Elizabethan and Jacobean Drama.* Chapel Hill: University of North Carolina Press, 1970.

Parker, Brian. "Jonson's Venice." In *Theatre of the English and Italian Renaissance*, edited by J. R. Mulryne and Margaret Shewring, 95–112. New York: St. Martin's Press, 1991.

Peacock, John. "Ben Jonson's Masques and Italian Culture." In *Theatre of the English and Italian Renaissance*, edited by J. R. Mulryne and Margaret Shewring, 73–94. New York: St. Martin's Press, 1991.

———. "Inigo Jones and the Florentine Court Theatre." *John Donne Journal* 5 (1986): 200–234.

Pieri, Marzia. "*Il pastor fido* e i comici dell'Arte." *Biblioteca teatrale* 17 (1991): 1–15.

———. *La nascita del teatro moderno in Italian tra XV e XVI secolo.* Turin: Bollati Boringhieri, 1989.

———. *La scena boschereccia nel rinascimento italiano.* Padua: Liviana Editrice, 1983.

Povoledo, Elena. "Ferrara." In *Enciclopedia dello spettacolo*, 5:173–86. Rome: Le Maschere, 1954–58.

Procter, Johanna. "The *Queenes Arcadia* (1606) and *Hymen's Triumph* (1615): Samuel Daniel's Court Pastoral Plays." In *The Renaissance in Ferrara and Its European Horizons*, edited by J. Salmons. Cardiff: University of Wales Press, 1984.

Proudfoot, Richard. "Shakespeare and the New Dramatists of the King's Men, 1606–1613." In *Later Shakespeare*, edited by John Russell Brown and Bernard Harris, 235–61. New York: St. Martin's Press, 1967.

Radcliff-Umstead, Douglas. "The Erudite Comic Tradition of the *Commedia dell'Arte*." In *The Science of Buffoonery: Theory and History of the Commedia dell'Arte*, edited by Domenico Pietropaolo, 33–58. Toronto: Dovehouse Editions, 1989.

Richards, Kenneth, and Laura Richards: *The Commedia dell'Arte: A Documentary History*. Oxford: Basil Blackwell, 1990.

Rosenberg, Eleanor. "Giacomo Castelvetro, Italian Publisher in Elizabethan London and His Patrons." *HLQ* 6 (1943): 119–48.

Rossi, Vittorio. *Battista Guarini ed Il pastor fido: Studio biografico-critico*. Turin: Ermanno Loescher, 1886

Salingar, Leo. "Elizabethan Dramatists and Italy: A Postscript." In *Theatre of the English and Italian Renaissance*, edited by J. R. Mulryne and Margaret Shewring, 221–37. New York: St. Martin's Press, 1991.

———. *Shakespeare and the Traditions of Comedy*. Cambridge: Cambridge University Press, 1972.

Salza, Abd-El-Kader. "Un dramma pastorale inedito del Cinquecento (*L'Irfile* di Leone De'Sommi)." *Giornale storico della letteratura italiana* 27 (1909): 103–20.

Schmidgall, Gary. *Shakespeare and the Courtly Aesthetic*. Berkeley and Los Angeles: University of California Press, 1981.

Schoenbaum, Samuel. *William Shakespeare: A Compact Documentary Life*. Oxford: Oxford University Press, 1977.

Scrivano, Riccardo. "Towards a 'Philosophy' of Renaissance Theatre." In *Comparative Critical Approaches to Renaissance Comedy*, edited by Donald Beecher and Massimo Ciavolella, 1–13. Ottawa: Dovehouse Editions, 1986.

Seaborg, Richard, ed. *Cyclops*, by Euripides. Oxford: Clarendon Press, 1984.

Sellers, Harry. "Italian Books Printed Before 1640." *The Library*, 4th ser., 5 (1924–25): 105–25.

Shawcross, John R. "Literary Revisionism and a Case for Genre." *Genre* 18 (1985): 413–34.

Siemon, James Edward. "'But it Appears She Lives': Iteration in *The Winter's Tale*." *PMLA* 74 (1974): 10–16.

Simonini, R. C. *Italian Scholarship in Renaissance England*. Chapel Hill: University of North Carolina Press, 1952.

Smith, Winifred. *The Commedia dell'Arte: A Study in Italian Popular Comedy*. New York: Columbia University Press, 1912.

Struever, Nancy S. *Theory as Practice: Ethical Inquiry in the Renaissance*. Chicago and London: The University of Chicago Press, 1992.

Sturgess, Keith. *Jacobean Private Theatre*. London and New York: Routledge and Kegan Paul, 1987.

Sutton, Dana F. "The Satyr Play." In *The Cambridge History of Classical Drama*, edited by P. E. Easterling and B. M. W. Knox, vol. 1, part 2, pp. 94–102. Cambridge: Cambridge University Press, 1989.

Taviani, Ferdinando. *La Commedia dell'Arte e la società barocca: La fascinazione del teatro*. Rome: Bulzoni, 1969.

Taylor, Michael. "The Pastoral Reckoning in *Cymbeline*." *Shakespeare Survey* 36 (1983): 97–106.

Tessari, Roberto. *Commedia dell'Arte: la maschera e l'ombra*. Milan: Mursia, 1981.

Thorndike, A.H. *The Influence of Beaumont and Fletcher on Shakespeare*. Worcester, Mass: Oliver B. Wood, 1901.

Tissoni, Antonia Benvenuti, and Maria Pia Missini Sacchi, eds. *Teatro del Quattrocento: Le corte padane*. Turin: UTET, 1983.

Todorov, Tzvetan. "The Origin of Genres." *New Literary History* 8 (1976): 159–70.

Toffanin, Guiseppe. *La fine dell'umanesimo*. Milan: Fratelli Bocca, 1920.

Tylus, Jane. "Colonizing Peasants: The Rape of the Sabines and Renaissance Pastoral." *Renaissance Drama*, n.s., 23 (1992): 113–38.

———. "Purloined Passages: Giraldi, Tasso, and the Pastoral Debates." *Modern Language Notes* 99 (1984): 101–24.

Uphaus, Robert W. *Beyond Tragedy: Structure and Experience in Shakespeare's Romances*. Lexington: University Press of Kentucky, 1981.

Vaughan, Alden T., and Virginia Mason Vaughan. *Shakespeare's Caliban: A Cultural History*. Cambridge: Cambridge University Press, 1991.

Voloshinov, V. N. *Marxism and the Philosophy of Language*. Translated by Ladislav Matejka and R. Titunik. Cambridge: Harvard University Press, 1986.

Waith, Eugene M. *The Pattern of Tragicomedy in Beaumont and Fletcher*. New Haven: Yale University Press, 1952.

Warren, Austin, and René Wellek, *Theory of Literature*. 3d ed. New York: Harcourt Brace Jovanovich, 1956.

Weinberg, Bernard. *A History of Literary Criticism in the Italian Renaissance*. 2 vols. Chicago: The University of Chicago Press, 1961.

Welsford, Enid. "Italian Influence on the English Court Masque." *MLR* 28 (1923): 394–409.

White, Hayden. "The Forms of Wildness: Archaeology of an Idea." In *The Wild Man Within: An Image in Western Thought from the Renaissance to Romanticism*, edited by Edward Dudley and Maximillian E. Novak, 3–38. Pittsburgh, Pa.: University of Pittsburgh Press, 1972.

Wickham, Glynne. "From Tragedy to Tragicomedy: 'King Lear' as Prologue." *Shakespeare Survey* 26 (1973): 33–48.

Wiles, David. *Shakespeare's Clown: Actor and Text in the Elizabethan Playhouse*. Cambridge: Cambridge University Press, 1987.

Williams, William Proctor. "Not Hornpipes and Funerals: Fletcherian Tragicomedy." In *Renaissance Tragicomedy: Explorations in Genre and Politics*, edited by Nancy Klein Maguire, 139–54. New York: AMS Press, 1987.

Wilson, Harold. "Philaster and Cymbeline." In *Shakespeare's Contemporaries*, edited by Max Bluestone and Norman Rabkin, 250–62. Englewood Cliffs, N.J.: Prentice-Hall, 1961.

Wittgenstein, Ludwig. *Philosophical Investigations*. Translated by G. E. M. Anscombe. New York: Macmillan, 1953.

Wright, Louis B. "Will Kemp and the *Commedia dell'Arte*." *MLN* 41 (1926): 516–20.

Yates, Frances A. *John Florio: The Life of an Italian in Shakespeare's England*. Cambridge: Cambridge University Press, 1934.

Yoch, James J. "A Greater Power Than We Can Contradict: The Voice of Authority in the Staging of Italian Pastorals." In *The Elizabethan Theatre, VIII*, edited by George R. Hibbard, 164–87. Port Credit, Ont.: P. D. Meany Co., 1982.

Young, David. *The Heart's Forest: A Study of Shakespeare's Pastoral Plays*. New Haven and London: Yale University Press, 1972.

Index